The Twentieth Century

The Twentieth Century is an exciting and intelligent guide to the literature and culture of the period. Its two-part organisation works effectively; the sections illuminate and communicate with each other. The modernist cities juxtaposed with the New York of the Harlem Renaissance are Joyce's Dublin and Fritz Lang's *Metropolis*, rather than the more familiar London and Paris. When London makes its appearance in Part 2 it's as the multicultural post-*Windrush* capital; which puts into a new perspective its earlier cosmopolitan claims. Conversely, the theme of memory is drawn out of *Dubliners* so as to anticipate and contrast with postcolonial memories of emigration. The choice of material is fresh. The directed readings are sure-footed and sensitive to a range of possibilities. The commentary is everywhere informed by contemporary critical developments, while remaining engaging and accessible. The illustrations are marvellous. The book is an admirable introduction, both to a set of challenging modern works, and to the discourses of modernity.

Max Saunders
Professor of English
King's College London

The Twentieth Century is superbly organised to lead students through a period of fundamental change in ideas and cultural productions. The well-written essays and thoughtful tasks will encourage students towards a complex and subtle understanding of this crowded period. The book is organised around two emblematic representations of the twentieth century: the modern city and migrant memory. While neither of these phenomena is uniquely 'modern', their textualisation intensified profoundly in the period under study. The choice of texts is inspired, and the multiple genres students are required to engage with will broaden an understanding of the issues. The significance and relevance of the texts to the discussion is carefully explained in the introductions and notes. The tasks are imaginatively and carefully organised, opening up the texts in engaging and challenging ways, while also introducing wide-ranging concepts that are indispensible to the student of literature.

Abdulrazak Gurnah
Professor of English
University of Kent

Reading and Studying Literature

This book is part of the series *Reading and Studying Literature* published by Bloomsbury Academic in association with The Open University. The three books in the series are:

The Renaissance and Long Eighteenth Century (edited by Anita Pacheco and David Johnson)
ISBN 978-1-84966-622-0 (hardback)
ISBN 978-1-84966-614-5 (paperback)
ISBN 978-1-84966-634-3 (ebook)

Romantics and Victorians (edited by Nicola J. Watson and Shafquat Towheed)
ISBN 978-1-84966-623-7 (hardback)
ISBN 978-1-84966-624-4 (paperback)
ISBN 978-1-84966-637-4 (ebook)

The Twentieth Century (edited by Sara Haslam and Sue Asbee)
ISBN 978-1-84966-620-6 (hardback)
ISBN 978-1-84966-621-3 (paperback)
ISBN 978-1-84966-620-4 (ebook)

This publication forms part of the Open University module A230 *Reading and studying literature*. Details of this and other Open University modules can be obtained from the Student Registration and Enquiry Service, The Open University, PO Box 197, Milton Keynes MK7 6BJ, United Kingdom (tel. +44 (0)845 300 60 90, email general-enquiries@open.ac.uk).

www.open.ac.uk

The Twentieth Century

Edited by Sara Haslam and Sue Asbee

The Open University

BLOOMSBURY ACADEMIC

Published by

Bloomsbury Academic
an imprint of Bloomsbury Publishing Plc
36 Soho Square
London W1D 3QY
United Kingdom
and
175 Fifth Avenue
New York
NY 10010
USA
www.bloomsburyacademic.com

In association with

The Open University
Walton Hall
Milton Keynes MK7 6AA
United Kingdom

First published 2012

Edited and designed by The Open University.

Printed and bound in the United Kingdom by Latimer Trend & Company, Estover Road, Plymouth PL6 7PY.

CIP records for this book are available from the British Library and the Library of Congress.

ISBN 978-1-84966-620-6 (hardback)
ISBN 978-1-84966-621-3 (paperback)
ISBN 978-1-84966-640-4 (ebook)

1.1

Contents

Preface

The Twentieth Century is the third book in the three-volume series Reading and Studying Literature, which aims to provide a chronological overview of the major literary periods. The other two books in the series are *The Renaissance and Long Eighteenth Century* (edited by Anita Pacheco and David Johnson) and *Romantics and Victorians* (edited by Nicola J. Watson and Shafquat Towheed). Together, these three books form the core teaching material for the Open University undergraduate module *Reading and studying literature* (Open University module code A230).

Ideally, the books should be read together as a linked survey of literature from the seventeenth century through to the twentieth century. However, *The Twentieth Century* stands on its own as an engaging and innovative introduction to a wide range of texts from across the period. As in the other books in this series, its subject is writing in English (with one textual exception) rather than 'English literature'. The first part of the book, 'Twentieth-century cities', examines the years 1900–1950, a literary period well known for its formal experimentations as well as for broad artistic interest in the real or imagined metropolis. Together, James Joyce's collection of short stories, *Dubliners*, Fritz Lang's film, *Metropolis*, and a range of New York poetry and prose fiction promote exploration of the urban contexts of the early twentieth century and how they were represented by writers and film directors of the time. The chapters offer guided reading of these exciting texts, looking at the thematic links and contrasts between them and focusing on questions of genre in order to develop skills of close reading and analysis.

The second part of the book, 'Migration and memory', is as generically various as Part 1, and features texts produced in a range of national traditions during the second half of the twentieth century. Sam Selvon's novel, *The Lonely Londoners*, Elizabeth Bishop's poetry (taken from the collection *Questions of Travel*), Brian Friel's play, *Dancing at Lughnasa*, and W.G. Sebald's semi-autobiographical set of fictive memoirs, *The Emigrants* (first published in German and then translated into English), all engage in different ways with the experience of migration and the uses of memory in the context of a newly global sensibility. Each of these writers explores the relationship between the present and the past as notions of national and individual identity are challenged by movement between countries and exposure to the wider world. Whereas the first part of the book considers the importance of locating texts in the literary period in which they were written, this second part explores the variety of national literatures and the related expansion of 'English' into 'Englishes'. As in Part 1, readings are closely guided and provide new opportunities to explore generic conventions and the individual thematic contributions of each author. Both parts of the book encourage readers to consider what these texts mean to us today, taking advantage of their increasing contemporaneity to explore new manifestations of the uses the creative present makes of the past.

Open University modules and text books are the products of extensive collaboration and involve the labour of numerous people. Sincere thanks are due to members of the A230 module team who did not write for this volume but contributed generously to the discussions that helped to shape it: Richard Allen, Delia da Sousa Correa, Jessica Davies, David Johnson, Clare Spencer, Shafquat Towheed, Dennis Walder and Nicola J. Watson; to the curriculum manager Rachel Pearce; the editor Hannah Parish; and the external assessor Michael Baron.

List of contributors

Sue Asbee is a Senior Lecturer in the Department of English at The Open University. She is author of chapters on Frank O'Hara and Allen Ginsberg in *The Popular and the Canonical* (2005) and Kate Chopin in *The Nineteenth Century Novel: Identities* (2001). She has also published articles and book chapters on the novelists Margiad Evans and Arnold Bennett.

Richard Danson Brown is a Senior Lecturer in the Department of English at The Open University. His publications include *The New Poet: Novelty and Tradition in Spenser's Complaints* (1999) and *Louis MacNeice and the Poetry of the 1930s* (2009).

Suman Gupta is Professor of Literature and Cultural History in the Department of English at The Open University. He has published ten monographs, most recently *Imagining Iraq: Literature in English and the Iraq Invasion* (2011), co-edited seven volumes, and authored over fifty papers, chapters in books and review essays.

Sara Haslam is a Senior Lecturer in the Department of English at The Open University and Deputy Chair of the Open University undergraduate module *Reading and studying literature*. She is the author of *Fragmenting Modernism: Ford Madox Ford, the Novel and the Great War* (2002), and editor of Ford's *The Good Soldier* (2010) and *England and the English* (2003). Further publications include *Life Writing* (2009, with Derek Neale) and articles and book chapters on Henry James, Thomas Hardy, the Brontës, modernism and the literature of the First World War.

Glenn Hooper is the author of *Travel Writing and Ireland, 1760–1860* (2005), and the editor of *The Tourist's Gaze: Travellers to Ireland, 1800–2000* (2001), *Irish and Postcolonial Writing* (2002) and *Landscape and Empire* (2004).

Anita Pacheco is a Senior Lecturer in the Department of English at The Open University and Chair of the Open University undergraduate module *Reading and studying literature*. She is the author of numerous articles and book chapters on Aphra Behn and the editor of *A Companion to Early Modern Women's Writing* (2002). Her book on Shakespeare's *Coriolanus* appeared in the 'Writers and their Work' series (2007).

Steve Padley is an Associate Lecturer with The Open University. He has also taught at the University of Cambridge and for the Workers' Educational Association. He is the author of *Key Concepts in Contemporary Literature* (2006).

Dennis Walder is Emeritus Professor of Literature in the English Department at The Open University. He is the author of *Dickens and Religion* (2007 [1987]). He published the first book on Athol Fugard in 1984, and has since edited Fugard's plays and produced a new study of the playwright (*Athol Fugard*, 2003). His other books include *Post-Colonial Literatures: History, Language, Theory* (1998) and *Postcolonial Nostalgias: Writing, Memory and Reputation* (2010).

Required reading

You will need to read the following texts in conjunction with this book:

Part 1

For Chapters 1 and 2: James Joyce (2000 [1914]) *Dubliners* (with an introduction and notes by Terence Brown), Penguin Modern Classics, London, Penguin.

The required reading for Chapter 4 can be found in 'Readings for Part 1'.

Please note you will also need the following DVD (for Chapter 3): Fritz Lang (dir.) (2010 [1972]) *Metropolis*, Masters of Cinema series, Germany, Ufa.

Part 2

For Chapter 5: Sam Selvon (2006 [1956]) *The Lonely Londoners* (ed. Susheila Nasta), Penguin Modern Classics, London, Penguin.

For Chapter 6: Elizabeth Bishop (2004 [1983]) *Complete Poems*, London, Chatto & Windus.

For Chapter 7: Brian Friel (1990) *Dancing at Lughnasa*, London, Faber and Faber.

For Chapter 8: W.G. Sebald (2002 [1996]) *The Emigrants* (trans. Michael Hulse), London, Vintage.

Part 1
Twentieth-century cities

Aims

The first part of this book will:

- introduce you to the literature and film of the first half of the twentieth century
- examine the treatment of the city in selected short stories, poetry, fiction and film
- explore the concept of 'period' in relation to the city texts featured.

Introduction to Part 1

Sara Haslam

Welcome to 'Twentieth-century cities', the first part of *The Twentieth Century*. This part of the book will look at texts from the first half of the twentieth century that are linked by their interest in the city, real and imagined. We begin with *Dubliners* by James Joyce (1882–1941), a collection of short stories published in 1914 and set in the Irish capital at the turn of the century. We then move on to examine the German silent film *Metropolis* (1927, directed by Fritz Lang (1890–1976)), a futuristic dystopian fantasy with an urban theme. We conclude this part of the book by studying a variety of New York texts published between 1920 and 1950. Poems by writers including Claude McKay (1889–1948) and Langston Hughes (1902–1967), and extracts from prose by, for example, Jack Kerouac (1922–1969), provide a sample of contemporary literary constructions of New York.

In 1944 the writer Elizabeth Bowen called the short story 'the child of this century' (quoted in Trotter, 2007, p. 1) because of the numbers of influential writers who contributed to its development from the turn of the twentieth century onwards. Cinema was of the same generation, and shared with the short story an experimental attitude to form. We focus on the short story and film for the majority of our study in this part of the book. It is hard to imagine exploring the literature of the city in this period without spending time on poetry too, however, and the writers you will encounter in Chapter 4 are mostly poets, or poets as well as prose fiction writers, and both genres feature here.

In addition to introducing you to city texts of the twentieth century, this part of the book will examine a concept central to literary studies – 'period'. Historical events and cultural artefacts relate to one another in important ways, and placing texts in context usually involves employing some notion of 'period'. Here and in the following chapters we shall use it as convenient shorthand for the classification of and reference to particular chunks of historical/literary time. All critics resort to such shorthand – in discussing the 'Renaissance' or the 'Romantic period', for example. But even cursory investigation reveals that periods are to a large degree arranged retrospectively and without nuance, can bear different names ('the Renaissance' and 'the early modern period' are both used, for example) and don't always begin or end in an agreed year. Such differences occur at a local level, but tend to become more dramatic when a range of national literatures (or traditions of film) is under scrutiny: periods are constituted differently according to where you stand when you are either conjuring them up or considering them. The 'Victorian age' or the 'Edwardian period' might express some organising principles about English/British literature, but neither translate well to texts produced at the same time in North America, say, for obvious reasons. Moreover, although the concept of 'period' assumes some fundamental similarities between contemporaneous texts, it is, in fact, not always easy to group them together in this way. In short, literary periods always need questioning, even while they constitute a useful analytical tool. We shall return to these ideas throughout this part of the book.

Our theme in Part 1 is the twentieth-century city. Since the Greek philosopher Plato (c.428–348 BCE) produced his treatise known as *The Republic* (c.360 BCE), the city has been a source of inspiration for, and backdrop to, Western literature. In one key text in that tradition, *Paradise Lost* (1667), John Milton (1605–1674) contrasted Eve's basic and pure rural affinity with the serpent's filthy, crowded, urban background. This particular binary opposition between city and country was re-energised from the mid-eighteenth century and the beginnings of the Industrial Revolution. Romantic writers often expressed their hostility to the idea of the city, as well as its reality, extolling the virtues of the 'natural' world in their poetry. In the very first lines of *The Prelude* (1805), William Wordsworth (1770–1850) recalled his grateful escape from the imprisoning, disenfranchising city to his regenerative experience of the countryside. The city was not always constructed like this. Though there were pastoral, anti-urban currents in the early modern period, the Renaissance view of the civilising effects of urban life and culture problematised the notion of rural perfection. *Utopia*, as conceived by Thomas More (1478–1535) in 1518, anticipated the potential of the great city, and Milton, among others, also celebrated the city as a site of refuge and liberty.

The city has played a prominent part in literature across many different periods, then, and has received a variety of treatments. The nature of each treatment will have been determined by the writer's aim, as well as historical contexts. Emily Brontë (1818–1848) picked on the shadowy urban port of Liverpool as the site of Heathcliff's birth for the exotic contrast it provided with the moors around Wuthering Heights. Many of her novel-writing peers concentrated more of their attention on city life. But towards the end of the nineteenth century, and the beginning of the period with which we are concerned here, a new critical intensity brought the city into different focus. European sociologists Emile Durkheim (1858–1917), Max Weber (1864–1920) and Georg Simmel (1858–1918), among others, formed its vanguard, but the effects permeated all aspects of contemporary culture. The city, and especially the metropolis (meaning a significant city, or capital), began to be taken as a subject in and of itself. Why should this be?

By 1920, the Western world was more urban than rural. In 1801, thirty-four per cent of Britain's population lived in cities; in 1911 it was seventy-nine per cent (Morris and Rodger, 1993, p. 3). Urbanisation increased particularly rapidly after 1850, propelled by the capitalist world market. It was the nineteenth-century bourgeoisie, as Karl Marx (1818–1883) pointed out, which created the enormous cities that defined the age (and, thereby, the conditions for its battle with the working class). Economic developments generated transformations of almost every other kind – cultural, social and artistic – sited primarily, and increasingly self-consciously, in the newly energised, expanding great cities. Artists and thinkers experienced, interpreted and re-theorised the city, concentrating on the ways that this material and social environment affected the human subject. They used the language of 'modernity' to do so. A densely populated, consumer-driven, experientially diverse modern metropolis at various stages of artistic development dominates the texts discussed in Part 1 of this book. Joyce's Dublin is still caught and held by the past; individual characters must, when they can, combat or escape the urban paralysis pervading *Dubliners*. The New York poets you will meet in Chapter 4 write, for the most part, out of the thrilling freedoms of a city whose moment has come – the sense of emancipation from previous restriction or repression is fundamental to much of their work. Fritz Lang visualises a future city in *Metropolis*, although his representation of the city is, of course, drawn from urban contexts familiar to the writers you will study here.

London was the site of the modern, according to the novelist Ford Madox Ford (1873–1939) in 1905, because it was 'wonderfully open-minded'. It was also 'tolerant', 'chaotic', crowded and immense (Ford, 2003 [1905], pp. 11–12). Such excitement in the face of modernity, particularly that frequently cited element, the urban crowd, was sometimes overwhelmed by other experiences of the twentieth-century city as fragmented, strange and lonely. Wyndham Lewis's contemporary painting *The Crowd* (1915) (see Figure 1), represents this sense visually. Lewis's city is geometrically labyrinthine and its crowd

Figure 1   Wyndham Lewis, *The Crowd*, 1915, oil and pencil on canvas, 21 × 15.4 cm. Tate Modern, T00689. Photo: © Tate, London 2011. © By kind permission of the Wyndham Lewis Memorial Trust (a registered charity).

massed together in ways that disguise and confuse perspective, as well as the nature of the figures' relationships, some of which seem hostile. An influential essay by Georg Simmel ('The metropolis and mental life', 1903) addressed the ways in which early twentieth-century metropolitan life had the potential to cause conflict. Money formed a prominent part of his analysis. Oswald Spengler (1880–1936), a German philosopher, assessed the modern city as both harnessing and producing a particular kind of energy, but he argued that it was ultimately enervating and parasitical, because it was money-based (1926, 1928). F. Scott Fitzgerald (1896–1940) was reading Spengler as he wrote *The Great Gatsby* (1926), a novel that features in Chapter 4 of this book. Scott Fitzgerald's representation of New York can be traced back to Spengler's vision of a dislocated human race migrating for scant reason to the tradition-less city, a modern 'Waste Land', as the poet T.S. Eliot (1888–1965) had termed it in a defining literary construction of the city in this period (1922). An atomised, quintessentially dystopic modern metropolis, as outlined here, produced the alienated urban characters that populated a wide range of contemporary writing and film. Eliot's famous insomniac, J. Alfred Prufrock, wandered a fog-deadened city, questioning his desire to 'disturb' it enough to make it live again: 'Shall I say, I have gone at dusk through narrow streets / And watched the smoke that rises from the pipes / Of lonely men in shirt-sleeves, leaning out of windows?' (Eliot, 1990 [1917], p. 13, ll. 70–2).

And yet, only eight years before Eliot published 'The Love Song of J. Alfred Prufrock', the *Manifesto of Futurism* (written by the Italian poet Filippo Tommaso Marinetti (1876–1944)) generated a hymn of extravagant praise to city streets, revelling in the crowds, noise, light and chaotic energy that were also used to express and define modernity. Point 11 of the *Manifesto*, which appeared on the front page of *Le Figaro* in 1909, begins as follows:

> We will sing of great crowds excited by work, by pleasure, and by riot; we will sing of the multicoloured, polyphonic tides of revolution in the modern capitals; we will sing of the vibrant nightly fervour of arsenals and shipyards blazing with violent electric moons; greedy railway stations that devour smoke-plumed serpents …
>
> (Marinetti, 1998 [1909], p. 251)

Futurism tethered the idea of the expanding city to a visionary and action-filled future, explicitly rejecting the past. To the Futurists, the city represented only opportunity, violent freedom and pleasure. Natalia Goncharova's painting *La Lampe Electrique* (1913), seen in Figure 2, was exhibited in Moscow in March–April 1914 in a show with a strong Futurist dimension. The depiction of a dazzling and diffuse electric light is an apt illustration of Futurism's 'electric moons'. The image is intended to display and to celebrate not just the source of the light, but its extent, the brightness and energy it brings to its urban setting: look particularly at the way the lines, both curved and straight, create the illusion of different kinds of movement in the painting. Many writers of the period worked with the idea of throwing light into dark places – particularly urban spaces – borrowing modernity's symbolic energy as they re-formulated their ambitions for representing the new age.

As we read and reread these city texts from a yet more urbanised twenty-first century vantage point, we contribute to evolving notions of this period too. The city is the dominant modern global social structure, and it is important to be aware of this context as we study the prose fiction, poetry and film that follow. It will inform our thinking as we consider which manifestations of early twentieth-century urban modernity, as introduced here, seem most to have inspired their authors/directors. The following chapters offer a series of related explorations of this question, though the discussion of Futurism may well bring *Metropolis* immediately to mind.

There were other related artistic movements and loose affiliations in the period, as there are in any literary period – they often become central to the later processes by which periods are named and shaped. When considering the first half of the twentieth century, such movements tend to be grouped under the heading 'modernism' (or 'modernisms'), a term that is widely used. Futurism is one example of a named movement; Imagism, which focused on poetry, was another. These named movements usually involved direct association between writers or artists: the Imagist poets, for example, agreed that poetry should use the language of everyday speech. Modernist writers more broadly were relatively independent of each other, and there was certainly no 'modernist' programme as such. What can be seen, looking back, is instead an often-shared focus on particular city-based themes or topics: modernity, technology, the crowd or the alienated human subject – as well as on experiments in technique. The short story, and film, as noted earlier, offered particular potential in this last respect. 'Make it new', the American poet Ezra Pound (1885–1972) said, in the slogan of the period. Far more often than not, as you will see in Part 1 of this book, this meant making it about the city too.

Figure 2   Natalia Goncharova, *La Lampe Electrique*, 1913, oil on canvas, 105 × 82 cm. Musée National d'Art Moderne, Centre Pompidou, Paris, AM4358P. Photo: Giraudon/The Bridgeman Art Library. © ADAGP, Paris and DACS, London 2010.

References

Eliot, T.S. (1990 [1917]) 'The Love Song of J. Alfred Prufrock' in *Selected Poems*, London, Faber and Faber.

Ford, F.M. (2003 [1905]) *England and the English* (ed. S. Haslam), Manchester, Carcanet.

Marinetti, F.T. (1998 [1909]) *Manifesto of Futurism* in Kolocotroni, V., Goldman, J. and Taxidou, O. (eds) *Modernism: An Anthology of Sources and Documents*, Edinburgh, Edinburgh University Press.

Morris, R.J. and Rodger, R. (eds) (1993) *The Victorian City: A Reader in British Urban History 1820–1914*, London, Longman.

Trotter, D. (2007) *Cinema and Modernism*, Oxford, Blackwell.

Chapter 1
James Joyce, *Dubliners*: city, theme and period

Sara Haslam and Glenn Hooper

Aims

This chapter will:

- introduce you to James Joyce's *Dubliners*, and explore in detail five stories from the collection: 'The Sisters', 'An Encounter', 'Eveline', 'Two Gallants' and 'The Boarding House'
- examine how Joyce represents the city of Dublin in *Dubliners*
- locate the short stories in *Dubliners* in relation to their literary and historical period.

Introduction

James Augustine Aloysius Joyce was born in Dublin on 2 February 1882 into a then prosperous family headed by John Stanislaus Joyce. John Joyce proved an unreliable provider, however, and the family was forced to move to a variety of addresses in Dublin in James's early years, as finances declined. The author lived in twenty-three different homes before he left Dublin. James Joyce was well educated, mostly at Jesuit schools, and took his degree in modern languages at University College Dublin. He went on to attempt a variety of careers, including medicine, teaching and music (as a singer). Although none of these ventures resulted in any permanent means of making a living, they did provide Joyce with a broad perspective on modern life and culture. His openness to new movements and technologies may be seen in his efforts to open Dublin's first cinema in 1909. Joyce published his first book, *Chamber Verse*, in 1907. After *Dubliners* (1914) came *A Portrait of the Artist as a Young Man* (1916) and *Ulysses* (1922), by which time he enjoyed international fame.

Dubliners is the only collection of short stories by this highly influential author, and is both a landmark in the development of the **genre** and a significant city text. Joyce wanted to present his city to the world because, as he explained in a letter to his publisher, no writer had yet done so, despite the fact that 'it has been a capital of Europe for thousands of years, it is supposed to be the second city of the British Empire and it is nearly three times as big as Venice' (quoted in the first footnote in Ellmann, 1983, p. 208). *Dubliners* was published in 1914, but the stories of which the collection is made up were written between 1904 and 1907. Each one seems, on the surface, to be a straightforward narrative of moments in the central characters' urban lives, written in an accessible form. But closer reading reveals effective stylistic devices and surprises, as well as an extraordinary richness of theme and topic, reflecting Joyce's own concerns in addition to those of contemporary British and Irish society at large.

The edition of *Dubliners* that is referred to in Chapters 1 and 2 is the Penguin Modern Classics (2000) edition, with an introduction and notes by Terence Brown. The stories that are discussed in detail are: 'The Sisters', 'An Encounter', 'Eveline', 'Two Gallants' and 'The Boarding House' (in Chapter 1), and 'Clay', 'A Painful Case' and 'The Dead' (in Chapter 2). You will be asked to read them at particular points in what follows.

Dublin and James Joyce

Figure 1.1   Sackville Street, Dublin, 1897. Photo: Francis Frith College/akg-images.

In 1907, when all the stories in *Dubliners* had been completed, Dublin was a rich mixture of radicalism and conservatism. The second city in the British Empire (as Joyce pointed out in the letter to his publisher, quoted above) due to its commercial significance, it had lost its own parliament in 1801. By the early twentieth century the city was a hotbed of nationalism. The political party Sinn Féin (meaning 'we ourselves') was founded in 1905, while the British Headquarters at Dublin Castle housed an armoury for 80,000 men. Readers of *Dubliners* are placed precisely in this context by Joyce's early reference to 'Great Britain Street' (p. 3; see also n. 10, p. 240), and many critics focus on the 'colonial setting' of his work (Kiberd, 1995, pp. 4–7, 330). The colonial perspective on Irish 'turbulence' is neatly summarised by a young English major in J.G. Farrell's novel *Troubles*, set a few years later than *Dubliners*, in 1919:

The Irish, as far as he knew, had always had a habit of making trouble. That was in the nature of things. As for the aim of their unruly behaviour, self-government for Ireland, that seemed quite absurd. … the important fact was this: the presence of the British signified a *moral* authority, not just an administrative one, here in Ireland as in India, Africa and elsewhere.

(Farrell, 1993 [1970], p. 57)

Figure 1.2   The Abbey Theatre, Dublin, 1913. Photo: Courtesy of the Abbey Theatre.

From 1880, Dublin had played an important role in the advance of the Gaelic revival that promoted a 'native' culture through literature, song and the Irish language. The famous poet W.B. Yeats (1865–1939) and playwright Lady Augusta Gregory (1852–1932) were its leading lights; they founded the Abbey Theatre (Figure 1.2), a driving force behind the revival, in 1904 – the same year that Joyce wrote 'The Sisters'. However, Dublin was also the site of a conservative flank that sought to prioritise a narrowly Catholic agenda, and objected to experimental or innovative works. These tensions between old and new, past and present – between what might be described as a backward-looking conservatism and a more forward-looking political and social agenda – complicate Dublin's relationship to its historical period, and this is something that will become apparent as we study this text. Such tensions erupted in the so-called 'Playboy Riots' that broke out at the Abbey Theatre in 1907, when audiences at John Millington Synge's innovative drama *The Playboy of the Western World* protested against what they considered to be an unjustifiable (and urban) slight upon traditional Irish peasantry in general, and modest rural womanhood in particular (see Figure 1.3).

Parts of this diverse city were infamous for their brothels and dissolute quarters, while others housed staunchly conservative 'purity' organisations dedicated to the rescue and rehabilitation of fallen women and the elimination of vice. Temperance organisations were common, and Joyce refers to several in the course of *Dubliners*. Religious tensions ran high, exacerbated by politics in many instances. Key businesses lay for the most part in Protestant hands (though the city was over eighty per cent Catholic), and sectarianism in employment preferment was commonly practised. The medical and educational systems were profoundly shaped by religious belief.

But Dublin was, above all else, an intimate city, with a population of only 290,000 in 1901 (London's was 3.9 million in 1880). Its complex relationship with modernity can be discerned from this fact too. After its rapid expansion in the eighteenth century, the city had entered a period of relative stagnation; the loss of its parliament was crucial here. Joyce describes the city as wearing merely the 'mask of a capital' in the story 'After the Race' (p. 39). The removal of much of the city's aristocracy to London left 'gaunt, spectral mansions' ('A Little Cloud', p. 66), empty monuments to previous wealth, and a cultural and financial vacuum – Dublin expanded slowly in comparison with many of her European neighbours, retaining visible links with her rural hinterland. Thus, although it embraced a limited modernity, offering a degree of anonymity and freedom in the manner of cities worldwide, Dublin was also small enough that people knew the reality of each other's lives, and shared a common set of social and political references. This fact underpins all the stories in *Dubliners*. The characters' concern that their actions will be observed and commented upon across the city was a reality of Dublin life. It is a key aspect of the urban context that had such a profound effect on James Joyce and, in turn, on the development of his writing.

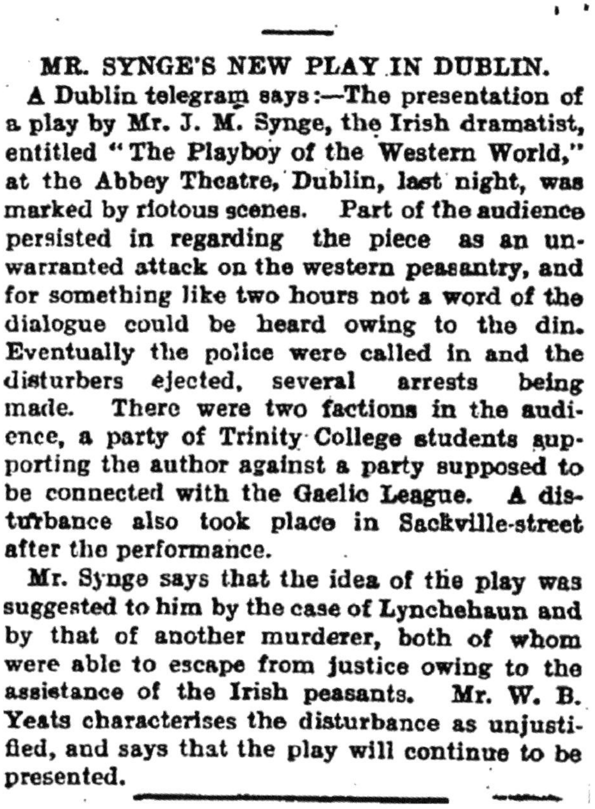

———

MR. SYNGE'S NEW PLAY IN DUBLIN.

A Dublin telegram says:—The presentation of a play by Mr. J. M. Synge, the Irish dramatist, entitled "The Playboy of the Western World," at the Abbey Theatre, Dublin, last night, was marked by riotous scenes. Part of the audience persisted in regarding the piece as an unwarranted attack on the western peasantry, and for something like two hours not a word of the dialogue could be heard owing to the din. Eventually the police were called in and the disturbers ejected, several arrests being made. There were two factions in the audience, a party of Trinity College students supporting the author against a party supposed to be connected with the Gaelic League. A disturbance also took place in Sackville-street after the performance.

Mr. Synge says that the idea of the play was suggested to him by the case of Lynchehaun and by that of another murderer, both of whom were able to escape from justice owing to the assistance of the Irish peasants. Mr. W. B. Yeats characterises the disturbance as unjustified, and says that the play will continue to be presented.

Figure 1.3 'Uproar in the theatre', *Manchester Guardian*, 30 January 1907, p. 7. Photo: © Guradian News & Media Ltd 1907.

Dubliners

Activity 1

Now turn to the contents page of *Dubliners*. Use the individual story titles to consider what themes or interests seem to link the stories. Can you group many of them together in this way?

Discussion

The city itself draws all the stories together, of course, and the collection is named after those who inhabit it. But smaller groupings are discernible in the story titles as well. There is a certain intimacy in the way first names appear as titles in two of the stories: 'Eveline' and 'Grace'. This seems to promise an in-depth and detailed portrayal of individuals' lives – linked, perhaps, to the idea of close observation introduced above. You may also have identifed an interest in family. 'The Sisters' begins the collection and 'A Mother' comes later on. Friendship, or sociability, seem prominent too in 'Two Gallants', 'After the Race' and, perhaps, in 'An Encounter'. Furthermore, the titles of two of the later stories in the collection could suggest a religious theme. 'A Mother' can be read for its likely **realist**, domestic tendencies but might also describe the Catholic focus on the Virgin Mary; 'Grace' suggests the favour of God (and, in fact, as you will see if you read it, this story turns out to be not about 'Grace', a person, but the Catholic Church). The potential for dual interpretations, which complicates this activity as you may have noticed, is present elsewhere, too (and is common throughout the collection). 'An Encounter' might also be read romantically; 'Clay' could be a character's name, but it indicates the earth as well, both literally and metaphorically. These 'double meanings' are one way in which Joyce's famously spare style in these stories can be highly productive. Coupled with the fact that *Dubliners* is made up of separate stories, offering multiple perspectives rather than, say, the sequential chapters common to a novel, they indicate that readers might well experience discontinuities and gaps in the text as a whole. We'll come back to this shortly, but it is something you could consider as you read on.

Joyce's tendency is to anatomise his city rather than to generalise in broad terms. The word 'Dublin' is absent until the fifth story; the reader gets to know it one view, one character, one story at a time. And yet the stories form a sequence, and they are most effective when read in this way. Joyce wrote to his eventual publisher, Grant Richards, on 5 May 1906, stating that 'I have tried to present [Dublin] to the indifferent public under four of its aspects: childhood, adolescence, maturity and public life. The stories are arranged in this order' (quoted in Ellmann, 1966, p. 134). So Dublin 'grows up' in *Dubliners* according to Joyce, and everything in each of the stories, from **narrator**, to subject, to formal technique, is designed to show its place in this order. With this in mind (as well as the overview of city texts provided in the introduction to this part of the book), you may wish to read the whole collection through at this point. If you would rather focus on the stories relevant to your study in this chapter, read 'The Sisters', 'An Encounter', 'Eveline', 'Two Gallants' and 'The Boarding House' now.

Joyce wrote most about this city after having left it. In 1904 he met Nora Barnacle, a young woman from Galway, recently arrived in Dublin where she worked as a hotel chambermaid. He first approached her in the street, and they agreed to meet again on 14 June, an appointment Nora failed to keep. Another meeting was arranged for 16 June: this was more successful, and they swiftly developed an intense relationship that resulted in their departure from the city in October. Joyce's distance from convention is marked in his relationship with Nora. They did not marry until 1931 (only ten years before Joyce's death), by which time they had two grown-up children.

Joyce visited Dublin three times after 1904, but never returned after 1912. He was intensely critical of what he saw as the narrow morality of many of its inhabitants. Declan Kiberd describes him as a 'world author', one who 'cut himself adrift from all cosy moorings', including those of a home city (1995, p. 327). Once cut adrift, Joyce proved how passionately interested in the city he could be. He set about constructing and reconstructing it in print. Joyce said of writing *Ulysses*, a later Dublin text:

> I tried to give the colour and tone of Dublin with my words; the drab, yet glistening atmosphere of Dublin, its hallucinatory vapors, its tattered confusion, the atmosphere of its bars, its social immobility; they could only be conveyed by the texture of my words. Thought and plot are not so important as some would make them out to be.
>
> (Joyce quoted in Igoe, 2007, p. 150)

Dubliners was the first stage in Joyce's engagement with the city from afar. It reflects his burgeoning obsession, born directly of his 'outsider' status. Now turn to the first story, to see how the process begins.

_____

Activity 2

Reread 'The Sisters'. In what ways does Joyce's narrator begin to convey the 'colour and tone' of Dublin?

Discussion

Specific shades of light and dark occur regularly through the story; they create the mood, and form some of the patterned contrasts that are also a notable feature. The reflected half-light of the opening helps to establish a religious tone and a heavy, near-death atmosphere. But as the narrator walks afterwards down the **alliterative**, and **allusive**, 'sunny side of the street', he muses that it is 'strange' that neither he nor the day is in a 'mourning mood' (p. 4). Something similar happens as he goes visiting at the house again after sunset but draws our attention to the 'tawny gold' reflection in the windows on his way in (p. 6). His feelings are not in line with what seems appropriate – our narrator has an oblique, even irreverent relationship to the events he recounts. He tells his tale in the first person (using 'I'), as you probably noted, and although it is not yet clear that the 'I' belongs to a child, a boldly questioning, though also fearful character is discernible from the start. Because our narrator is outside the house, rather than inside, we also know we are not in the hands of a centrally placed narrator, but someone more peripheral instead. The effect this has on you as a reader is worth considering – perhaps it seems an unusual or destabilising technique, or perhaps you are more aware of a sense of freedom and playfulness in the narrative as a result.

Three individual words stand out from the very first paragraph on p. 1, and contribute a great deal to Dublin's 'colour and tone' as Joyce is presenting them. These words are italicised, and the narrator draws further attention to them, relating them to one another. '[P]aralysis' refers most immediately, we might think, to the man who has had the stroke, for whom there is 'no hope' – but also think back to the muted light of this story, and the description of Dublin's contemporary 'stagnation' above. '[S]imony', as noted in most editions of the text, refers to the sin of making a profit from the sale of religious pardons or blessings. It both stresses Joyce's interest in religion in the city, specifically in what happens when the material world collides with the spiritual, and is linked to 'paralysis' by our narrator, as is the final word, 'gnomon', which means the pointer on a sundial. More significantly, in terms of how Joyce intends to convey the colour and tone of his city, 'gnomon' also refers to the part of a geometric shape that remains after a section has been taken away. This is how we might interpret those strange gaps and silences that persist in the story, particularly in dialogue, which help to conjure Dublin's 'tattered confusion' (see pp. 2 and 5 for early examples). The rumour and intrigue about the priest are never quite explained or put to rest. And why do 'the sisters' take so long to appear? Eventually we realise our narrator is a child – who does not, as we've seen, know it all. He understandably wanders off the subject, and contrasts with 'old Cotter' in several ways, notably in his ability to relate the drab aspects of Dublin life, but also to transform them in a brilliantly naive way – in the scene where he juxtaposes the corpse and the flowers, for example. His fellow characters' **malapropisms** (or humorous misuses of words) help create some additional absurdity in this particular story.

Important aspects of the 'colour and tone' of Dublin have been precisely conveyed by this first story, and will recur in other stories, as we shall see. And yet much remains indistinct. We do not learn the name of the youthful narrator, who himself did not know every relevant detail of the story he tells. Furthermore, Father Flynn's death itself does not form its climax, though the boy's feelings for him seem strong and genuine. From the beginning and that title which deflects readers away from the central, but unnamed, scandal, uncertainty is the predominant tone: Joyce did say in the quotation above that 'Thought and plot are not so important as some would make them out to be'. Our narrator is interested, alert and intensely involved in his story – but he is young, and cannot or will not process all that he feels and sees. He lacks a panoramic vision. The first-person **point of view** limits the matter of the narrative to what the **first-person narrator** knows, of course, and our narrator might be described as particularly 'limited' in some ways. The Dublin we start with is very much this narrator's idiosyncratic version, made up of 'dusky golden light', 'the flowers' and 'cream crackers' (pp. 6, 7). In the following section we'll explore some of the literary contexts of the period that helped to produce him.

Dubliners: modernity and modernism

Dubliners appeared in the same year that the First World War began. This fact is often noted by critics reading Joyce as part of the fundamental transformations in literature that were characteristic of the period. '[M]odernism in Ireland', writes the critic Emer Nolan, 'certainly began with Joyce' (2005, p. 163). 'Modernism', as a literary term, became current around the time *Dubliners* was published to describe new and experimental literature, including that written by Joyce. More generally, modernism can also be defined as the aesthetic and cultural reaction to and context of modernity. Modernism and urbanism go together, as noted in the 'Introduction to Part 1'. In this section we'll use *Dubliners*, a city text planned and constructed over ten years from the turn of the twentieth century, to explore this idea in more detail, beginning with a discussion of modernity, and moving on to modernism – all with particular reference to the Dublin of this period.

Figure 1.4   Gino Severini, *Le Boulevard*, 1910–11, oil on canvas. Photo: Estorick Collection, London, UK/The Bridgeman Art Library. © ADAGP, Paris and DACS, London 2011.

In contrast to the planned and more obviously modern cities of continental Europe, Dublin looked in the early twentieth century very much as if it had evolved in a haphazard manner. Kiberd remarks that:

> Unlike Paris, with its radial system of boulevards, centrally planned by Baron Hausmann in the nineteenth century, Dublin as a city is scarcely planned at all. No single mind or imagination lies behind it. It has never been destroyed and rebuilt in such a pattern – and apart from those Georgian squares at its very centre, it is more an agglomeration of villages like Ranelagh, Rathmines, Rathgar, Clontarf, Killester, Marino, all of which eventually got 'joined up'. When James Joyce called it 'the last of the intimate cities', he was in all likelihood recalling fondly this very villagey feel.
>
> (Kiberd, 2005, p. 293)

Kiberd suggests that it was, in fact, the complex nature of Dublin that led Joyce to treat it 'as a site of the modern' in his work (2005, p. 293). It was a city, yet based still on a village structure, and bound firmly at that time to its rural past – permitting both intimacy and anonymity among its inhabitants. We know that Dublin's development followed an unusual trajectory, and Joyce was exploiting a unique and fertile context in this respect. But in assessing the city as a 'site of the modern', comparison (as well as contrast) with Paris helps. Georg Simmel (see the 'Introduction to Part 1') regarded the metropolitan city of the early twentieth century as the site of a new kind of urban consciousness. This consciousness was inflected primarily by intimacy – he was interested in the sociology of the senses – and by the psychological effects of city living, especially in busy, crowded spaces. The predatory roving of Corley and Lenehan in 'Two Gallants', as well as Joyce's use of smell and sight, touch and taste, might well come to mind. Modern cities, as theorised by those such as Simmel, offered the ideal situation for the linked figure of the *flâneur*, literally a stroller, a wanderer, but also an observer. This figure was key to the literature of the period, and appears in many guises, as we shall see. Dublin's small scale, the open and public intimacy of its streets, provided Joyce with an arena similar in some ways to the boulevards and department stores of Paris, in which the *flâneur* was particularly susceptible to all the visual and aural stimuli the developing city could offer. Commercial engagement – the pleasure to be taken from the observation or purchase of a swiftly increasing range of commodities – was a notable feature of the *flâneur*'s activity at this time (Benjamin, 2002, pp. 14–26; Hahn, 2007).

The discourse of modernity often focuses on speed and light and travel, on the technological advances of the early twentieth century rather than its shops and boulevards. But the word 'modernity' was, in fact, coined by the French poet Charles Baudelaire (1821–1867) in the mid nineteenth century. He defined it as the transient, and contingent, and his writing on the subject was a foundational formulation of the modern in both literature and art. In his essay 'The painter of modern life' (1863), Baudelaire (like Simmel) focuses on the crowd, on his *flâneur*'s enjoyment and ownership of his urban surroundings:

> The crowd is his domain, just as the air is the bird's, and water that of the fish. His passion and his profession is to merge with the crowd. For the perfect idler, for the passionate observer it becomes an immense source of enjoyment to establish his dwelling

in the throng, in the ebb and flow, the bustle, the fleeting and the
infinite.

(Baudelaire, 1998 [1863], p. 105)

It is after Baudelaire, but in the context of a modernity that he helped
to shape, that what critic Richard Lehan calls the two 'major themes of
modernism' begin to emerge (1998, p. 77). Lehan's two themes are the
artist and the city, and, related as they are to the *flâneur*, they converge
in the observer who brings a distinct, highly subjective consciousness to
the urban, sometimes alienating, settings of modernist fiction and poetry
(1998, p. 77). One of the best-known examples, Clarissa Dalloway, can
be found in a novel by Virginia Woolf (1882–1941); in *Mrs Dalloway*'s
opening line, she 'said she would buy the flowers herself' (Woolf, 2009
[1925], p. 3). Mrs Dalloway sets out on her walk from the political
centre of the city – and empire – in Westminster, taking in the most
exclusive, expensive areas of London's commercial centre too. Woolf
foregrounds the relationship between the *flâneur* (or in this case
flâneuse) and metropolitan commerce in her novel.

The consumerist pleasures available to the characters in *Dubliners* are, of
course, more limited. Joyce's shops are less grand, the range of goods
more narrow, the finances of its inhabitants more precarious. The
related sense of closeness to a previous period – a rural past – also
affects the urban journeys in Joyce's text, as we have seen, influencing
the sense of modernity. (This will become most obvious as we discuss
the later stories in Chapter 2.) Nonetheless, in Dublin at the turn of the
twentieth century, 'everyone was a *flâneur*' (Kiberd, 2005, p. 294). In
'The Sisters', even the smallest narrator is shown lingering over the
'theatrical advertisements' in the shop windows as he wanders, an
activity that helps to dispel the 'mourning mood' (p. 4). Joyce designed
the stories in *Dubliners* to reflect the city's wide streets as open locations
of financial/social exchange as well as their sometimes intimidating
possession by individual characters. (The eighteenth-century Wide Street
Commission had established a street pattern of ready access and
spacious vistas: Dublin was a 'walker's city', as Terence Brown notes on
p. xvii of your edition of *Dubliners*.) With the exception of 'Eveline',
'The Boarding House' and 'The Dead', where the dramas are mainly
played out in domestically limited situations, the stories are characterised
by constant movement across the city, with men and women both
enjoying and literally exercising a new-found freedom – impossible for
women in an earlier period.

Joyce's interest in modernity is clearly signalled in *Dubliners*, as are his credentials as a modernist author. Added to his choice of an urban theme, and use of the short story genre (to be explored below), aspects of his technique are fundamental here as well, of course, and feature in the discussion that follows: his experimentation with the mix between **realism** and **symbolism**, for example, and the challenge of uncertainty posed by all of the stories in their different ways. Modernist authors were also known for their attention to previously taboo subject matter. Joyce struggled to get the collection published because of publishers' fears of obscenity charges. In 1907 Grant Richards argued with Joyce over his choice of language and references to sex. Joyce took his work to another publisher, who similarly requested changes and cuts, and Joyce was forced to return to Richards, who eventually published the (edited) collection in 1914.

The short story was becoming an increasingly popular genre in the period – favoured by publishers in the literary marketplace and the reading public. For modernist writers, focus on this genre was also a very effective way of signalling aesthetic distance from the nineteenth-century novel. Usually much shorter than a novel ('Eveline', as you will see, is only five and a half pages long, while 'The Dead' weighs in at fifty pages in the edition we're using), the tight focus demanded by a short story made it easier to 'anatomise' a city, to return to that word we used earlier. Collecting fifteen examples together, as Joyce does in *Dubliners*, produces a diverse, complex range of individualised views of the city overall.

From childhood to church: 'An Encounter' and 'Eveline'

In this section we will explore further stories from *Dubliners* in detail. Central themes (such as religion, sex and paralysis) emerge in more than one story, and your work on each of them will enable you to develop a sense of these connections. It is also important to maintain awareness of the specific genre Joyce chose. Joyce originally set out to write and publish separate stories, but he chose in the end to put them together in *Dubliners*. The variety is crucial to their overall effect, and yet the stories also speak to each other in their portrayal of this city. The recurring themes mentioned above contribute here, and Joyce's own key to the structural organisation of the text, quoted earlier, is worth repeating to emphasise the importance of the relationship between the stories and their progressive order: 'I have tried to present [Dublin] to the indifferent public under four of its aspects: childhood, adolescence, maturity and public life. The stories are arranged in this order' (Joyce quoted in Ellmann, 1966, p. 134). The next two stories we shall discuss take us from childhood to adolescence in his scheme.

Activity 3

Reread 'An Encounter'. Describe some aspects of the childhood Joyce is representing here. What does it add to our developing sense of Joyce's Dublin?

Discussion

As 'An Encounter' begins we are clearly placed in a schoolboy world. Boys' magazines, and tales of the 'Wild West' (p. 11), are ranged against the classical Latin to be learned in the classroom. 'Low' and 'high' culture are in active conflict. 'Escape' is key here, from all that the adult world represents ('eight-o'clock mass' (p. 11), Latin text books) into 'wild sensations' and 'chronicles of disorder' (p. 12). Our narrator is clearly a child, therefore, but you may have noticed that 'we' is more prevalent than 'I' in the telling of his tale. This in itself is an interesting distinction between this story and 'The Sisters', suggestive of a broader, older focus – in keeping with the later subject matter. The narrator styles himself – and his desires – as unruly, but he is also discerning, preferring the 'sometimes literary' (p. 12) detective story, to the more obviously populist Wild West adventure. Yet despite the effects of an education he cannot help but display, the frustrated quest for freedom from the dominating world of adults is a genuine one. He can't sleep due to his excitement the night before he and his friends are to meet for their own adventure; his absolute pleasure and peace while waiting alone on the bridge might be described as one of the abiding images of the collection. Once the boys are joined there are high-spirited games, some of which introduce echoes of the imperialist theme (cowboys versus Indians, for example (see also n. 8, p. 246)). These games culminate in the boys being shouted at by the working men at the Liffey riverside, and, additionally, in schoolboy dreams brought on by this 'spectacle of Dublin's commerce' (p. 15). They imagine running away, joining the trade on those big ships.

Quickly, though, as the day becomes 'sultry', the tone gets darker. There is a growing sense of futility even as we are introduced to the idea that the boys may actually have something to escape from. Mahoney chases, but does not catch, a cat, and the final encounter of the story unsettles with its indistinct paedophiliac overtones. That the man is sexually threatening is clearer to those reading the story than it is to the boyish narrator – despite the fact that he, or at least Mahoney, knows what we do not (whether the man masturbates at the end of the field). But, true to the point of view Joyce has used to tell the story, the narrator's half-innocent, half-knowing 'agitation' (p. 20) is forgotten quickly enough as they move on, and we are left at the conclusion with a completely different, also unanswered, question about the boys' relationship instead. By the end of 'An Encounter' we have learned more about how Dublin might look and feel from a boy's fleeting perspective; school, or school avoidance, friendship, curiosity, and the unsettling feeling of being out of one's depth, have all featured here. We have also had our thoughts directed to the Liffey as a route into, but more significantly out of, the city.

'An Encounter' relates ideas of escape very much to childhood. By the time we get to 'Eveline', in which escape is also a theme, Joyce's treatment of childhood is over. He conveys this development formally. The first-person narrator he has used in 'An Encounter' and 'The Sisters' is left behind. 'Eveline' is the shortest story in the collection, and is told using a **third-person narrator**. Focus on this particular example of the genre proves particularly productive in the consideration of Joyce's treatment of **plot**.

Activity 4

Reread 'Eveline' and make notes on its plot as you do so. What happens in the story?

Discussion

'Eveline' is a story in which very little happens. There is hardly any action or movement of any kind. You may well have found it difficult to write down many plot events, even at the conclusion (can we be sure what exactly happens here?). Reading it just after 'An Encounter', you might have noted that the physical energy of the earlier story is entirely absent; a 'plot', in so far as it consists of events linked together in a relationship of cause and effect, is thin on the ground too. 'Eveline' develops as a series of thoughts and reminiscences, on the narrowness of existence, and the possibility of escape from Dublin, rather than as a sequence of occurrences. But the consequences of inertia are made plain. If Eveline does not take action, and somehow transform her encounter with Frank into forward movement, her life at the age of nineteen will be over. At the docks, when she stands on the brink of happiness, it seems she cannot do so, and, as far as we can tell, Frank is swept away from her on board the ship that was to take her to a better life. Eveline's silent appeal to

God 'to show her what was her duty' (p. 33) is apparently met with paralysis, and she is incapable of speech, sight or movement. In one of Joyce's more cruel descriptions, Eveline is rendered inhuman: 'She set her white face to him, passive, like a helpless animal. Her eyes gave him no sign of love or farewell or recognition' (p. 34).

'Eveline' is a good example of Joyce's interest in *Dubliners* in conveying the inner consciousness of his characters. The third-person narrator tells the story almost entirely from Eveline's point of view; it is her thoughts, feelings and perceptions that we are exposed to. What matters here is not action or plot, but the perceptions and psychology of the character. 'Eveline' is a deliberately modified emigration story, in that its **protagonist** stays put. Its anti-climactic and even uncertain conclusion (as noted above, we can't be entirely sure what happens at the close of the story) can be compared with that of 'An Encounter', in which the subject changes more than once but is never neatly disposed of (see the remark in the discussion to Activity 3 about the 'unanswered question' as to the boys' relationship). Joyce's refusal to provide his readers with narrative closure or the satisfaction of a happy ending is characteristic of modernist writing. In conjunction with his subject matter, it suggests by the end of the fourth story that his Dubliners will not go very far, and will not be transformed, despite their dreams. The short story form Joyce has chosen is put to good modernist use elsewhere, too: there are other oblique endings throughout the collection which, though often including a moment of vision or realisation for the protagonist, almost never form a satisfying or neat conclusion, as such. (Such moments of vision are often described as 'epiphanies' in any discussion of Joyce's writing, a term we will come back to, and one he himself adapted with regard to his later books.) Joyce manipulates readers' expectations as to plot while providing his own take on Dublin's effects on its citizens at this time.

The constituencies Joyce represents in these early stories are, respectively, boys and young women. These are the Dublin inhabitants to whom he is giving a voice, and he does so realistically (in particular, see his use of Dublin slang in 'An Encounter') and without nostalgia for childhood (think about the intended cruelty to the cat). The narrator of 'An Encounter' is busy growing up, which makes the lack of an evident conclusion to the story a strikingly effective technique. The boys' experience of life is related to Eveline's, through powerlessness and the sense of paralysis, for example, but there is far less physical expression, the outlook is bleaker, and so the stakes become higher overall in the woman's tale. This is signified, perhaps, by the fact she is given a name. Joyce is most concerned in 'Eveline' with examining the tremendous pressures brought to bear upon unmarried women in Ireland in this period. Through a forceful combination of societal expectations and religious obligations, many women were placed in Eveline's position, expected to sacrifice any chance of happiness for the good of others. It was not uncommon for the youngest daughter in the family to remain unmarried, in order to take care of ageing parents, only to spend her own old age alone. Religious veneration for the Virgin Mary played a potent part in this expectation, where women were to direct themselves uncomplainingly towards service, seeking their reward in heaven. In this case, Eveline feels herself further bound by a deathbed promise made to her mother, to keep the family together as long as possible. This kind of promise was regarded as absolutely binding in Ireland, and Eveline shoulders the burden, despite seeing clearly that it means she will replicate her mother's own wasted life. This must have been especially poignant for Joyce. He had returned to Dublin in 1903 because his mother was terminally ill and, although beside her as she died, he refused his uncle's request to kneel in prayer. In 'Eveline', the deathbed scene becomes not a source of active defiance, as it was in Joyce's own case, but the death knell for the family's second female generation.

The role of the Catholic Church in circumscribing women's lives is subtly signalled in the story. As Eveline glances around the room, her eye passes over the photograph of an unnamed priest, and a print of Blessed Margaret Mary Alacoque (p. 30). The priest is notable for the fact that he lived in Melbourne, Australia – one peripheral character, then, who managed an escape from the city. The woman, by contrast, was a member of the seventeenth-century nobility, venerated by the Catholic Church because of her life of extreme sacrifice. Despite her wealthy background, she chose a path of mortification and denial (what the Church terms 'corporal mortifications': painful exercise, scourging and extreme physical punishments) to purify herself, and devoted herself to charitable work and prayer. Eveline has not made that choice, but has had it thrust upon her. She is just as effectively paralysed – look again at the story's end – growing up in one sense only, while remaining a child, experientially, at the same time.

The theme of paralysis links many of the stories in *Dubliners*, and you should consider its different manifestations as you reread them. The city as Joyce represents it seems to possess a particular power to limit individual action: it is the past, in particular (in the form of family and Church tradition), that holds on to Eveline. Dublin's intimacy as discussed so far means that freedom for the weak and vulnerable would necessitate dramatic action of the kind way beyond such characters' scope. The obsession with superficial respectability and conformity underlines the hopelessness of their case. Eveline is unable to defy her father because of his patriarchal authority, just as the boy in 'An Encounter' is helpless to run away from the obscurely menacing man who engages him in an uncomfortable and inappropriate conversation. Later characters experience something more like freedom, qualified though it may be.

'Freedoms' of the city and epiphany: 'Two Gallants' and 'The Boarding House'

Eveline's failure to leave Dublin may also be read as the essence of Joyce's relationship with the city. In his own life he believed that he could only find happiness and, more importantly, recognition, outside that capital. Yet, like Eveline, he was ambivalent about breaking the powerful ties to Dublin. It may have been suffocating, parochial and restrictive (sex, scandal and excitement belong to London, Paris and Berlin, we learn from various stories in this collection), but it was also the single most creative element in his life. Indeed, it was precisely because Dublin offered examples of sectarianism, and dramatic and divisive social and sexual politics, that it proved an enduring source of inspiration.

The two main characters of the next story we will discuss in detail offer a definite contrast to the youthful protagonists we have met so far. We have moved on to 'maturity' in Joyce's structural model of the text. Their cocksure ownership of Dublin's streets was considered so scandalous that the story was almost omitted from the collection altogether.

Activity 5

Reread 'Two Gallants'. What does the story reveal about sexual mores in early twentieth-century Dublin?

Discussion

'Two Gallants' is a story in which traditional expectations of romantic and sexual relations are overturned. It is a shocking tale for what it reveals about the nature of contemporary sexual, and indeed broadly human, relations. The two central characters, Lenehan and Corley (whose suggestive name, spoken, as Joyce tells us, with an aspirated first letter, echoes 'Whorley'), have no professions or incomes, and survive with varying degrees of success by sponging off their acquaintances. Such material could be treated humorously, but Joyce does not take this option. 'Two Gallants' delineates the complete degradation of its characters. Corley is a detestable creature, physically repulsive, ignorant and vulgar. He depends upon favours, connections and a low-level patronage for his living. Most dramatically, he prostitutes himself to domestic servants whom he solicits in the city. His modus operandi is to mislead deliberately the women he picks up (none of whom he recalls by name) as to his real identity, and his intentions of forming some sort of recognised relationship with them. He prides himself on their mistreatment.

Such transactions could only take place in the city because it offered the necessary anonymity, as well as a plentiful supply of clients. Dublin had several notorious red-light districts in this period (where sex was both the commodity for sale, and on view, or 'advertised'), the most famous of which was 'Monto' (see Figure 1.5). This area, on the inner-city's north side, close to the docks and the army barracks, had an estimated 1,600 prostitutes by 1900. But Joyce depicts an unusual, and for many a more unsettling, element of the trade. Although the concept of men marrying for money was not unknown, the notion of a man experimenting with what was regarded as an exclusively female profession was a bold literary step.

Joyce was on more solid contemporary ground with 'Two Gallants' in the analysis of the economics of modern city life, and its potentially demeaning consequences for all. Georg Simmel's essay, 'The metropolis and mental life', includes a whole section on the metropolitan attitude to money. Simmel argues that this attitude 'hollows out the core of things, their peculiarities, their specific values and their uniqueness and incomparability in a way which is beyond repair' (Simmel, 1998 [1903], p. 55). In this reading, human relations are stripped down to merely economic essentials in – or by – the modern city, resulting in matter-of-factness and indifference, both of which characterise the gallants'

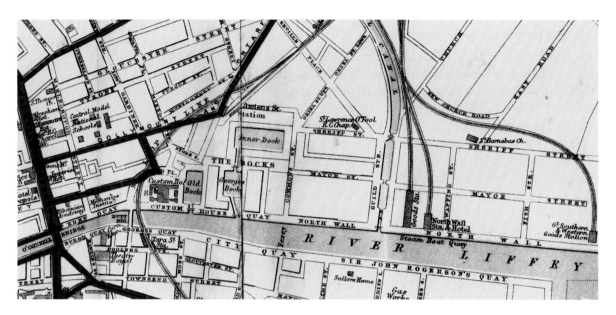

Figure 1.5   Dublin, city map in the 1912 edition of *Black's Guide of Ireland*, London, A & C Black. Photo: Shane Wilson. Ellmann tells us: '... the brothel area, "Monto", [was] so-called from Montgomery Street [in the upper left-hand corner of the map]. Monto was labeled about 1885 by the *Encyclopedia Britannica* as the worst slum in Europe. It was concentrated chiefly in Mecklenburg Street, which became Tyrone Street and is now a dreary Railway Street' (1983, p. 367).

approach to their peers. It may be hard to feel sympathy for the pair. But Joyce's two protagonists are also, like the women they prey on, victims of the financial climate, through the poverty of choice that confronts them. Joyce uses circles symbolically throughout to show how: Terence Brown's notes point out the two gallants' circular, repetitive movement across the city, as well as the significance of the final 'dead-end' (n. 69, p. 266). Equally potent is the round coin of the story's climax, small as it is, indicating the depressing limits and effects of their ambition – their degree of entrapment in a monetary economy of its kind, at that time. Though the coin is of low value, the woman could ill afford to part with it, and Corley has sold himself for little reward. The characters of this story show that the city can induce a kind of paralysis not only in those who, like Eveline, are more physically restricted, but also in those who move through it with more apparent ease. The contemporary idea of modern urban 'freedom' is endlessly qualified in this as in other tales.

Corley's character was a means through which Joyce broke new ground in this story, as we have suggested. Many Victorian novels featured prostitutes, but they were invariably tragic figures, or the proverbial prostitute with a 'heart of gold', an inherently good working-class character whose essential nature rose above her sordid profession (the best-known example being Nancy in Charles Dickens's *Oliver Twist* (1838)). They aroused the reader's sympathy, even as they largely remained irredeemable. The 'sauntering' Corley, who knows better than to spend any money on any of his girls, and who feels no regret that the one woman he had genuine feelings for is now a prostitute – because of him, Lenehan indicates – is cut from very different cloth (pp. 46–7).

Activity 6

What techniques does Joyce use to characterise Lenehan and Corley in 'Two Gallants'? Concentrate your answer on the first three pages of the story.

Discussion

The **characterisation** of Lenehan and Corley is colourful, physically unforgiving and rich. The second paragraph dissects Lenehan as to his ruddiness, wheeziness, expressiveness, but underlying 'ravaged' nature (p. 43), as keenly as if he had been some kind of medical specimen. Corley's 'head', we are similarly told, was 'large, globular and oily; it sweated in all weathers' (p. 45). Based on their physicality, Joyce's characterisation is also built out of the contrasts between the men. Corley is aggressive, rude and stereotypically 'burly' (p. 45) and masculine, barging his friend off the pavement, and forcing him to run breathlessly throughout their venture. Lenehan is, on the other hand, feminised. He trips along in Corley's wake, hanging upon his words, and is dependent upon his favour for survival. Appropriately enough, all these two characters have is each other – they both rely heavily on mutually comprehended Dublin slang – but even this relationship is complex, and ultimately doomed. In language that evokes significant religious imagery, Lenehan, the 'disciple' (p. 55), begs Corley at the conclusion for proof of his success.

Like doubting Thomas, who believed only when he saw the wounds on Christ's palm, Lenehan has to see what is hidden in Corley's hand. Following the religious theme, the 'small gold coin' (p. 55) is also reminiscent of the fee that Judas received for selling Christ to the Jews. Having betrayed the unnamed woman, and themselves, the two men appear set on the same path, with no possibility of redemption.

Joyce creates in 'Two Gallants' two male characters who are markedly adept at evading any sense of responsibility. The next story in the collection continues the theme of the sale of sexual favours for gain. The politics may be differently configured, but this story also invites analysis of the absence of strong, positive male role models in Joyce's text, and of the effects of industrialisation, and colonialism, on the contemporary notion of the family. Richard Lehan suggests that Joyce, and other European writers of this time, 'were considering in literary terms what Marx and Engels had taken up in economic terms' (1998, p. 107). In *Dubliners*, this consideration includes:

> the breakdown of the family as the young leave the land; the effect of this transformation on women; the rise of the criminal as an urban type; the rise of urban institutions like the boardinghouse [where cheap rented accommodation could be found], which in the city substitutes for the nuclear family.

> (Lehan, 1998, p. 107)

We turn to 'The Boarding House' now.

Activity 7

Reread 'The Boarding House' and identify what this story tells us about sex and the family in the city, in comparison with 'Two Gallants'.

Discussion

There was no family network in 'Two Gallants'. Here, the family is the way into the tale. But sex is still for sale – in the house, rather than on the streets. The shiftless Mr Mooney has gone 'to the devil' (p. 56) and Mrs Mooney is in charge. Her superficially respectable front conceals her role as '*The Madam*' (p. 57). The horror in this tale is that it is her own daughter whom she effectively encourages into prostitution. The story opens with a succinct picture of a woman whose most formidable weapons in her fight for advancement are Dublin's rigid social codes, which she can manipulate to her advantage. She has disposed of her drunken husband, enlisting the help of her priest to ensure that she retained her home, children and business assets. Mrs Mooney made her case directly to the Church (divorce in Ireland in this period was expensive and difficult to obtain). Her 'separation', which has no legal basis, will nevertheless carry sufficient moral weight to mean that her husband will have no claim upon her. The factual rights or wrongs of the situation are of no account – the irony of the Church's support for such a woman is left to the reader to note. Mrs Mooney 'dealt with moral problems as a cleaver deals with meat' (p. 58), Joyce writes in a devastating **simile**, evoking Mrs Mooney's earlier career as a butcher, and placing Polly, the 'meat', on the same level as the goods her mother has previously sold. Her daughter is a commodity to be displayed as attractively as possible to secure the highest bidder. The 'disreputable sheriff's man' (p. 57), calling unsolicited to the office where Polly worked, would not fulfil that function. So Mrs Mooney brought her home, where she would have 'the run of the young men' (p. 57). Doran's first sexual encounter with Polly occurs following her bath, when she approaches him in her nightdress on the pretext of relighting her candle. The opportunity thus offered to Polly to show her potential as a wife confirms Mrs Mooney's shrewdness (p. 58).

Joyce's explicit rendering of Mrs Mooney's thoughts is, perhaps, the most expressive of all his techniques in this story. She embraces all the outward signs of respectability, but is shown to be a conniving and ruthless individual, who actively sets out to trap a husband for her daughter, regardless of love or even suitability. Rather than offering protection to her offspring, the mother in this story is head of a disturbing and sexually dysfunctional nuclear family – seemingly experiencing the lack, as noted above, of a strong and positive male character. If, as Lehan suggests above, the boarding house became in this period the urban equivalent of a nuclear family, Joyce's twist in this story is to experiment with sexuality, and with notions of masculinity and femininity within that new 'family' as well.

Boarding houses were a significant part of Dublin life. At the turn of the twentieth century, one-third of the city's population was not Dublin-born, and many of these workers lived in boarding houses. Joyce himself had occupied a series of rented rooms in Dublin, and was well aware of the dramatic possibilities they offered. Young people, away from parental supervision, and beyond the communities that had known them from birth, were liberated in ways that were impossible at home – though, as further evidence of its paradoxical nature as 'home', Polly sings 'I'm a ... naughty girl' in her own 'front drawing-room' (p. 57). Mrs Mooney's guest house teeters on the fringes of respectability: the mention of the 'artistes' (p. 56) who frequent it underpins its dissolute character, and the description of the Sunday night entertainments, at which Polly performs, are highly suggestive of a brothel instead. We are considering this story in the section entitled '"Freedoms" of the city and epiphany'. Dublin certainly offered chances for sexual licence, as indicated by Doran's review of his earlier life: 'As a young man he had sown his wild oats, of course' (p. 61). But as we have seen in other stories, it also constrained individuals' lives, through its parochialism, narrow-mindedness and, as Joyce amplifies in this case, ubiquitous and overpowering institutionalised scrutiny. The priest to whom Doran makes his confession extracts every humiliating detail of the affair, leaving him with no choice but to marry Polly. Doran is trapped by his Church, his employer, and his fear of what people will say of him. Despite the intensely private nature of his dilemma, it feels simultaneously true that the whole city knows his situation, and despises him for it. Not even the most private of transactions – says Joyce – can be concealed in this city at this time.

Activity 8

Look carefully at the conclusion of the story (from 'Polly sat for a little time ...' on p. 63 until the end of the story). How would you describe what happens to Polly's character as the story comes to a close?

Discussion

One thing you may have noted in response to this question is that paralysis is not uniform in *Dubliners*: some characters – like Polly here – are transformed in this text. When Doran leaves his room for his unpleasant interview with Mrs Mooney, Polly is left weeping on his bed. Then we witness a remarkable alteration, as she slowly and deliberately brings her perturbation under control, forgetting or repressing her agitation and the reason behind it. She is taken out of real time and placed in a dream-like zone, a 'revery' (p. 64). As we watch, we realise that the outcome of the confrontation was never in doubt: Mrs Mooney was always, as she puts it herself, going to 'win' (p. 60). Doran has been shown to be, aside from his earning power, an incidental element in the plot. What is on one level shockingly precise in Joyce's story is made to resonate much more widely by this particular, and intense, technique. Polly's patient transformation, and her 'vision', show her knowledge and acceptance of her place in this city world as Joyce depicts it – where marriage has nothing to do with love. She grows into this world before our eyes.

We might well identify Polly's experience as an example of the prominent Joycean technique noted earlier, the '**epiphany**'. (Joyce was borrowing and updating the biblical association with the Magi's discovery of the infant Christ in his naming of the term.) This technique was dedicated to producing moments of intensity and revelation in his characters, often towards the close of the narrative. Terence Brown debates in the introduction to the edition of *Dubliners* we're using whether Polly's experience is an example simply of intense realism, or the more revelatory and notably climactic 'epiphany' (pp. xxxiii–xxxvi). Critics disagree, in fact, as to whether there are examples of the epiphany in this short story collection at all, or if they only emerge in later works. (Joyce himself conspicuously avoided employing the term in relation to *Dubliners*.) Nonetheless, it is useful to bear it in mind as one possible aspect of his technique in this text, and Polly Mooney's resonant transformation is certainly treated very differently from Mr Doran's plodding and mundane realisation as to his fate:

> The harm was done. What could he do now but marry her or run away? He could not brazen it out. The affair would be sure to be talked of and his employer would be certain to hear of it.
>
> …
>
> It was not altogether his fault that it had happened.

(pp. 61, 62)

We shall return to the subject of epiphany in more detail in Chapter 2.

Conclusion

In this chapter you have studied several stories in detail, and considered how each is articulated within Joyce's collection to anatomise Dublin life. You've thought about some recurrent themes, and the way they establish connections between the stories. (If the idea of these recurrent themes interests you, you may want to turn briefly to 'A Mother', from the 'public life' section of the text, to compare its representation of an equally determined and ambitious mother with Mrs Mooney's story.) We noted Joyce's wordplay, and his deployment of dual meanings, in the titles of some of the stories. The multifaceted 'gnomon' was discussed as a key term for the collection and its uncertainties. Joyce often combines the literal and the symbolic and, as you will see when you read 'The Dead', the biblical roots of two characters' names (Gabriel and Lily) join them together through matters of sex and/or childbirth, even before we hear them converse. Other techniques have emerged too. We saw that colours are important, and contribute to what is often an intensely visual experience of reading the text, for example in the characterisation of Lenehan, Corley and the woman in 'Two Gallants' (pp. 47–9). Particular colours are often used symbolically, and one of Joyce's favourites is the colour brown. Where this is used, he is signalling his themes of paralysis, decay and corruption, or making a largely negative assessment of character. Consider how often the colour summarises a character's life or expectations in the stories you have read, and look out for it too in the stories in Chapter 2. Sense impressions more broadly are also vital to his cityscape, as we have suggested – sounds and smells, and physical contact or the experience of its lack. We have also considered Joyce's use of different types of narrators, his skill in representing the inner consciousness of his characters, and the way in which his stories seem intent on withholding the pleasures of a tidy resolution of the plot or the gratification of a happy ending. In Chapter 2, we continue our examination of Joyce's treatment of Dublin and of the techniques he employs in anatomising the city.

References

Baudelaire, C. (1998 [1863]) 'The painter of modern life' in Kolocotroni, V., Goldman, J.A. and Taxidou, O. (eds) *Modernism: An Anthology of Sources and Documents*, Edinburgh, Edinburgh University Press, pp. 102–9.

Benjamin, W. (2002) *The Arcades Project*, Cambridge, MA, Harvard University Press.

Ellmann, R. (ed.) (1966) *The Letters of James Joyce*, vol. 2, London, Faber and Faber.

Ellmann, R. (1983) *James Joyce*, Oxford, Oxford University Press.

Farrell, J.G. (1993 [1970]) *Troubles*, London, Phoenix.

Hahn, H. (2007) 'Boulevard culture and advertising as spectacle in nineteenth-century Paris' in Cowan, A. and Steward, J. (eds) *The City and the Senses: Urban Culture Since 1500*, Aldershot, Ashgate, pp. 156–75.

Igoe, V. (2007) *James Joyce's Dublin Houses and Nora Barnacle's Galway*, Dublin, Lilliput Press.

Joyce, J. (2000 [1914]) *Dubliners*, Penguin Modern Classics, London, Penguin.

Kiberd, D. (1995) *Inventing Ireland*, London, Jonathan Cape.

Kiberd, D. (2005) *The Irish Writer and the World*, Cambridge, Cambridge University Press.

Lehan, R. (1998) *The City in Literature: An Intellectual and Cultural History*, Berkeley, CA, University of California Press.

Nolan, E. (2005) 'Modernism and the Irish revival' in Cleary, J. and Connolly, C. (eds) *The Cambridge Companion to Modern Irish Culture*, Cambridge, Cambridge University Press, pp. 157–72.

Simmel, G. (1998 [1903]) 'The metropolis and mental life' in Kolocotroni, V., Goldman, J.A. and Taxidou, O. (eds) *Modernism: An Anthology of Sources and Documents*, Edinburgh, Edinburgh University Press, pp. 51–60.

Woolf, V. (2009 [1925]) *Mrs Dalloway*, Oxford, Oxford University Press.

Further reading

Fagan, T. (2000) *Monto: Madams, Murder and Black Coddle*, Dublin, Printwell Press.

Ferriter, D. (1994) *The Transformation of Ireland, 1900–2000*, London, Profile.

Finegan, J. (1978) *The Story of Monto*, Dublin, Mercier Press.

Hutchins, P. (1950) *James Joyce's Dublin*, London, Grey Walls.

Igoe, V. (1994) *A Literary Guide to Dublin: Writers in Dublin – Literary Associations and Anecdotes*, London, Methuen.

Jeffreys, S. (1985) *The Spinster and Her Enemies: Feminism and Sexuality, 1880–1930*, London, Pandora Press.

Kiberd, D. (2009) Ulysses *and Us: The Art of Everyday Living*, London, Faber and Faber.

Mercier, V. (1962) *The Irish Comic Tradition*, Oxford, Oxford University Press.

Nicholson, V. (2008) *Singled Out: How Two Million Women Survived Without Men after the First World War*, London, Viking.

Simmel, G. (1997) 'The sociology of space' in Frisby, D. and Featherstone, M. (eds) *Simmel on Culture: Selected Writings*, London, Sage.

Chapter 2
James Joyce, *Dubliners*: paralysis, memory and 'The Dead'

Sara Haslam

Aims

This chapter will:

- develop the close textual analysis of James Joyce's *Dubliners* and explore in detail three further stories from the collection: 'Clay', 'A Painful Case' and 'The Dead'

- examine additional ways in which Joyce represents the city of Dublin in *Dubliners*, linked to paralysis and memory in particular

- consider in more detail the notion of 'period' in reference to the text.

Introduction

In this chapter we will explore three further stories from James Joyce's *Dubliners*, including the longest and most famous, 'The Dead'. While the theme of paralysis, as introduced in Chapter 1, is developed here, we shall also be devoting attention to Joyce's use of memory, and particularly the ways in which it helps to counter the prevalence of paralysis in the collection. Memory is also important when considering *Dubliners* with reference to ideas about period, as we shall see. If you have not yet done so, you should read 'Clay', 'A Painful Case' and 'The Dead' now.

Single Dublin life: 'Clay' and 'A Painful Case'

Maria, the protagonist of 'Clay', confirms the limited opportunities available to single women in the city. In this period, a woman's destiny was largely regarded as marriage and motherhood, and spinsterhood as a failure. However, from the turn of the twentieth century, increasing numbers of women had begun to press for access to education and to wider employment opportunities, and to envisage lives for themselves beyond marriage. Maria clearly reflects on this as she confidently 'arranged in her mind all she was going to do and thought how much better it was to be independent and to have your own money in your pocket' (p. 98), and then moves across the city, buying small treats for her friends. Dublin was indeed opening itself up to professional and working women: women could attend Trinity College Dublin (from 1904) and the National University (from 1908), and were entering the workforce in large numbers, thanks to wider employment opportunities as secretaries and clerical workers.

Activity 1

Reread 'Clay'. What kind of narrator does the story have?

Discussion

You have probably identified that 'Clay' has a third-person narrator. It is reassuringly present throughout the paragraphs on the opening page (for example, 'Maria was a very, very small person indeed but she had a very long nose and a very long chin' (p. 95)). Moreover, these early paragraphs straightforwardly inform us as to several different aspects of Maria's physical appearance, character and life, in what seems to be a clear omniscient (or all-seeing and all-knowing) style.

As discussed in Chapter 1, the term 'point of view' signifies the perspective from which a story is told. A first-person narrator brought us into *Dubliners* – the 'I' of 'The Sisters' – and we saw events through his eyes. The narrative was consequently limited to what the boy knew. By the time of 'Eveline', as also noted in the last chapter, Joyce was using a third-person narrator – of a particular kind. The narrator of 'Eveline' tells the story for the most part from the protagonist's point of view. We are going to think about this kind of narrator in more detail now because it features in the main in 'Clay' too. You do not have to read on very far in 'Clay' to see how little even-handedness there is in Joyce's approach to the telling of this tale. To return to the term used above in the discussion, the narrator rarely seems to be 'omniscient', in fact. The narrative is often filtered through Maria's consciousness: what we get is her particular view of reality, and events are ordered according to her experience of them. So we can hear Maria's 'voice', rather than that of an omniscient third-person narrator, in these lines:

> She arranged in her mind all she was going to do and thought about how much better it was to be independent and to have your own money in your pocket. She hoped they would have a nice evening. She was sure they would but she could not help thinking what a pity it was Alphy and Joe were not speaking.

(p. 98)

This technique, which involves a very close correlation between the narrative voice and the voice of a character, is usually known as **free indirect style** (sometimes called 'free indirect speech'). The novelist and critic David Lodge gives a useful illustration of the difference between free indirect style and other forms of representing characters' speech and consciousness:

For readers who may not be familiar with this term, let me give a very simple example. *'Is that the clock striking twelve?'* Cinderella exclaimed. *'Dear me, I shall be late.'* That is a combination of direct or quoted speech and a narrator's description. *'Cinderella enquired if the clock was striking twelve and expressed a fear that she would be late'* is reported or indirect speech, in which the same information is conveyed but the individuality of the character's voice is suppressed by the narrator's. *'Was that the clock striking twelve? She would be late'* is free indirect speech. Cinderella's concern is now a silent, private thought, expressed in her own words, to which we are given access without the overt mediation of a narrator. Grammatically it requires a narrator's tag, such as 'she asked herself,' 'she told herself,' but we take this as understood. Hence it is termed 'free'. The effect is to locate the narrative in Cinderella's consciousness.

(Lodge, 2002, p. 37)

Dubliners is well known for its use of free indirect style. It is a common narrative strategy in those tales that are not told in the first person. One major effect of Joyce's employment of free indirect style is that there is no narrator passing comment, or making overt moral judgements, on events as they unfold. (See Lodge's more general phrase above about the lack of 'overt mediation of a narrator'.) Joyce switches from first-person narration as his main characters 'grow up', and therefore might reasonably be expected to know more about their world, and their narratives. By then choosing in later stories to present the action through the consciousness of the older characters, he also denies to his third-person narrators the God-like knowledge of the omniscient narrator – and to the readers of their stories any certainty that might go with it.

The lack of omniscience and overt moral judgement are, therefore, notable features of all the tales in this collection, and, in general, apply to modernist narrative styles. Writers such as Joyce rejected omniscience, in the main, along with any idea that readers had to be told what to think. Maria, on whom we rely for the story in 'Clay', is carefully positioned on the periphery of life, close to the most important elements of human relationships, yet never a part of them.

It is her restricted view of sex, for example, that is privileged by the free indirect style. But filtering the narrative through Maria's consciousness does not mean that we only see the world of the story through her eyes. Rather, because Joyce has let us know that her perspective is limited (as limited in its way as the perspective of 'The Sisters' and 'An Encounter'), we are able to see more than she sees, or at least to suspect that her perception of events going on around her is less than acute. For example, when Maria is at the Halloween party, it seems obvious to us that Joe gets drunk and loses his temper, yet Maria, oblivious, but still filtering the narrative, 'was delighted to see the children so merry and Joe and his wife in such good spirits' (p. 101). The limited point of view helps to ensure that frequently in this story – as well as in others – we cannot be wholly certain what is happening. Joyce's skilful deployment of the third-person narrator and devices like free indirect style give to the story the opacity for which the collection as a whole is famous.

The *Dublin by Lamplight* laundry, mentioned in 'Clay' (p. 96), was a Protestant institution for so-called 'fallen women': unmarried mothers and prostitutes who worked in the laundry in order to redeem themselves. There were many such organisations in Dublin in this period, and several had a reputation for vigorous proselytising. These inmates, in sharp contrast to Maria, are sexual veterans, and their brief descriptions are vividly coloured. They quarrel among themselves, they come to the kitchen hungry for food and company; their arms are 'red' and 'steaming'; they laugh and joke throughout the meal that Maria serves them, and toast her with a clattering of their huge mugs on the table (pp. 96–7). They occupy a diminished position in society's eyes, and we see them at a distance thanks to the dominance of Maria's perspective, but they are vibrant, vital figures, compared with Maria in her drab brown raincloak. Her single, independent life seems without joy or pleasure. Her 'nice tidy little body' is looked at without desire or affection, save by herself (p. 97). She is continually overlooked in the story, in fact. The 'colonel-looking gentleman' (p. 98) who gives up his seat for her therefore precipitates a flood of emotion: flustered by his attention she leaves her independently purchased and carefully chosen present of plumcake on the tram.

Maria's arrival at Joe's house, viewed through her own eyes, of course, seems one of welcome integration into the family. In the story's crucial scene, she takes part in a traditional game to predict the future.

At Maria's turn, the 'next-door girls' have included a dish of clay, to signify death: this is the saucer that Maria selects. Wrapped in a 'bandage' that suggests the linen shroud in which she will be buried, Maria stands helpless until the game is rearranged so that she selects 'the prayer-book' – predictably enough (p. 101). Also predictably, she seems oblivious to the realisation among the others that she will face her death alone. But with her subconscious editing of '*I Dreamt that I Dwelt*' (p. 101) (she avoids singing the verse about suitors 'upon bended knee' – see Appendix III, p. 234), Joyce complicates the narrative perspective at the story's conclusion still further, suggesting that Maria is, in fact, aware on some level that she has missed out on life.

'A Painful Case' is a companion story to 'Clay' and its position as the subsequent tale in the collection is an effective one. Mr Duffy is a single, lonely man, whose name derives from the Irish for 'black' or 'dark'. He lives in the suburbs, however, and this less notably urban story is enacted with a far smaller cast than Maria's.

Activity 2

Reread 'A Painful Case'. Whose is the 'painful case' of the title?

Discussion

'A Painful Case' applies the term to Mrs Sinico, as you probably noted. The story's title is taken from the newspaper report of the inquest after her death, borrowing its legal overtones (pp. 109–11). But perhaps your reading of the text also suggested Mr Duffy as a potential subject, leading to a second, quasi-medical interpretation of the phrase.
Mr Duffy's existence is minutely detailed by Joyce, in all its painful constraints, frustrations and repressions. His stunted relationship with the rest of the world is suggestive of a psychological case study, something by Joyce's contemporary, Sigmund Freud (1856–1939), perhaps – known at the time for his work on the psychosexual problems of the neurotic Viennese middle class. This could mean a reader's sympathies are divided between the two characters, each of whom experiences serious degrees of loneliness and isolation. Perhaps your reading of the story left you with this impression. By contrast, if you felt some bias in the narrative – privileging one 'painful case' over the other – maybe it was because Mrs Sinico was not, in fact, alone in her life. She had family. Duffy did not. Point of view is more telling still. Mr Duffy's is the central consciousness of the story. Mrs Sinico never offers her perspective on

events. Men controlled her life, and they narrate her death: the Deputy Coroner, the train driver, the railway porter, the policeman, the doctor, the newspaper reporter and her husband combine with a powerful and patriarchal eloquence. Duffy's condemnation of Mrs Sinico – firstly, for her one passionate gesture when she takes his hand (p. 107), secondly, for her drunken death (p. 111) – is another male verdict on a constrained female life. Joyce experiments with this constraint by providing Mrs Sinico with the only line of dialogue in the story (p. 105), as you may have spotted. But her husband seems entirely indifferent to his wife's unhappiness, and her daughter wishes only that her mother would 'join a league' (p. 111) – that is, take a pledge against alcohol in a temperance society. Joyce does provide further insight into contemporary women's lives in this story, but this is Mr Duffy's 'case'. Frightened and threatened by sex, the drive in him becomes distorted and unhealthy. We watch the results.

The theme of paralysis is employed by Joyce here in a slightly different manner from the way he uses it elsewhere in the collection. On a superficial level, Duffy seems to be entirely in control of his life, with rigid routines and a dislike of novelty and disruption. However, the reader quickly sees that these routines are a protection. He is, in fact, paralysed by fear of contact, of what a close friendship, let alone a lover, might mean in his emotionally impoverished life. His peculiar analysis of the impossibility of loving relationships (p. 108) is merely a means of excusing himself from any normal human interaction. Like Eveline, Duffy has been offered one chance at happiness, which he has spurned, and Joyce suggests that he will never have another.

'A Painful Case' also differs from the other stories in the collection because Mr Duffy appears to be genuinely heedless – or, more accurately, unwitting – as to social expectations. Though he is revolted by Mrs Sinico's drunkenness, even casting judgement on her fitness to live due to her 'habits' (p. 111), Duffy rarely considers the possible impropriety of his relationship with her. It is he who forces their meetings to be relocated to her house where they continue to talk, unconscious 'of any incongruity' (p. 106). His rejection of her is based upon his own bizarre standards (irreparably assaulted when she takes his hand), rather than society's attitudes to fidelity in marriage. In some ways, this makes his pitiful appearance at the story's end even more pathetic: standing in the Phoenix Park, aware of the prostitute and her client waiting for him to move on, Duffy is finally envious of rather than dismayed by this manifestation of what he has denied himself – and her. (Look back at the section on p. 113 from 'When he gained the crest …' to '… the syllables of her name' now.) Here we experience a rare example of an unambiguous climactic ending in the stories we have read so far. 'Those venal and furtive loves filled him with despair', the narrator tells us (p. 113). The feeling that Duffy has carefully excised from his life floods back in. This is his 'epiphany': he is outcast from – a typically extraordinary version of – 'life's feast' (p. 113).

Activity 3

Think about the settings of 'A Painful Case', and what they add to your understanding of the Dublin Joyce is representing in the collection.

Discussion

Despite all we have learned about the 'intimacy' of Dublin, and the ways in which social interaction is eminently possible in this period for Joyce's observant, wandering characters, he places this compelling portrayal of growing intimacy outside the city walls. Yes, the 'lonely road' to Chapelizod in one sense simply mirrors, and helps to create, these two characters' separate isolations. Yes, there is less scrutiny here – especially because Mrs Sinico's husband is often absent. But it is for more reasons than these that it is in her 'little cottage outside Dublin' that they become close (p. 107). They become simultaneously ahistorical in some senses. It is as though they are being naturalised and reclaimed by the rural environment – the 'warm soil' of companionship of a previous age. The complexity of modernity, when Dublin is the context, is at its clearest in this late tale (and is important, too, in 'The Dead', which we will come to in the next section of this chapter). Mrs Sinico and Mr Duffy push back the modern world, re-creating an earlier period. They sit in the dark, eschewing the lighted lamp; he withdraws from politics; she becomes his confessor; his mental life is 'emotionalised' and so he begins to change.

Chapelizod, Dublin.

Figure 2.1   Chapelizod, Dublin, *c*.1904. Photo: Archive of Irish Heritage Giftware – www.irishhistoricalpics.ie.

Mrs Sinico's passionate gesture – itself painfully modest – brings an end to these developments, proving at the same time how limited Duffy's adaptation would have been. He displays no ill effects after their separation, or in fact until he is faced with the newspaper article that relates her death. Joyce takes a page and a half over this event, reproducing it completely for the reader, signifying its very modern significance to his plot (newspapers' reporting of scandal caused much public debate). Once Duffy's revulsion has been indulged, the way is open to the operation of a more interesting human process that has received very little treatment in the collection so far: memory.

Memory – by its nature more obviously relevant as Dublin 'grows up' – leads to the epiphany in this story, and though it is limited, personal, and ultimately questioned by Mr Duffy, its function here prepares us for the role it plays in the last story of the collection, which is also, of course, concerned with the dead.

'The Dead'

Joyce himself described his narrative style as one of 'scrupulous meanness' (quoted in Ellmann, 1966, p. 134). In the edition of *Dubliners* that we're using, Terence Brown relates this 'scrupulous meanness' to the 'troubling indeterminacy' of Joyce's employment of free indirect style (p. xlii) and the ultimately fragmentary nature of the portraits of life he provides. He also relates it to the gaps in the text – those aspects Joyce's narrators neglect to, or cannot, explain. We may also apply Joyce's phrase to the almost 'bloodless' character of some of his prose – think of the final description of Eveline, or, indeed, the fact that we're not shown Mrs Mooney's interview with Mr Doran at all. But, to counter all this, there is the youthful confidence with which the boys range across their city in 'An Encounter' – curtailed though it may be – and the astonishing liveliness of the dialogue in these stories, in Corley's tales, for example. Epiphanies disrupt the tone too, creating intense bursts of resonant energy as characters experience their revelations. 'Scrupulous meanness' describes very neatly some aspects of Joyce's text, but does not summarise it. Might something similar be said about 'paralysis'? In the same letter in which he set out his model for the structure of the text (quoted in Chapter 1, p. 18), Joyce declared famously that his 'intention was to write a chapter of the moral history of my country and I chose Dublin for the scene because that city seemed the centre of paralysis' (quoted in Ellmann, 1966, p. 134). Paralysis is a dominant theme in this example of city literature, as we have seen. With it very much in mind, we now turn to the final story of the collection to assess how far 'The Dead' challenges, or reinforces, those representations of Dublin life and culture to which Joyce has treated us so far.

'The Dead' was written in 1907, so was not yet the concluding part of the Dublin-based text James Joyce was taking to publishers in 1906. But Joyce already had a notion of the story he would build around Dublin teacher and book-lover Gabriel Conroy. He knew some time before he began to write that a party would be at the centre of his tale. Other decisions and details took longer. Joyce complained in a letter to his brother that he had been put off writing while he 'watched' (from Rome, where he had been based since the summer of 1906), the outcome of the so-called 'Playboy Riots' at Dublin's Abbey Theatre in February 1907 (described at the beginning of Chapter 1). They made Joyce pause because the playwright John Millington Synge was following advice from W.B. Yeats that he himself had rejected, to go 'back to the land' and find inspiration as part of the Gaelic revival. The pointed depiction of the very modern, 'frank-mannered talkative' Miss Ivors in 'The Dead', with her 'large brooch' bearing an 'Irish device', and her planned excursion to the Aran islands, is an obvious intervention in a dispute Joyce was frustrated to miss out on (pp. 187, 189).

In addition to this contemporary outbreak of the politics of art, Joyce's biographers point out that a substantial amount of his own autobiographical experience was being processed as part of writing 'The Dead'. What he himself had 'seen and heard', as he put it in a letter to Grant Richards, is strongly present in both character and event (Joyce quoted in Schwarz, 1994, p. 63). Though this is true of all the stories in *Dubliners* – the creative result of the Dublin life he observed in such detail – it is most comprehensively realised in this last and longest tale. Elements drawn from three generations of Joyce's own family in Dublin find their way into the text. And the courtship of Nora Barnacle in Galway by a boy, Michael Bodkin, who subsequently died, was also part of the rich and suggestive store of factual material he sifted through as he prepared to write.

Finally, Rome itself, with its embodied history, its grandeur and ruins, affected Joyce greatly as he focused his mind on that other Catholic city which he would represent in 'The Dead'. He expected to be impressed, but less predictable were the nightmares that seemed fed by a sense of Rome itself as overwhelmed by death. He wrote about the city as a giant cemetery, a crumbling monument to the past, in letters at the time. Rome came to remind him 'of a man who lives by exhibiting to travellers his grandmother's corpse' (Joyce quoted in Ellmann, 1966, p. 164). These thought processes helped to generate the active conflict between past and present we find in 'The Dead', as well as the often ambiguous self-locating of its characters in their historical period. Both of these aspects serve to remind us of the precarious modernity of Dublin as represented by Joyce – itself, perhaps, related to the fact that many of its inhabitants hadn't been in the city very long. A rural, or 'villagey' past, to use Kiberd's word (2005, p. 293), was very much part of Dublin's modern urban character. And in 'The Dead', Gabriel Conroy's sense of gloom about the modern age counters his cosmopolitan urges; the independent, sassy and self-aware Molly Ivors roots herself in the traditional past.

At around fifty pages, 'The Dead' is the longest of the stories in *Dubliners* by some distance. It is different, then, in its scope from those others that you have studied so far and offers a more complex take on

Dublin as 'the centre of paralysis' than its companions. One might expect this, perhaps, of the conclusion to the collection. But there is also much that you will recognise as you read. The character of Dublin itself, and the nature of urban experience more generally, are as important here as they have been up to now.

'The Dead': the party

Activity 4

Reread 'The Dead', from the beginning to the point in the story where Gabriel is shown to be 'waving his hand to her in deprecation' (towards the end of p. 178). In what ways do the setting and focus of this opening section echo the depiction of Dublin that you have been exploring so far?

Discussion

The narrow focus of the story as it opens, on Lily and the 'little pantry' and 'bare hallway' of which she is currently in charge, certainly conjures up other dark and spare Dublin settings. Entrance to the house is signalled by a 'wheezy hall-door bell' (p. 175), which announces the arrival of each guest while suggesting he or she is about to lose an ongoing battle for oxygen despite (or because of) the welcome the waiting Morkan sisters are eager to give. This sense of ground-floor constriction is reinforced by the sight and sound of the 'gossiping and laughing and fussing' women peering down over the banisters (p. 175). Their anxious scrutiny is explained shortly by the image of the potentially 'screwed' Freddy Malins, who might arrive before Gabriel, the favourite nephew (p. 176). The city as Joyce has represented it so far is also recognisable in the early sense of tight networks of characters, closely related to one another by blood, but also by behaviour. The party is an annual event of some considerable standing: routine and ritual have been set firm over years of practice, as all the participants have aged but remained in close proximity to one another, and to the city centre. And finally, when the conversation settles between Gabriel and Lily, and he tries to engage her 'in a friendly tone' (p. 177) in a discussion of her prospects, the brutal candour of her responses immediately punctures the polite exchange, echoing those earlier depictions of the narrowness of women's existence, in 'Eveline', for example. No, Lily is not being educated. No, she is not about to be married. She is bitter enough, though, to allude to sex (she is a very different character from Eveline), forcing Gabriel to confront the realities of her likely exchanges with men she knows and embarrassing him both with this image and its distance from the casual and unthinking gaiety of his original question (pp. 177–8).

Lily is trapped and bitter despite her youth; drunken Freddy Malins needs managing; the aunts are anxious and old; the snow is falling as the guests arrive. This is all very much like Dublin as Joyce has drawn it earlier on. The gold coin which seals the end of the exchange between Lily and Gabriel, buying him some renewed ease of mind, may not be quite as tarnished as that which graces Corley's palm in 'Two Gallants', but, providing another of those threads that structure the collection, it says similar things about economic and sexual realities in the city at that time. Gabriel, bright enough to be aware of some of these at least, finds they dampen his evident affection for – perhaps attraction to – Lily, and is eager to make good his escape. He is 'almost trotting to the stairs' that will take him up to the party (p. 178). The action follows him, leaving Lily behind.

On 25 September 1906 Joyce wrote a letter to his brother Stanislaus. He was trying to get *Dubliners* published, and he was prone to making judgements on its merits and defects, often as part of a more general assessment of his work. This letter provides an example that is particularly useful in approaching 'The Dead':

> I have often confessed to you surprise that there should be anything exceptional in my writing and it is only at moments when I leave down somebody else's book that it seems to me not so unlikely after all. Sometimes thinking of Ireland it seems to me that I have been unnecessarily harsh. I have reproduced (in *Dubliners* at least) none of the attraction of the city for I have never felt at my ease in any city since I left it except in Paris. I have not reproduced its ingenuous insularity and its hospitality. The latter 'virtue' so far as I can see does not exist elsewhere in Europe. I have not been just to its beauty: for it is more beautiful naturally in my opinion than what I have seen of England, Switzerland, France, Austria or Italy.
>
> (Joyce quoted in Ellmann, 1983, p. 231)

Joyce had a deep affinity for city living. Though the reviewers did not write much about the collection on publication, their most positive comment tended to be directed towards 'The Dead', for its sympathy and exactness at recording contemporary urban life (Deming, 1970, pp. 62, 60). As the quotation above suggests, Joyce had experienced a wide variety of urban environments for a man of his age and time – especially when you consider that his funds had to be procured from donors or borrowed from friends. He first left Dublin for Paris via London in 1902, living there briefly at the end of the year and returning for longer in 1903. In 1904 he and Nora started off in Paris, then travelled to Zurich and on to Pola (250 km south of Trieste) before settling in Trieste in the spring of 1905 where, aside from the time in Rome in 1906–7, they would be based for much of the next ten years. In addition to his need for travel, and also for the particular energy he drew from these different city environments, we know that distance from Dublin – 'outsider' status – was what was required. Joyce began to judge the work that resulted comparatively, as his experiences in mainland Europe (including the teaching and the reading he was doing) developed his mind. In this key letter to Stanislaus, then, he indicates what might be taken as a new aim for his treatment in the last story of *Dubliners*, one that would complicate Dublin's reputation as he has constructed it so far in the collection with representation of its 'ingenuous insularity and its hospitality', and its beauty as well. In the remainder of this chapter we will explore the story from this angle. The modern Irish tourist industry, and the city, after all, have a firm and upbeat hold on James Joyce. The house in which 'The Dead' was set, 15 Usher's Island, Dublin 8, was a museum, and John Huston filmed some of his version of the story on location there in the 1980s. It is now opposite the James Joyce Bridge, an intensely modern construction (as Figure 2.2 shows), opened in 2003. Joyce's text both remade Dublin, and itself is being remade through time. Despite what we have learned so far about the collection, perhaps we may assume that Joyce moves on in ways which suggest a different side to the city from what early reviewers persisted in simplifying as 'sordid' or 'drab' (Deming, 1970, pp. 59, 60).

Activity 5

Reread 'The Dead' from where Gabriel leaves Lily (p. 178) as far as Freddy's arrival (p. 185). As you read, focus on the variety of Dublin life Joyce represents. Do the aspects Joyce described in his letter to Stanislaus ('ingenuous insularity', 'hospitality' and 'beauty') quoted above seem most prominent here, or is it Gabriel's separateness that claims your attention as the friends and family meet?

Figure 2.2   James Joyce Bridge, Dublin. Photo: Declan O'Doherty/www.declanod.wordpress.com.

Discussion

Aunt Julia and Aunt Kate are tightly attuned to the party they are giving, and all that they know of their guests – there is precious little anonymity here. And yet the first thing that strikes me about Gabriel at this point is Joyce's presentation of his difference from his immediate society. He's depicted as a demanding parent, seeking to push his children on, but more tellingly he has his mind on 'the continent', originator of the goloshes he now makes his wife wear whenever it is wet. They are only his latest fad. The associated humour is immediately countered by the effect the discussion is shown to have on Aunt Julia, who doesn't know what goloshes are. Her 'mirthless eyes' reflect suspicion of newfangled objects like these which she transfers to her nephew and his direction in life (p. 180). The goloshes represent a rift in their experience, and specifically in their relationship to the city in which they live – their purpose is to insulate Gabriel from his environment, after all. Aunt Kate's fussing over domestic detail does not paper over the crack, and the resulting tension is only broken because Aunt Julia announces Freddy Malins. His arrival coincides with a burst of cathartic applause from the drawing-room, and the sense of a party returns, briefly. Freddy is important because he helps to show, very early in the story, how vital it is that this entertainment, this party, is properly managed. There are rules as to what comes upstairs, and what stays downstairs. Gabriel is instructed to keep Freddy downstairs if he is drunk and unruly, and this is reminiscent of the speed with which Gabriel made for the stairs in the opening scene.

Gabriel, then, is tasked with repression and control. Once he is dispatched, you may have noted how often Joyce resorts to numbers to describe the behaviour of the company: they fall into traditional patterns to do predictable things – most obviously, of course, the formal dances. As soon as Freddy has been integrated successfully, it is the arrangement of the Lancers (the military association is only too appropriate once their sparring begins) that brings Gabriel face to face with Molly Ivors. Markedly, it is here that his control begins to slip. Their brief but heated argument raises issues of nationalism that were fundamental to Joyce's conception of the story, as noted above, and remain important for the remainder of the text. Again, Gabriel is shown regularly to place himself outside Dublin society, and Irish society, in mind first of all (his reviewing for an English newspaper; his love of books and other European languages) and then in body too (his anticipated annual cycling holiday to the continent). The partnered dance he and Molly are joined in means that their conversation is also managed, punctuated by their regular coming together and moving apart. But the ground they cover, politics and history and language and nationhood, still transforms Gabriel, agitating him to the extent that he blurts out that he is 'sick of [his] own country' (p. 190) and reveals his proprietary attitude to his wife's identity. When Miss Ivors asks '[s]he's from Connacht, isn't she?' and Gabriel replies '[h]er people are' (p. 189), he communicates in three short words contempt for his wife and where she comes from – the symbolic 'west', site of many ideas central to the Irish revival, including those related to language and nationhood – as well as for rural Ireland. Gretta is excluded from his planned European tour; conversely, she would form an explicit part of the reason to take the trip to the predominantly Irish-speaking Aran Isles. The ramifications are not fully understood until the last section of the story, when the scene shifts to the Dublin hotel. But brilliantly, Joyce manages to recalibrate the tension and energy that has amassed here, redirecting nearly all of it towards a mid-point climax to the story, replete with that elusive hospitality and generosity: the spread at the supper table.

It is worth having another look at the description of the supper table, just to revel in its sumptuous difference from the 'plate of peas' in 'Two Gallants', or even the 'plumcake' in 'Clay' (pp. 51, 98). In fact, the table itself cannot contain the delights on offer at this house on Usher's Island, which spread to the top of the piano. And it is the lack of containment – and constraint – that is the key here, especially when contrasted with the somewhat ordered nature of some of the previous description in this story. Joyce's sentences lengthen accordingly, out of the dialogue and away from the conflict; the punctuation softens ('A fat brown goose lay at the end of the table and at the other end, on a bed of creased paper strewn with sprigs of parsley ...' (p. 197)), and we can feel enjoyment, as well as anticipation, in the writing. The feast (a symbolic word, as Mr Duffy in 'A Painful Case' knew), as portrayed by Joyce, is a positive riot of colour, texture and shape. We already suspect that the quality will be high too: 'Though their life was modest they believed in eating well' (p. 176). This hospitable spread performs a magical, levelling function. The characters can be moved as one body, united by their hunger, as Mary Jane, reclaiming the floor from religion, pacifically suggests. Only one character is immune. Molly Ivors refuses to break bread with the assembled company, and though she goes away laughing, her exit at this point means that her debate with Gabriel remains unresolved – leaving the way for its reappearance in the second half of Joyce's story. Her laughter should not disguise the seriousness of the issues she has raised. The Irish were, as Declan Kiberd points out, the first English-speaking people to decolonise in the 1900s (2005, p. 147). And in Ireland, as Molly knows, it was language that served to distinguish ruler from ruled.

Activity 6

Reread the rest of Joyce's depiction of the supper, from 'Gabriel took his seat boldly ...' (p. 197) to its end (p. 207). What subjects emerge in the conversation? Can they be linked in any way to Gabriel's after-dinner speech?

Discussion

At first, appropriately enough, conversation is about food. The general noise and laughter is testimony to the continued sense of well-being that Mary Jane introduced along with supper. 'A chorus of voices', harmonious and pleasant, soon leads into the main topic of conversation: music. This is in keeping, of course, with the musical theme of the

Figure 2.3   Theatre Royal, Dublin, *c*.1920. Photo: © RTÉ Stills Library.

evening, and much of what we know so far of Dublin as well as Joyce's own background. While the resident opera singer criticises his peers in Dublin's theatres, it doesn't take long before the pleasures of the present, including the focus on eating and laughter, are abandoned. There is a march to the past, via collective memory, and we become mired there. Mr Browne's '[t]hose were the days' (p. 199) sums up the view of the table. Dublin has been left behind by London, Paris and Milan as a contemporary city of music, and these inhabitants at least regret it greatly. (As Terence Brown's notes point out, the high period of opera in Dublin was between 1840 and 1880 (see n. 60, p. 312).) With the exception of the younger, more modern Mary Jane, the guests refuse to be deprived of their regret, which quickly becomes a more ponderous nostalgia. While Bartell D'Arcy gamely offers modern singers as examples of excellence, such as the real-life Italian tenor Enrico Caruso (1874–1921), his chances of convincing his listeners are few. Kate Morkan insists on the greatness of one Parkinson, whom D'Arcy has never heard of, and even Browne never heard sing. ('Parkinson' has never been identified by critics, and while it is possible Joyce is signalling Miss Morkan's confusion because of her age, I think a joke is more likely – Parkinson is so far in Miss Morkan's beloved past that he has receded from all view.) Mrs Malins changes the subject by talking of Mount Melleray, County Waterford, in which monks offer hospitality and care for alcoholics like Freddy, who is shortly to visit them. The table is drawn away from its busy comment on Dublin's terminal decline and joins the monks in their active anticipation of bodily death (the final paralysis) instead. It is recounted that they sleep in their coffins 'to remind them of their last end' (p. 202).

At this point, for the first time, there is 'a silence of the table' (p. 202). Gabriel Conroy uses it to collect his thoughts, which he does partly by imagining how the house looks from the street outside to those who do not number among the evening's guests. Though in his imagination those without his aunts' walls are keenly aware of the music, and the warmth of the lights at the window, he also visualises them breathing 'pure' air. He puts them swiftly out of his mind, however, because when he begins his speech, it is as though he is delivering a manifesto on Dublin and its inclusive hospitality – though one that he locates firmly in the past, evoking dead generations and reminding us of the contradictions in his cosmopolitan stance. Gabriel builds to a rhetorically impressive conclusion to this first section:

> Of one thing, at least, I am sure. As long as this one roof
> shelters the good ladies aforesaid – and I wish from my heart
> it may do so for many and many a long year to come – the

tradition of genuine warm-hearted courteous Irish hospitality,
which our forefathers have handed down to us and which we
in turn must hand down to our descendants, is still alive
among us.

(p. 204)

'The Dead': the past and memory

Although the feast has undoubtedly been wonderful, as experienced by
the gathering, any energy in the life of the tradition Gabriel describes
struggles to be heard or felt. The timescales almost swamp it. (Try
reading the lines in the quotation above aloud to see what I mean.)
And it is snuffed out completely by what follows. Gabriel's morbid
conclusion, an attack on the modern age, is partly designed as a retort
to the absent Miss Ivors. The whole section is riven with ironies (some
of which have already been noted) – not the least of which is modern,
'hypereducated' (p. 204) and lively Molly's adherence to a movement
which is a revival. Her vision of modernity clashes violently with what
is currently Gabriel's own more outward-looking version, and even
though he has his goloshes, history would be shown to move forward
with Molly Ivors' nationalism. Underscoring Joyce's complex patterning
of past and present in this section is Gabriel's phrase, 'I will not linger
on the past' (p. 205). 'Of course you will', we may well think, and then
Gabriel does, by introducing staples of Greek mythology to end his
speech. Freddy Malins steps in, and he alone holds us in the present,
away from the deadening past, as he beats time with his fork.

There is no gentle transition to the world after the party. The outside
air that in Gabriel's imagination was 'pure' is now 'piercing' (p. 207).
The group is about to disband, but before this finally occurs different
combinations of characters cohere again in two important scenes. They
make a contribution to the theme of the city's 'paralysis' in *Dubliners*, as
well as to Joyce's particular presentation of the past and the present –
or ideas as to period more generally – in this tale.

Activity 7

Reread the description of the leave-taking, from 'The piercing morning ...' (p. 207) up to and including the round of 'good-nights' from Gabriel and Gretta (at the top of p. 214). Where do you see the theme of paralysis being developed, and what new aspects of the past does Joyce introduce, and to what effect?

Discussion

One of the most quoted sections of 'The Dead' is that which tells the story of Johnny the horse. Despite the humour the characters all find in the telling – some of which is self-deprecating – Joyce would have had to strive long and hard to find a more effective symbol of a native population restricted in its growth and development than the poor horse which could only go round in circles because that was what it was used to in its work. (The circles described by the 'Two Gallants' are not dissimilar.) Dublin's inability to keep up with mainland Europe was one message that we took from the party; Johnny reinforces the message that Dublin prevents its inhabitants from going anywhere too. How far this is an accurate portrayal of the characters of 'The Dead' needs to be thought about (though it seems appropriate enough regarding earlier characters in the collection). The Morkan sisters, after all, have travelled some distance from 'Back Lane'. They keep a relatively generous table and though they rent their 'dark gaunt' rooms, these rooms are well furnished (p. 175). Nonetheless, Johnny is a prominent part of the family mythology, and by extension of Dublin mythology, and the fact that Gabriel paces round the hall in his goloshes as he mimics him, raises a poignant question as to how accurate a symbol of his gradual migration to the continent these ludicrous objects actually are. Laughter is a constant backdrop to this section: its genuineness, despite everything, helps to set this story apart from its companions. The hilarity is raised a notch by a cabman who doesn't know where he is going and is confused further by the contradictory directions he is given. Joyce is staying with his paralysis theme – but injecting it with humour too.

In the second of the scenes paralysis is relevant again, but it is given a twist when Gretta is shown as caught to such a degree by her response to music that she is transported out of real time altogether, evoking a quasi-religious, distant 'grace and mystery' to her husband (p. 211). In this modified epiphany, what has been concealed and is now revealed is not comprehended by its audience. As Gabriel watches his wife listen to D'Arcy singing a traditional, unaccompanied Irish song (it is important that the other music played at the party has been adapted and is therefore less authentic), he does not understand what is being communicated to him about Gretta's past emotional life. He parcels up his inept intellectualising in the name of a picture, *'Distant Music'*, the clichéd tone of the title signifying his lack of genuine appreciation in this scene.

Gabriel will learn later what the song 'in the old Irish tonality' (p. 211) meant to his wife, and why the way she soon comes back 'to life', stimulating so immediately the resurgence of Gabriel's desire for her, makes her distant from him, in both time and space, instead of bringing her close. And as we shall see in the closing pages of the story, memory does not have to function as a barrier, isolating one character from another in this way.

Gretta's intense experience, produced by an immediate sense interacting with her memory, is mirrored now by one of Gabriel's own as they walk through Dublin together. He is freed for his fantasy by the presence of Bartell D'Arcy, with whom Gretta is walking ahead, leaving him to watch her and indulge the starburst of memories invading his consciousness. A few years later, in 1919, Virginia Woolf's essay 'Modern fiction' would theorise modernist experiments such as this passage in *Dubliners*, in which fiction records the working of an 'ordinary', active and impressionable mind as it receives an 'incessant shower' of innumerable experiential/sensory atoms (Woolf, 2008 [1919], p. 9). Whereas Woolf's statement of modernism is focused on the present tense, on the 'trivial, fantastic, evanescent' stimuli affecting her imagined subject, Joyce's happy victim is at the mercy of the past; not the deadening tread of the past, as heard in his after-dinner speech, but the enlivening, audacious, heartbreakingly generous simultaneity of it. Love comes back; desire comes back; tenderness comes back, all with memory. It is an interesting take on modernity: one more example of Joyce's nuanced approach to period in this text.

Activity 8

Reread the section on pp. 214–15 from 'She was walking on before him …' to '… galloping to their honeymoon'. How does Joyce emphasise the significance of Gabriel's experience?

Discussion

What strikes me immediately about this section of the story is the effectiveness of the tense Joyce uses throughout. Gabriel's 'ordinary mind' is not so different from Woolf's after all. The past continuous tense means that nothing he's remembering ever, technically, ends. The past seems to merge with the present. Compare these examples to see what I mean: 'he was caressing' instead of 'he caressed' (which it would be in the simple past tense); 'the curtain was shimmering' instead of 'the curtain shimmered'; 'they were standing' instead of 'they stood' (p. 214). All is held together by this powerful and individually inhabited time frame, to the extent that when a cab comes and collects them, Gabriel knows that he is 'galloping to catch the boat, galloping to their honeymoon', travelling back into that same past (p. 215).

Figure 2.4   The Gresham Hotel, Dublin, *c*.1900. Photo: Courtesy of The National Library of Ireland, L_CAB_02253.

As the story comes to a close, this sense of the present and the past interacting through and in the characters intensifies still more. We know from the beginning of 'The Dead' that Gabriel and Gretta are spending this night in a hotel. As far as Dublin locations go, the Gresham represents the height of exclusive anonymity – right at the city's heart (see Figure 2.4). In this context, it has the potential to free Gabriel from all of Dublin's constraints. Leaving the claustrophobic house on Usher's Island, there is more than a hint of the adolescent escaping scrutiny in Gabriel's anticipation of his night with Gretta. The 'wild impulse of his body' (p. 217) is in response to their specific location: 'as they stood at the hotel door, he felt that they had escaped from their lives and duties, escaped from home and friends and run away together with wild and radiant hearts to a new adventure' (p. 216).

The sexual encounter this seems to be leading to would be a logical conclusion to a collection based in what we have come to know as an intimate city. Gradually, since the end of the party, Joyce's narrative focus has been narrowing until Gabriel and Gretta alone (the only couple in the story) are its subjects. Unusually, they have some privacy too. His desire, at least, has received detailed treatment over the previous pages, and we expect the sexual tension to be cathartically released once the porter goes out with his candle. (Joyce is careful to tell us that Gabriel 'shot the lock to' (p. 217).) But, in fact, things go wrong very quickly. His thoughts of sex are almost immediately stifled. In the story's final section we are overtaken by other more compelling pasts: Gretta's, which is made up of anything but her lived relationship with her husband, and then that of Ireland itself. The terms of Gabriel's quarrel with Miss Ivors, and notions of the paralysis of Dublin, return.

Activity 9

Reread the last part of 'The Dead', from 'A ghostly light …' (p. 217) to the end. When you get to the final line, use it to reflect on the section as a whole. In what ways are 'the dead' invoked? In what ways are 'the living'? Is the city an important aspect of either?

Discussion

Though Gabriel's sexual impulse is not realised in this final section of the story, there is physical contact between the couple that might be seen, initially, as a vivid affirmation of their relationship. As this contact is between husband and wife, it is different from all other physical interaction in the story so far. But both characters get their bearings by looking out of the window first. It is almost as though they can only connect after having disrupted the unfamiliar exclusivity of the scene, by drawing Dublin back in. Quickly it becomes apparent why. They are not close; they are strangers. Gabriel's 'astonishment' at Gretta's outburst of feeling shows why. And we as readers anticipate the explanation of her earlier intense response to the song, which is as yet unknown to her husband. Their relationship – including its basis in modern Dublin life and society – is a sham. Gretta's emotional life takes place in what is another period: a rural past. It is entangled with the memory of a rural boy, now dead, who haunts her consciousness, and will now haunt Gabriel's too. Her particular 'revival' (and think back to how Joyce describes her total stillness in response to the song) is not so different from Molly Ivors' fight for her 'own land'. Gretta's route to the west, that partly symbolic region

Molly tries to persuade Gabriel to visit in the summer instead of mainland Europe, is memory-bound, and more personal, that is all. Dublin itself is crucial as a catalytic backdrop in this final section of 'The Dead', therefore. It also makes possible Gretta's distinction between her rural past, which has precedence in her consciousness, and the urban present, which neither she nor Gabriel finds stimulating in comparison with memory. Eventually, though, Dublin assumes a yet more important role. In Gabriel's own epiphany, which forms the climax of the story, and the collection as a whole, Dublin becomes the most immediate site of this rather last-minute revival as, building on his new and 'strange friendly pity' for his wife (p. 223), he experiences a more general generosity and communality of spirit, joining in imagination the past and the present, the living and the dead, the west and the city that lies just outside the window, all of it under the same snow.

The snow wraps up this story. It arrives with the first guests at the party, and is falling again as Gabriel goes to sleep, muffling footsteps and much other sound, too, in between. Does it contribute more to the deathly atmosphere, or to the sense of inescapable connectivity between all the constituents of Gabriel's half-dream? Each reader may well have a different answer to this question, and that answer may also change with each new reading of the text. There is no doubt, though, that 'the west' is ranged close to Dublin as part of the conclusion of *Dubliners*. Personal memory and the national past combine to produce this effect in 'The Dead'. Joyce chose to expand upon the nature of Dublin's life and culture by bringing up close the experience of those such as Michael Furey – 'poor Michael Furey' (p. 222), a singer, a Galway boy, who loved Gretta so much he braved death – as he wrote this final tale.

Dubliners: portrait of a city

The American poet Ezra Pound (1885–1972), who met Joyce first in London, was a great advocate of and support to the writer. He reviewed *Dubliners* in July 1914, including the following paragraph as part of his assessment of the collection:

> [Joyce] gives us Dublin as it presumably is. He does not descend to farce. He does not rely upon Dickensian caricature. He gives us things as they are, not only for Dublin, but for every city. Erase

the local names and a few specifically local allusions, and a few historic events of the past, and substitute a few different local names, allusions and events, and these stories could be retold of any town.

(Pound quoted in Deming, 1970, pp. 67–8)

Pound, like other reviewers mentioned in this chapter, was certain of Joyce's realism. Unlike others, though, he didn't argue with it, suggesting that Joyce should have done something different instead. As you conclude your work on James Joyce, I'd like you to interrogate the other claim he makes here more closely – that what Joyce tells us about Dublin holds true of all cities.

Activity 10

Think about Pound's point of view as expressed in his review (quoted above). How far does it seem to you, from all you have learned of the portrayal of Dublin in this collection as a whole, to be an accurate reflection of Joyce's representation of this city?

Discussion

In some ways I agree with Pound's assessment, or at least I can see why he is making the claims that he does for the text. The characters in *Dubliners* strive with economic, social, physical and moral difficulty, of a kind that can be found in other urban-based fiction of the period, as well as of earlier periods. (Joyce's influences included the French realist novelist Emile Zola (1840–1902), for example, whose Paris-based fiction established him as the leader of the French naturalist school.) And yet, this does not do complete justice to the Dublin that Joyce represents in these stories. Specific myths, locations and characteristics of this city permeate each of the stories in the collection, rendering them uniquely about Dublin. Crucially, too, as we discovered in our reading of 'The Dead', the city's relationship to a wider Ireland, and the contemporary Gaelic revival that was helping to construct views of both Dublin and the rural west, informed Joyce's storytelling as well, as did many of his own experiences and those of people he knew. All this combines to suggest that, in fact, *Dubliners* is highly time- and place-specific, while containing recognisable aspects of other literature of the city as it is discussed, for example, later in this part of the book.

Conclusion

Following this reading of Joyce's collection of short stories, do you find that he did, finally, expand upon his presentation of Dublin in ways that made you aware of the 'attraction' the city held for him? Its triumphs, miseries and cruelties were well treated earlier on, but surely it is 'The Dead', in particular, that Tom Paulin had in mind when he said that Joyce 'redeems his Dubliners' in the collection (see the back cover of *Dubliners*). Redeeming his Dubliners involved redeeming his Dublin too.

Dublin is without doubt Joyce's focus in this collection, as is the backward-looking paralysis he believed it central to. Joyce's realism in depicting this city at this time, beset by the past and complicated in its relationship to its period as a result, is also unquestionable. But the energy and originality of Joyce's attention to an urban theme; his aesthetic rather than narrowly moralistic focus; his technique, including the deployment of ambiguity, experimentation with perspective, as well as his interest in representing consciousness, all mark this clearly as a modernist text. Finally, and most importantly, perhaps, Molly Ivors' confident laughter, and Gabriel's epiphany, during which 'generous tears' fill his eyes, remind us of Dublin's particularly nuanced, yet definite, route to modernity too.

References

Deming, R.H. (ed.) (1970) *James Joyce: The Critical Heritage*, London, Routledge.

Ellmann, R. (ed.) (1966) *The Letters of James Joyce*, vol. 2, London, Faber and Faber.

Ellmann, R. (1983) *James Joyce*, Oxford, Oxford University Press.

Joyce, J. (2000 [1914]) *Dubliners*, Penguin Modern Classics, London, Penguin.

Kiberd, D. (2005) *The Irish Writer and the World*, Cambridge, Cambridge University Press.

Lodge, D. (2002) *Consciousness and the Novel: Connected Essays*, London, Secker and Warburg.

Schwarz, D.R. (1994) *James Joyce: The Dead*, New York, St Martin's Press.

Woolf, V. (2008 [1919]) 'Modern fiction' in *Virginia Woolf: Selected Essays*, Oxford, Oxford University Press, pp. 6–12.

Further reading

Ferriter, D. (1994) *The Transformation of Ireland, 1900–2000*, London, Profile.

Hutchins, P. (1950) *James Joyce's Dublin*, London, Grey Walls.

Igoe, V. (1994) *A Literary Guide to Dublin: Writers in Dublin – Literary Associations and Anecdotes*, London, Methuen.

Igoe, V. (2007) *James Joyce's Dublin Houses and Nora Barnacle's Galway*, Dublin, Lilliput Press.

Jeffreys, S. (1985) *The Spinster and Her Enemies: Feminism and Sexuality, 1880–1930*, London, Pandora Press.

Kiberd, D. (1995) *Inventing Ireland*, London, Jonathan Cape.

Kiberd, D. (2009) Ulysses *and Us: The Art of Everyday Living*, London, Faber and Faber.

Lehan, R. (1998) *The City in Literature: An Intellectual and Cultural History*, Berkeley, CA, University of California Press.

Maddox, B. (1988) *Nora: The Real Life of Molly Bloom*, Boston, Houghton.

Miles, S. and Miles, M. (2005 [2004]) *Consuming Cities*, Basingstoke, Palgrave Macmillan.

Nolan, E. (2007) *Catholic Emancipations: Irish Fiction from Thomas Moore to James Joyce*, Syracuse, NY, Syracuse University Press.

Chapter 3
Fritz Lang, *Metropolis*

Suman Gupta

Aims

This chapter will:

- study ideas about and representations of cities with reference to the film *Metropolis*
- examine how a futuristic fantasy might be used to explore a range of social concerns of a specific period
- introduce you to ways of critically engaging with a visual medium, film.

Introduction

Metropolis (1927), directed by Fritz Lang (1890–1976), is the only futuristic dystopian fantasy, with elements of science fiction, which features in this book. This may be a genre with which you are already familiar: numerous popular novels – for example Aldous Huxley's *Brave New World* (1932), George Orwell's *Nineteen Eighty-Four* (1949), Ray Bradbury's *Fahrenheit 451* (1953), Philip K. Dick's *Do Androids Dream of Electric Sheep* (1968) and Margaret Atwood's *Handmaid's Tale* (1985) – and films (all of these have been turned into popular films) may come to mind. Where an imagined utopia evokes a world that is in some sense perfect, the dystopian fantasy visualises the ways in which utopian aspirations can go awry and lead to undesirable consequences. Both utopias and dystopias are naturally imagined from a present, and reflect the hopes and fears of the contexts in which they are imagined. Themes that have appeared repeatedly in science fiction and dystopian fantasies include principles of government, the manner in which institutions and individuals wield power, the nature of interpersonal and sexual relations, and interactions between humans and machines.

This part of the book, and consequently this chapter, lays a particular emphasis on early twentieth-century thinking about cities. *Metropolis* is a natural candidate for attention given this emphasis. Quite apart from the title, it presents vivid and influential images of city architecture and spaces, social arrangements and populations. It also both draws upon existing critical ideas about cities (of artists, philosophers and cultural theorists) and encourages further thinking in a general way, by visualising a future city and thus dislocating preconceptions about familiar real cities. The metropolis of the film brings together, somewhat uneasily as I shall show, real cities with futuristic, dreamlike and abstract visions of cities. Consequently, through *Metropolis* you are able to contemplate the theme of cities and urbanity in a somewhat different light from that illustrated in the discussions in Chapters 1 and 2 of Joyce's realistic portrayal of turn-of-the-century Dublin.

This does not mean that *Metropolis* is in any way less determined by period and location. It was commissioned by the largest German film studio of its time – Universum Film AG (Ufa) – and first screened in 1927. The film was preceded by a 1925 novel version by Thea von Harbou (Lang's wife at the time), who also wrote the **screenplay**. But in this instance the novel was a tried-and-tested publicity device for the film, managed by Ufa's marketing department, rather than being the inspiration for it (for further information, see Bachman, 2000). *Metropolis*'s social and aesthetic perspectives are recognisable in what is now referred to as the Weimar Republic, covering the period in German history between the Versailles Treaty of 1919 (which ended the First World War) and the appointment of Adolf Hitler as Chancellor in 1933. The film is, however, not narrowly localised – in fact, its futuristic vision and fantastic qualities were designed for a broad appeal beyond its obvious time and place. At times, the film self-consciously plays on images associated with and imagined for different periods – past, present and future. Critically engaging the film in terms of its historical context consequently draws attention to methods of periodising texts in general. Such methods are a matter of consistent interest for this book as a whole (obviously following a chronological structure), and for this part in particular.

For the purposes of this part of the book, I have assumed a few significant emphases and delimitations in discussing *Metropolis*. These are determined not only by the argument of this chapter but also by existing knowledge about and critical appraisals of the film, some of which are highlighted below.

First, though existing scholarship on *Metropolis* is often concerned with how it was made, this chapter does not go into that. The film was one of the largest and most expensive productions undertaken by Ufa and reputedly led to the studio's near-bankruptcy. It has been regarded as representative of the Weimar period film industry's aspirations, and is often gauged alongside other films of the time – particularly Lang's. Pioneering techniques for creating special effects were used in it. But none of that has a bearing on this chapter. Here I am concerned with the analysis of themes and ideas in the film.

Second, you will notice when watching the film (which is a new edition) and reading the original plot summary that large chunks of the original film are missing. In fact, the film started being snipped and tampered with almost immediately after its first screening in January 1927 in Germany. When it was taken to America later that year, playwright Channing Pollock was employed to abridge it and render it amenable to American viewing habits. Large parts of the film were cut (including scenes considered risqué). Similar cuts were made to the German version by the Berlin board of censors later in 1927, and since then this is the version that has largely been available. The restoration of the original version (which is the one on the DVD) has been a prolonged process of research with some missing bits being discovered in

Argentina as recently as 2008. One way of taking these facts into account, and the pragmatic path here, is not to regard any film version of *Metropolis* as a fixed definitive version. Different audiences had different versions to view and understood the film accordingly, and none of the versions and viewings can be regarded as more or less authentic.

Third (which happily fits with the second), in part because of the variously truncated forms in which the film was received, and more significantly because of numerous inconsistencies in the plot, critics have generally tended to pay only secondary attention to the story. This doesn't mean the story has been disregarded (not at all), but it has often been regarded as the weak scaffolding that is paradoxically held up by the complexity and power of the images – the building blocks. As Spanish film-maker Luis Buñuel was to put it in 1970: 'That which it recounts is trivial, overblown, pedantic and outdatedly romantic. But, if to the tale we prefer the "plastico-photogenic" background of the film, then *Metropolis* will fulfil our wildest dreams, will astonish us as the most astonishing book of images it is possible to compose' (2000 [1970], p. 106). That is roughly the view the discussions below also take: your attention is drawn primarily to certain images, but without losing sight of the story.

With this chapter's (and this part's) thematic interest in cities and conceptual interest in periodising in mind, my approach to *Metropolis* is divided into four sections: 'Real and imaginary cities', 'Humans and machines', 'Gender and desire' and 'Politics and aesthetics'. Before we consider these, however, there is an introductory section on how to read a film.

The version of the film that is referred to in this chapter is the most recent (November 2010) version, in the 'Masters of Cinema' series. You should watch the film in its entirety to familiarise yourself with the story before reading the chapter, and re-watch sections as and when instructed to in the chapter.

On reading a film

This chapter differs from others in this book in that it addresses entirely a recorded visual text, a silent film, rather than a written literary text. For other performance-based works, such as films with sound and plays, you are likely to have had the advantage of a printed text; as far as this chapter goes, however, there is no equivalent written text to refer to. Activity 1 is designed to give you a sense of how to begin analysing films. The activities that follow thereafter will help you further hone your skills at reading and interpreting this film in terms of its visual character.

Activity 1

Go to the main menu of the DVD. From 'Chapters' select Chapter 6 ('The new tower of Babel'), and watch it carefully – several times if necessary – especially from the point when the tower begins to be shown after Freder jumps into a cab (00:17:40). Make a list of the visual strategies through which your view of the tower is developed within the few seconds of this chapter. What are your impressions of the scene described here through a series of moving images?

Discussion

You might have noted some of the following:

1   Your gaze was directed at the scene on the screen in four subsequent **shots** (i.e. continuous unedited strips of film), which gradually drew you back from being close to the tower to finally being at a distance from where the whole tower can be seen. Also, each shot shifted the perspective slightly, so that you don't see the tower from the same direction while you are taken further away from it. You appear to have different vantage points: in the first shot you are looking straight ahead from somewhere in mid-air; in the second you are looking slightly upwards at a somewhat different view; in the third you are looking down (perhaps from a window) to ground level; and in the fourth you are back in mid-air but at a distance from the first shot. In fact, the view of the tower that is thus developed is not consistently one person's from one location; you had the advantage of looking from different viewpoints and different locations. Whatever the impression conveyed in this chapter of the film, it is not an individual or subjective one. Rather, the tower is presented, and therefore the supraterranean (as opposed to subterranean) Metropolis, in an objective manner or as the aggregate of different perspectives that are cobbled together.

2   From the first shot you were made aware of relative proportions that suggest the great magnitude of the built structures. In the first shot you would have registered the only appearance of people in the chapter, walking along an aerial pavement that cuts diagonally across the scene at a transverse to an aerial carriageway. The sense of people being dwarfed by the enormity of the buildings is magnified in the second shot, from a perspective where people are no longer visible but trains and aeroplanes seem equally dwarfed. By the fourth

shot, when the whole tower is brought to view, you have a sense of an intimidating gigantic construction.

3   The chapter might have struck you as describing an intense and busy scene. Each shot is composed of a dense collection of straight lines and geometric structures (buildings, rows of windows, vehicle tracks of various kinds), which grows denser as the perspective shifts, and ultimately seems almost more than the eye can quite take in. The compressed lines of the fixed structures in each shot form a grid that accentuates the density of movements: people, cars, trains and aeroplanes drift back and forth along the lines constantly. The entire effect is one of concentration: a concentration of buildings, intersected by a concentration of pathways for traffic and people in three-dimensional space, bearing a heavy concentration of moving objects.

4   A powerful impression of order is conveyed in the scenes. As the first shot of the supraterranean Metropolis comes up, the eye is drawn to the ordered movement of people on the aerial pavement, in regulated little phalanxes at a steady marching pace. The grids of straight lines that compose the scenes have an implicit order. The movements in the shots present a sort of to-and-fro rhythm, crossing the screen back and forth along predetermined paths – so that when, in the second shot, an aeroplane curves and moves in your direction there is something unexpected and threatening about it. In the first shot three squat pylons on the aerial carriageway flash beams of light before a car approaches, suggesting some kind of surveillance. And, after registering the phalanxes of people in the first shot, the viewer sees no other for the remaining three, as if all humanity is absorbed into the all-subsuming constructions and machineries of Metropolis.

It is quite possible that you have made other or further observations. Close attention to even such a short span of this film clarifies, at any rate, the differences from reading a written text closely. Where the written text is necessarily available in a linear sequence as words follow words and sentences follow sentences, in film a great deal of interrelated information is packed in simultaneously in each shot and in consecutive shots. Also, where words and sentences are essentially abstract significations and need to be interpreted accordingly, each image and sequences of images appear to be as immediate as looking around. And yet, these, too, involve selections and juxtapositions that also need to be interpreted. By and large, most people are habituated now to gathering information from moving images, from films and television shows, and you will face little difficulty in adapting yourself to 'reading' and interpreting a film as you might read and interpret a literary text. Nevertheless, it is worth bearing in mind that you are adopting more of an analytical perspective here towards a film than you might habitually. You need to adapt your gaze to take in the development of the film both in normal time (as its story unfolds before your eyes) and in momentary details (a concentration of simultaneous information that is visible in a moment). And you will find it useful to be sensitive to how the viewer's gaze is positioned, how different shots are selected and put together, how scenes are organised within the boundaries of the screen (the manner in which objects and persons and backgrounds are arranged in relation to each other), and how all those are modified by actions and movements. These facets of the visual experience bear upon the kinds of things you usually undertake in critical reading of literary texts: for example how the plot and characters develop, what symbols are employed, how contexts are evoked.

Real and imaginary cities

Fritz Lang had often acknowledged that the inspiration for *Metropolis* came from a visit to New York with Ufa director Erich Pommer in October 1924. Shortly after returning to Berlin he published an essay entitled 'Was ich in Amerika sah' ('What I saw in America') (11 December 1924). In it he wrote:

> [Where is] the film about one of these Babylons of stone calling themselves American cities? The sight of Neuyork alone should be enough to turn this beacon of beauty into the center of a film … Streets that are shafts full of light, full of turning, swirling, spinning light that is like a testimony to happy life. And above them, sky-high over the cars and trams appear towers in blue and gold, in white and purple, torn by spotlights from the dark of night.
>
> (Lang quoted in Bachmann, 2000, p. 4)

Four decades later, his strongly visual sense of that visit to New York remained vivid, and in a 1966 interview with Gretchen Berg he observed:

> *Metropolis*, you know, was born from my first sight of the skyscrapers of New York in October 1924 … while visiting New York, I thought that it was the crossroads of multiple and confused human forces,

blinded and knocking into one another, in an irresistible desire for exploitation, and living in perpetual anxiety. I spent an entire day walking the streets. The buildings seemed to be a vertical sail, scintillating and very light, a luxurious backdrop, suspended in the dark sky to dazzle, distract and hypnotize.

(Lang quoted in Berg, 2003 [1966], pp. 68–9)

Lang was obviously struck by the visual spectacle of the New York cityscape, the play of lights and colours inspired his admiration, and it seemed 'a beacon of beauty' and a 'testimony to happy life'; he felt that it was all, so to speak, out of this world. His view was essentially an aesthetic one, as if looking at a painting or sculpture, and he was mainly concerned with shades and colours and lines and shapes. What is interesting in the first quotation is the manner in which beauty translates into happiness. The achievement of beauty and happiness are aspirational norms, and unsurprisingly Lang's view of New York seems to gesture towards the futuristic vision of at least the supraterranean Metropolis. At the same time, contradicting that aesthetic appraisal, there's a sort of foreboding in both quotations (forebodings can also be about the future). This foreboding is not so much about what Lang actually *saw* in New York, but about what he suspected lay behind the shining surfaces and bustle, and more importantly in his own associations and feelings. The comparison to Babylon in the first quotation is a telling one: Lang obviously had the biblical associations of Babylon in mind. Though in Akkadian (the extinct Semitic language of Akkad in ancient Babylonia) *babilani* meant 'Gate of God', the biblical Hebrew *babel* meant 'confusion' and consequently the Greek form Babylon in the Bible is associated with confusion or disorder. Indicatively, the biblical Babel myth is given a full recounting in *Metropolis* (Chapter 16). In the second quotation above Lang effectively enumerates the associations of Babylon when he talks of confusion, anxiety and feeling bedazzled.

Lang was far from alone in being impressed thus by New York. Several artists, especially those associated with the Precisionist Movement in America in the 1920s (which depicted industrialised and urban landscapes in cubist forms), developed a distinctive aesthetic vision from their encounters with New York. Consider, for instance, Figures 3.1 and 3.2. Figure 3.1, by the architect and artist Hugh Ferriss, is entitled *The Four Stages*, from 1922, and Figure 3.2, by artist Louis Lozowick, is entitled simply *New York*, from 1925. Interestingly, Lozowick's view was probably

Figure 3.1   Hugh Ferriss, *The Four Stages*, *c.*1922, charcoal on paper, in Ferriss, H. (1929) *The Metropolis of Tomorrow*, New York, Ives Washburn, p. 81.

not unlike Lang's – though he had emigrated to America in 1906 he established himself as an artist in Berlin in the early 1920s, and that is where he started painting American cities from memory before returning to America in 1924.

Figure 3.2   Louis Lozowick, *New York*, 1925, lithograph, 29 × 23 cm. British Museum, London, 1993. Photo: © Trustees of the British Museum. Reproduced courtesy of the Lozowick family.

Activity 2

In your view, how do Figures 3.1 and 3.2 compare with the images of the supraterranean Metropolis (such as the one you focused on in Activity 1, and elsewhere) in the film? Make brief notes of similarities and differences as you see them.

Discussion

It seems to me that there is an unmistakable similarity between Lozowick's depiction of New York and the picture of Metropolis that comes with the film's opening credits, and between Ferriss's future New York and the images of Metropolis you examined in the previous activity. Lozowick and Ferriss employ design techniques for their visions of the city, with somewhat different emphases: Lozowick resolves the view of the city into geometric patterns that are evenly balanced within the frame; Ferriss arranges geometric forms in complex layers so as to magnify the central building and endow it with a disproportionately solid weight and presence. The balance of Lozowick's picture is more intriguing than disturbing, and draws the eye in. The deliberate thrust of Ferriss's imposing building is meant to diminish the viewer, to stick out in the field of vision and make him or her feel insignificant and conquered. Both render their city visions devoid of humans: the city is reduced to a particular sort of aesthetic – a pure design perspective. Lang's supraterranean Metropolis (as observed in the previous activity) could be thought of as a wedding of Lozowick's and Ferriss's techniques in these pictures: also largely devoid of humans, intriguing in the balance of geometric patterns on some shots, threatening in the imposing enormity of certain structures (especially the new tower of Babel) in others. The ambiguities of Lang's view of New York are contained in that mixture of design perspectives; the exaggerations of resolving into patterns or magnifying give the images of Metropolis their superlative futuristic character.

Though the most powerfully visualised cityscape of *Metropolis* is of what I have called the supraterranean level, there are obviously other levels. If you think of yourself as a pedestrian with access to all levels of Metropolis, you would also encounter exterior views of the city at the terra firma or ground level and the subterranean level. The shots from the film I am asking you to look at in Activity 3 show some of the views you may have at ground level. And for the subterranean level – they show all of the workers' city (do try to disregard all the water splashing around) – go to Chapter 19 from 1:57:44 onwards.

Activity 3

Look at the following shots (time codes are given in parentheses):

1   The cathedral front: Chapter 22 'Head, hands, and heart' (2:24:00).

2   Art deco boards: Chapter 14 'The thin man' (1:17:00).

3   Rotwang's house: Chapter 9 'The machine-man' (00:38:09).

4   Club Yoshiwara, Chapter 14 'The thin man' (1:09:44).

With these images before you, what do you think is the purpose of dividing the city into these levels and what are the relationships between the levels?

Discussion

Where the supraterranean is presented in terms of the aesthetic of design perspectives (as a designed visual construct, so that even when it is not being deliberately shown to the audience it is framed like a background picture in Joh Fredersen's office window), the psychological and social aspects of Metropolis – its human dimensions – are concentrated at the ground and subterranean levels. (And in the interiors, but I leave a proper consideration of the interiors to you and do not touch on them here.) Here, there are familiar views to contemplate, specific architectural styles and motifs that suggest the historical past, familiar everyday views, the forms of human fantasies. The Gothic cathedral is evocative both of religious feelings and of a distinct architectural style; the art deco style posters remind us of what was modern in Lang's time; Rotwang's house is a sort of fairy tale witch's cottage; the entrance to Club Yoshiwara is a fantastic Oriental-style structure; the workers' city, underground, presents the drabness of, say, Britain's less imaginative public housing. The complexities of social classes and histories and psyches are concentrated at these levels, literally underpinning the pristine aesthetic design perspective of the supraterranean Metropolis.

The images of the ground and subterranean levels appear as fairly disparate, not immediately linked in terms of social relations or social rationales with each other or with the supraterranean Metropolis. If the latter works as an aesthetic of design perspectives, the former work also primarily in aesthetic terms – but not of the supraterranean sort. The ground and subterranean images are evocative of forms and associations that audiences are familiar with: these are historical and our-world images. They stir feelings and bring to mind associated ideas and impressions because they are already out there, on the streets, in the neighbourhood, in books and albums and galleries. In other words, their impact in the film is also predominantly an aesthetic one, but drawn from a complex of histories and artefacts and environments with which we are familiar.

This tactic of dividing the beautiful future world from its darker subterranean aspects is reminiscent of H.G. Wells's *The Time Machine* (1895) where in a future world the consuming class, the Eloi, live on the surface of the earth and the working class, the Morlocks, live underground. In fact, H.G. Wells wrote an extended review of *Metropolis* in 1927 which famously began with the words, 'I have recently seen the silliest film …', and acidly observed that while symbolising social relations in that supra and subterranean fashion might have been excusable in the late 1890s, it made no sense in the 1920s (2000 [1927], pp. 94, 95). Wells's readers at the time wouldn't have expected any other response: with the publication of his *A Modern Utopia* (1905), it had become clear that he was thinking of social relations on a planetary scale rather than in such constricted spaces as cities.

It is tempting to think of the vision of a future city in *Metropolis*, with its touch of Wells's *The Time Machine*, as somehow drawing upon concepts of utopias (ideal societies) and dystopias (dysfunctional societies). This is understandable. Philosophers of ideal societies have often focused on cityscapes, and imagined aesthetically pleasing and happy dispensations as prevailing in a city environment or an enclosed built-up space. In Wells's *A Modern Utopia* the tendency to think of utopias in enclosed spaces was explicitly criticised and eschewed (1905, pp. 11–12). Dystopian possibilities were also often discerned in urban settings. When, around the time of *Metropolis*, the overlapping of utopian aspirations and dystopian outcomes began to be overtly explored in fiction, it was visualised primarily in terms of city images – as in the enclosed cities of Yevgeny Zamyatin's *We* (English publication, 1924) or of Aldous Huxley's *Brave New World*. So, the very idea of an imagined future city seems to be associated with the business of conceiving utopias and dystopias. Moreover, such imaginings have often presented the utopian landscape effectively in terms of design and order.

However, it seems to me that Lang's film, in fact, doesn't go as far as actually presenting a utopian or a dystopian concept of a city; it merely presents images which seem to gesture in that direction. But these images do not come together in a tight rationale about social relations and political order, as all the above-mentioned literary utopias and dystopias do. The consistency of political principles and social and economic arrangements form the *raison d'être* of those, and aesthetic perceptions are a conditional or secondary matter; whereas in *Metropolis* the aesthetics of the images dominate and the social rationales and arrangements are weakly developed. There isn't a consistent social or political rationale articulated in the film – an assertion that becomes clearer when we look closely at further aspects of the film below.

Humans and machines

The relationship between machines and citizens seems to be central to society and politics in Metropolis, and images that explore this relationship in the film are widely regarded as being richly suggestive.

Activity 4

Have a careful look at the following two scenes from *Metropolis*:

1   All of Chapter 5 'Moloch!'.
2   Chapter 18 'Death to the machines!' and 19 'The city is drowned' (from time 1:53:21 to 1:55:16).

Compare and contrast the two scenes, and make notes on your inferences.

Discussion

Superficially, the two scenes appear to present the workers' relation to the machines with opposing effect: in the first, the Moloch Machine overcomes and kills the workers; in the second, the workers celebrate the destruction of the Heart Machine. In the first scene, the workers are *within* the Moloch Machine, as much part of the machine as a cog or wheel; in the second, the workers stand at a distance from the Heart Machine, the dancing audience for the drama of the machine's self-destructive pyrotechnics. In other words, in the first the workers seem to be passive victims of the machine, and in the second they are active in destroying the machine. The counterpoint between the two scenes, if that's what it is, is emphasised by various visual resonances between them. The machines themselves are structurally similar: the forms of each recall the other. The factory premises through which they are approached are identical. Both machines malfunction through a similar mechanism, portended by the overflowing of a cylindrical liquid gauge. However, despite the apparently opposing thrusts of the two scenes, in fact the relation of the machines to the workers is actually the same – in both, the machines effectively destroy workers. In the first scene, workers' lives are taken, and in the second, the workers' city is flooded. And in neither scene do the workers really exert an independent will: in the former they are at the behest of the machines, within their autonomous and uncontrolled workings, and in the latter the workers are manipulated by Joh Fredersen and egged on by the mechanical false Maria to destroy the Heart Machine, and it is the false Maria who makes the Heart Machine malfunction.

Despite appearances, then, the workers are presented in both scenes – and indeed throughout the film – as a passive and manipulated population. In fact, it is arguable that if the machines are presented as the opposite of human, then the workers are rather ambiguously presented as barely human, as more a counterpart of the machine than representative of humanity. In various scenes the dehumanised presentation of workers stands out. Whether as fodder for the Moloch Machine or as a baying crowd before the Heart Machine, they are portrayed with the mixed qualities of order and unpredictable destructiveness that are also the qualities of the machines.

Correspondingly, the machines are not portrayed as purely instrumental things either but as possessed by some kind of demonic animus. Freder's vision of the Moloch Machine transforming into a sphinx-like man-eating monster is a crystallisation of this animus. Similarly suggestive of having a life of its own, the surge of electricity that crackles around the Heart Machine before it blows up reminds us of the electric lightning bolts with which Rotwang had animated the robot to become the false Maria (in Chapter 15). The machines seem to have their own animating spirit.

The encroachment of machines on the human world is constructed in obviously normative terms – a normativeness drawn from religious associations. Machines are, to put it glibly, bad. The machine is monstrous, like a man-eating Moloch. The name Moloch evokes biblical fear of a pagan god who calls for human sacrifice (mentioned, among other places, in Leviticus 18:21 and 20:2–5), who appears as a fallen angel among Satan's generals in Milton's *Paradise Lost*: 'First MOLOCH, horrid king besmear'd with blood, / Of human sacrifice, and parents' tears' (2000 [1667], Book 1, lines 392–3). Machines in *Metropolis* control people rather than being controlled by people. Even those who do seem to control the machines, such as Joh Fredersen and Rotwang, are not really quite on top of them and seem to be infected by them. Fredersen's infection is, obviously, his inability to empathise with the workers; Rotwang's is materialised on his body, in his mechanical hand. It is clear that the workers are not in control of the machines or, for that matter, themselves. They appear throughout en masse, mostly in an indistinguishable collective rather than as individuals. They are either shown as regimented and mechanical groups (beginning with Chapter 2 'Shift change') or as seething atavistic crowds (in a prolonged sequence from Chapters 18 to 20), or as the pliable audiences for the real Maria's exhortations or the false Maria's machinations.

Importantly, however, all the above observations on the manner in which machines are depicted, and on the relations between machines and humans (particularly workers), need to be put into perspective in terms of the peculiarity of *Metropolis*'s machines. It is a curious feature of the film that there is no indication whatever of the functions of the different machines. No hint is given of what the Moloch Machine or the Heart Machine or the myriad other machines produce or what sort of work they perform. Thus, the usual definition of 'machine' seems not to be quite met; these machines appear to serve a purely symbolic purpose for the film. To some extent they characterise the opposite of the human, the unfeelingly mechanistic as opposed to the emotionally humane. Slightly at variance with that, they can be taken as symbolising an aspect of the human – the rationalistic, ordered, controlling drive of human society and power. Both these nuances are especially effectively conveyed in Rotwang's creation of the false Maria: a machine that is the opposite of the human Maria, and at the same time a machine that seems like an emanation of all too human fantasies. And playing with both nuances, machines symbolise the negative aspects of human society and human psyche, and inspire a sort of religious dread.

Underpinning these symbolic nuances, the machines in *Metropolis* straightforwardly fall in with the aesthetic structure of the film. In fact, the apparent purposelessness of the machines has the effect of accentuating the audience's sense of their forms and rhythms. Just as the various levels of Metropolis are characterised through aesthetic perception, so too are the machines of Metropolis. Various critics have noted this. With regard to the depiction of Rotwang's creation of the machine Maria (Chapter 15 'False Maria'), for instance, film critic Siegfried Kracauer observed that, 'In the brilliant laboratory episode, the creation of a robot is detailed with a technical exactitude that is not at all required to further the action', and that such scenes demonstrate no more than 'Lang's penchant for pompous ornamentation' (1947, p. 149). More recently, Michael Cowan (2007) has observed that the influence of contemporary philosophers like Ludwig Klage led Lang to insert deliberately a series of rhythmic movements in *Metropolis*. Thus the rhythms of the machines and clocks, and movements of people and bodies, and indeed of the filmed images themselves, cohere into an aesthetic whole in *Metropolis*.

The film's concern with the relation of humans to machines seems to chime in with long-standing political and social anxieties by the time it was made. It may recall Karl Marx's observations (especially in *Capital*, Volume 1) on the inevitable development of mechanisation and automation in industrial production, and the deleterious effects these have on workers. Some of these effects were becoming clear in the 1910s and 1920s, as assembly lines were successfully introduced in the Ford Motor Company's factories (they were to be hilariously satirised in Charlie Chaplin's film *Modern Times* (1936)), the influence of engineer and management-guru Fredrick Taylor's 'scientific management' theories spread, and a growing working-class movement and workers' unrest were evidenced. Numerous literary and philosophical works examined the relations between humans and machines accordingly: notably, the Czech playwright Karel Čapek's play *R.U.R.* (*Rossum's Universal Robots*) (1921), which explored the possibilities of mass-producing humanoid machines or 'robots' (Lang's false Maria was probably inspired by this). While such ideas and events seem to resonate with the images of machines in *Metropolis*, the latter cannot be regarded as a pointed intervention in such concerns. Marx's observations about the alienating effects of mechanisation on workers, in fact, have no resonances with Lang's vision of Metropolis. Marx's observations derived from a clear understanding of capitalist systems of production and consumption, and Lang's film is unforthcoming about such systems in Metropolis. The film's depiction of machines in relation to humans has primarily an aesthetic and normatively religious thrust, with little attempt at clarifying the economic and industrial system which determines that relationship.

However, the relation of humans and machines has continued to be a constant preoccupation since the 1920s, and sometimes even politically aware and avowedly unreligious thinkers seem to come close to evoking a *Metropolis*-like vision. Philosopher Bertrand Russell's comments, for instance, on the dangers of overemphasising the 'cog' function (the usefulness) of people in society may come to mind:

> You can only justify the cog theory [of people] by worship of the machine. You must make the machine an end in itself, not a means to what it produces. ... It no longer matters what the machine produces ... In time men will come to pray to the machine. ... This really won't do. The idolatry of the machine is

an abomination. The Machine as an object of adoration is the modern form of Satan, and its worship is the modern diabolism.

(Russell, 1952, pp. 59–60)

At a rhetorical level this sounds very like *Metropolis*. But *Metropolis* doesn't dig deeper than religious and aesthetic effect, and Russell's comment is neither religious nor simply rhetorical – it leads into a complex argument on how society should be organised and should conduct itself. However, though the arrangements of Metropolis are not clearly laid out, it is possible to argue that the film does have a distinctive political position: this is discussed in the following two sections.

Gender and desire

The depiction of gender and sexual relations in *Metropolis* is arguably a politically charged matter. This has to do as much with what is depicted as with how it is depicted.

Activity 5

Watch the following chapters attentively:

1   Chapter 11 'Sermon and prophecy' (you can fast forward over the Babel section (00:52:40 to 00:55:22) here, as I return to it in the next section).

2   Chapter 16 'Delirium and the dance of the whore of Babylon', from 1:30:10 to 1:33:24.

3   Chapter 18 'Death to the machines!', from 1:39:52 to 1:42:60.

For each chapter, chart out how the female characters are presented to your gaze (i.e. the view of the camera) and in terms of the gaze of those in the film.

Discussion

These chapters present the obviously opposed stereotypes of woman as 'saint' (Chapter 11) and 'whore' (Chapters 16 and 18), discussed respectively point-wise below.

1   Chapter 11: These episodes – covering Maria's sermon and her second and more intimate encounter with Freder – are largely composed according to the logic of looks, in terms of who is looking

and what he (mostly) or she (rarely) sees. So, Chapter 11 begins with Freder raising his eyes (we have a face-on shot of him looking) and then moves to Maria at a distance, centred in every imaginable way (we see what he sees). Then Joh Fredersen and Rotwang are shown taking their vantage point above the scene (they are the beholders now) and soon the shot moves to Maria talking to the workers from above (we see what they see). For a brief moment before Maria begins her Babel sermon we have a shot of a large group of workers (all male) looking intently, and then a close-up of Maria looking straight at them (we see both sides looking at each other). After the Babylon sermon, there is a carefully composed exchange of glances between Maria, Freder and some workers, where each shot quickly establishes not only the gaze of the speaker/listener (glaring, intense, ecstatic, humbled) but also the view. Finally, after the workers leave, there is a gradual transition from the technique followed so far. Here a personal exchange between Maria and Freder begins in a similar way (interspersed with exchanges between Fredersen and Rotwang) – the audience is shown Freder/Maria looking at/seeing each other in a series of shots as they move closer. But when they are close together, our view is moved away so that both are seen in semi-profile (sometimes from Freder's side and sometimes from Maria's), and finally both are seen, kissing and parting, in close-up full-profile. In these chapters there is a shift from the camera following the looking/seeing of different characters to presenting its own perspective (from the side) of Maria and Freder in full profile. In that shift Maria is transformed from the workers' saint to Freder's lover.

2   Chapters 16 and 18: These are complex episodes to do with the public appearances of the false Maria, in each of which several strands are woven together. I focus here particularly on scenes of the false Maria's interaction with her audiences, at Club Yoshiwara and in the workers' city. The Chapter 16 segment moves back and forth between the dance in Club Yoshiwara and Freder's delirious vision of Death's dance. The entirely male audience of the club becomes fixated by the dance in semi-profile to begin with; as the dance progresses, the technique of moving the camera view back and forth between looking (the young men face on) and being seen (the dancer from the front) takes over. The viewers and the viewed are brought closer and closer as the camera moves back and forth, till the viewers become condensed into an image of eyes covering the screen. In a structurally similar fashion, the Chapter 18 segment weaves together Rotwang's conversation with the real Maria and the false Maria's rabble-rousing address to the workers. The latter is clearly meant to echo Maria's sermon in Chapter 11, and most of the techniques used there are, ironically, repeated here. By way of a transition from the

Club Yoshiwara scene, the false Maria is first imaged as speaking amidst the faces and eyes of workers, all facing the camera. Then the false Maria begins her speech in exactly the same setting as the sermon. As this unfolds we find our eyes following the workers and the false Maria looking at/seeing each other again, but also being seen from above once (in an echo of Rotwang's and Fredersen's view in Chapter 11), and being seen in semi-profile (in an echo of the real Maria and Freder's meeting in Chapter 11). Where Maria's sermon held the audience at some distance, here the false Maria draws the workers towards her – a quick succession of edits shows us these moves from a range of perspectives.

Close attention to how the camera works in *Metropolis*, and consequently how the audience's (our) view is directed, gives an overwhelming sense of the gendered nature of seeing within the film or of viewing the film. In these scenes it is predominantly men who look, especially as a collective, and women who are seen. This connection of gendered looking and gendered appearance is performed, so to speak, by the camera and therefore by the film's audience. It is a dominant and collective male gaze that perceives and interprets and effectively constructs Maria as either the real saint or the fake whore, as a comforting or dangerous presence. The film doesn't simply mould the audience's view through a tacit presumption of the male gaze; it brings this gendered gaze explicitly to awareness. The reverence of the workers for the real Maria, the lust and passions aroused by the false Maria at Club Yoshiwara or in the workers' city, are not only due to the presentation of the two Marias as females but because of how men look at females – as an audience we both see the collective eyes of the male gaze and partake of their vision. The charge of desire, whether religious or lustful, in these scenes is heightened and constantly sexualised by that deliberately constructed awareness of the predominant and predominantly collective male gaze.

In fact, this awareness is not confined to these scenes. Chapter 3 ('The sons' club') has young men playing in a gigantic stadium, and Chapter 4 ('The eternal gardens') finds them frolicking with scantily but elaborately clothed women – the sphere of pleasure is divided between men competing with each other and men being pleasured by women. Freder beholds Maria for the first time at the moment when he is about to kiss one of his frolicsome female cohorts – he is transfixed by the sight of her.

It seems clear that Freder transfers his sexual attentions to the more elevated target of Maria. It also seems clear by the end of the film that the collective male gaze not only constructs femininity, but also leads to men acting upon women accordingly and aggressively. Indicatively, the resolution of the film is reached by the witch-burning of one Maria by a group of men (led by Grot) and the rescuing of the other by the heroic Freder. The dominance of men over women in the film is, perhaps, most trenchantly conveyed in Rotwang's creation of the false Maria. According to Andreas Huyssen:

> Clearly the issue here is not just the male's sexual desire for woman. It is the much deeper libidinal desire to create that other, woman, thus depriving it of its otherness. It is the desire to perform this ultimate task which has always eluded technological man.
>
> (Huyssen, 1981/2, p. 227)

The various ways in which looking/seeing is thematised in the film while the camera manipulates the audience's view creates a sort of complicity between the vision of *Metropolis* and the audience's gaze. In a way, the sexualised desire of the male gaze spills around and beyond the obvious encounters of men and women in the film and attaches to other images and scenes. A sort of sexualised desire seems to extend to the depiction of machines too, and ultimately to the envisioning of the cityscape of Metropolis itself. Gabriela Stoicea's description of the machines in the opening sequence makes the point succinctly:

> Vertical phallic-like pistons combine with endlessly spinning wheels and other rotating devices to create the impression of a pulsating rhythm with clear sexual overtones, underscored toward the end of the sequence also by the dramatic cadence of a clock, which grows to dominate the musical score.
>
> (Stoicea, 2006, pp. 23–4)

Such sexually suggestive imagery appears constantly, and seems to spread across the vision of *Metropolis* in all directions. Towers and caverns, pistons and spouts, the to-ing and fro-ing of bodies, the cadences of visual composition merge with the sexualised male gaze that dominates in the film. The male gaze and its desire are implicit in the very aesthetic composition of *Metropolis*.

Politics and aesthetics

Just as the aesthetic of the film – the carefully structured way in which images are composed and linked up – is intricately connected with the film's gender and sexual politics, so, too, is it implicit within the more obviously foregrounded political concern: the relation between workers and bosses.

Activity 6

Revisit Chapter 11 and watch the Babel episode from 00:52:40 to 00:55:22, the content of Maria's sermon. Then select Chapter 22 ('Heads, hands, and heart') and watch from 02:23:54 until the end credits. How do these scenes create the impression that a harmonious mutual understanding between bosses and workers is established at the end?

Incidentally, Maria's account of the Babel myth bears little relation to the biblical account. The biblical Tower of Babel story (to be found in Genesis 11:1–9) describes briefly the aspirations of a people united by one language to build a tower, which was understood by God as overweening ambition. He therefore thwarted the project by 'confound [ing] their language, that they may not understand one another's speech' (Genesis 11:7).

Discussion

The perception that a harmonious mutual understanding is established in the 'Finale' is based on presumptions set up in the earlier scene. In Maria's Babel sermon God doesn't play any role; she imagines internal conflict between the planners of the tower or the 'head' (represented by one person in a colourful chiton) and the workers or the 'hands' (represented by lots of bald men), so that the latter overwhelm the former and the tower remains only partially built. This is essentially a vision of a neat social order, where planners (best thought of as one person) and workers (always a multitude) coexist in social strata that do not overlap. Since they don't overlap, Maria recommends that a 'mediator' is necessary – a 'heart' is needed – to sort things out and avert the disaster of Babel. This recommendation becomes the **leitmotif** of the film. The neatly divided situation in Babel clearly obtains in Metropolis; Maria prophesies the imminent appearance of a 'mediator' as a messiah, which (rather disappointingly) turns out to be Freder; and in the 'Finale', Freder fulfils the prophecy by making the 'head' – his father Joh – and the chief 'hand' – Grot – shake (happily both use their hands) and stop Metropolis from suffering the fate of Babel. As a structural scheme contained *within* the plotting of the film, this may be regarded as satisfactory in various ways. There is a neat structural fit between the presumptions set up in the Babel episode and the 'Finale' of the film: the neatly divided social order remains the same in both, and yet progress has been made from a failed tower to a hopeful future city. Out of a dystopian aesthetic the utopian possibility is found and affirmed. Carefully composed shots in the 'Finale' also suggest satisfying fits: the workers march in wedge formation towards the cathedral arch with its sharp wedge-shaped frontispiece, like a jigsaw piece about to move into its designated space. That the accord is reached in a temple, under the stony gaze of apostles, would also be reassuring to many.

Despite the accord and apparent harmony with which the film concludes, on numerous later occasions Lang expressed dissatisfaction with the head–heart–hand leitmotif: 'It is absurd to say that the heart is the intermediary between the hands and the brain, that is to say, the employer and the employee. The problem is social and not moral' (quoted in Berg, 2000 [1966], p. 69). In fact, what seems structurally fitting within the logic of the film looks quite different if the historical context – the period of the Weimar Republic – is taken into account. This was a particularly politically divided period in Germany, marked by an ongoing power struggle between left and right – communists and fascists – even in the phase of the relative stability of the mid-1920s when the film was made. Just a few years later the decisive rise of Hitler and Nazism would take place. Numerous cultural historians of the Weimar Republic (such as Gay, 1968/9; Durst, 2004; Kolb, 2005 [1984]) have noted a turning away from political concerns in favour of purely aesthetic artistic and mass cultural productions in the Weimar period, and the implicit politics of that proclivity. The emphasis on the aesthetic structure and perspective of *Metropolis*, which I have variously noted in the previous sections, exemplifies the zeitgeist Lang worked within. The most influential reckoning with its implicit politics came in film critic Siegfried Kracauer's book, *From Caligari to Hitler* (1947), shortly after the Second World War. This was an examination of the cultural ethos of the Weimar Republic as revealed by films made at the time, and an accounting for the rise of Nazism in the 1930s thereby. The critique of

Metropolis's resolution, far from harmonious, given by Kracauer is worth quoting at length:

> On the surface, it seems that Freder has converted his father; in reality, the industrialist has outwitted his son. The concession he makes amounts to a policy of appeasement that not only prevents the workers from winning their cause, but enables him to tighten his grip on them. His robot stratagem was a blunder inasmuch as it rested upon insufficient knowledge of the mentality of the masses. By yielding to Freder, the industrialist achieves intimate contact with the workers, and thus is in a position to influence their mentality. He allows the heart to speak – a heart accessible to his insinuations.
>
> In fact, Maria's demand that the heart mediate between hand and brain could well have been formulated by Goebbels. He, too, appealed to the heart – in the interest of totalitarian propaganda. At the Nuremberg Party Convention of 1934, he praised the 'art' of propaganda as follows: 'May the shining flame of our enthusiasm never be extinguished. This flame alone gives light and warmth to the creative art of modern political propaganda. Rising from the depths of the people, this art must always descend back to it and find its power there. Power based on guns may be a good thing; it is, however, better and more gratifying to win the heart of a people and to keep it.' The pictorial structure of the final scene confirms the analogy between the industrialist and Goebbels. If in this scene the heart really triumphed over tyrannical power, its triumph would dispose of the all-devouring decorative scheme that in the rest of METROPOLIS marks the industrialist's claim to omnipotence. Artist that he was, Lang could not possibly overlook the antagonism between the breakthrough of intrinsic human emotions and his ornamental patterns. Nevertheless, he maintains these patterns up to the very end: the workers advance in the form of a wedge-shaped, strictly symmetrical procession which points towards the industrialist standing on the portal steps of the cathedral. The whole composition denotes that the industrialist acknowledges the heart for the purpose of manipulating it; that he does not give up his power, but will expand it over a realm not yet

annexed – the realm of the collective soul. Freder's rebellion results in the establishment of totalitarian authority, and he considers this result a victory.

(Kracauer, 1947, pp. 163–4)

Kracauer's historically nuanced reading of *Metropolis* shouldn't need any explanation. It is particularly significant that he finds the implicit political slant of the film in its aesthetic structure.

Conclusion

Kracauer's 1947 reading of Weimar films generally, and *Metropolis* in particular, has subsequently coloured the views of film critics and social historians. Many have been unable to dismiss the taint of totalitarian sympathies from the film, and moral attitudes to the film have thereafter circulated around it. Some have felt outraged. Talking of the ideological confusions of Weimar youth, historian Peter Gay observed:

And how could they find clarity amid the general cacophony, the conflicting appeals, the blood-tingling assemblies of the Nazis, and the general condition of the sick Republic? The popular media, above all the films, were calculated mainly to sow confusion … As early as 1927, the greatly over-rated director Fritz Lang brought out the tasteless extravaganza, *Metropolis*, which would be of no importance had it not been taken so seriously and acclaimed so widely.

(Gay, 1968/9, p. 148)

A bitter diatribe against the film follows. Others have teased out a denunciation of totalitarianism rather than sympathy for it, and applauded the film. Jerold J. Abrams, for instance, felt that *Metropolis* closely anticipated the groundbreaking critique of totalitarian reasoning offered by left-wing Frankfurt School philosophers Max Horkheimer and Theodor Adorno in their book *Dialektik der Aufklärung* (*Dialectic of Enlightenment*), which also appeared in 1947. According to Abrams:

Lang presented perfectly, in some of the greatest moving images ever put to screen, the entire philosophical movement of Adorno and Horkheimer's *Dialectic of Enlightenment* – anticipating them by almost two decades. Living in Hitler's Germany, Adorno and Horkheimer watched the Enlightenment become totalitarian, revert to mythology, and descend into insanity. As witnesses to the rise of Hitler's fascist totalitarianism, they had the philosophical benefit of watching it happen. But Lang envisioned the same mad totalitarian-mythology fusion long before Hitler came to power. Few films – indeed, few works of art – can claim such clarity of philosophical vision.

(Abrams, 2008, p. 169)

Most have taken Buñuel's view (quoted in the introduction to this chapter), and focused on the images of the film, their aesthetic effect, their psychological resonances, and underplayed their context-specific social and political content. In this strain *Metropolis* has had an abiding impact on film and literature since. Deliberate allusions to images and visual motifs from *Metropolis* are found scattered across a simply enormous number of films and texts now.

You can test whether your engagement with the film *Metropolis* feeds usefully into your engagement with literary texts and representations of cities in the next chapter, which returns you to where my discussion of this film began – New York.

References

Abrams, J.J. (2008) 'The dialectic of enlightenment in *Metropolis*' in Saunders, S.M. (ed.) *The Philosophy of Science Fiction Film*, Lexington, KY, University Press of Kentucky, pp. 153–70.

Bachmann, H. (2000) 'Introduction: the production and contemporary reception of *Metropolis*' in Minden, M. and Bachmann, H. (eds) *Fritz Lang's* Metropolis: *Cinematic Visions of Technology*, New York, Camden House, pp. 3–45.

Berg, G. (2003 [1966]) 'The Viennese night: a Fritz Lang confession, parts one and two' in Grant, B.K. (ed.) *Fritz Lang Interviews*, Jackson, MS, University Press of Mississippi, pp. 50–76.

Buñuel, L. (2000 [1970]) '*Metropolis*' in Minden, M. and Bachmann, H. (eds) *Fritz Lang's* Metropolis: *Cinematic Visions of Technology*, New York, Camden House, pp. 106–8.

Cowan, M. (2007) 'The heart machine: "rhythm" and body in Weimar film and Fritz Lang's *Metropolis*', *Modernity/Modernism*, vol. 14, no. 2, pp. 225–48.

Durst, D.C. (2004) *Weimar Modernism: Philosophy, Politics, and Culture in Germany 1918–1933*, Lanham, MD, Lexington Books.

Gay, P. (1968/9) *Weimar Culture: The Outsider as Insider*, London, Penguin.

Huyssen, A. (1981/2) 'The vamp and the machine: technology and sexuality in Fritz Lang's *Metropolis*', *New German Critique*, no. 24/25, pp. 221–37.

Kolb, E. (2005 [1984]) *The Weimar Republic* (trans. P.S. Falla and R.J. Park), Abingdon, Routledge.

Kracauer, S. (1947) *From Caligari to Hitler: A Psychological History of the German Film*, Princeton, NJ, Princeton University Press.

Metropolis, film, directed by Fritz Lang, Germany, Ufa, 2010 [1927].

Milton, J. (2000 [1667]) *Paradise Lost*, London, Penguin.

Mindon, M. and Bachmann, H. (eds) (2000) *Fritz Lang's* Metropolis: *Cinematic Visions of Technology*, New York, Camden House.

Russell, B. (1952) *The Impact of Science on Society*, London, Routledge.

Stoicea, G. (2006) 'Re-producing the class and gender divide: Fritz Lang's *Metropolis*', *Women in German Yearbook*, vol. 22, pp. 21–42.

Wells, H.G. (1905) *A Modern Utopia*, Lincoln, NB, University of Nebraska Press.

Wells, H.G. (2000 [1927]) 'Mr Wells reviews a current film' in Minden, M. and Bachmann, H. (eds) (2000), *Fritz Lang's* Metropolis: *Cinematic Visions of Technology*, New York, Camden House, pp. 94–100.

Chapter 4
New York: poems and stories

Sue Asbee

Aims

This chapter will:

- introduce you to some American and African-American writing about New York in the first half of the twentieth century
- encourage you to develop your understanding of ways in which cities are represented in fiction and poetry
- develop your skills of close analysis in poetry and prose
- consider the use of new and traditional forms and techniques of writing in relation to the period.

Introduction

New York at the beginning of the twentieth century was constantly changing. In 1908 the Singer Building dominated the skyline at a height of 612 feet (187 metres), while only five years later the Woolworth Building outstripped it, becoming the world's tallest at 792 feet (241 metres). The American Radiator Building went up in 1924, the Bank of Manhattan Trust and the Chrysler Building in 1930, swiftly followed by the Empire State Building in 1931, each taller than the last. But skyscrapers and relentless construction work were not alone in declaring this city's difference from any other in the world at the time: London's West End had had gaslight since 1807 – New York had gaslight too, but in 1882 the first power plant opened and the streets were illuminated by electric light. Broadway was known as 'The Great White Way' as early as the 1890s. Odette Keun, a European arriving in New York several decades later in the 1930s, describes the way that:

> as soon as dusk falls, Broadway bursts into a scintillation which has no equal in America or anywhere else in the world. In an illumination more blinding than a tropical day at its zenith … All around you is the apotheosis of electricity. It makes your head reel, for that blaze and riot of light isn't static: it flares, flows, writhes, rolls, blinks, winks, flickers, changes colour, vanishes and sparkles again …
>
> (Keun, 1939, p. 61)

Many of these lights were illuminated advertisements testifying that trade and consumerism were (as they remain) the vital centre of the city, while the coming of electricity radically changed the way inhabitants and visitors saw the city, as 'brightly lit interiors of apartments and offices became visible to people passing in the streets or on elevated trains' (Sharpe, 2008, p. 5).

Of the vast amount of writing about New York that dates from 1910 to 1950, I shall begin by selecting poems and biographical extracts that represent the strangeness and the excitement of arrival in the city. Short poems are included in the chapter itself, whereas longer ones, along with some prose extracts, are reproduced as Readings 4.1–4.12 in 'Readings for Part 1' at the back of this part of the book. You should read these as and when you are instructed to do so within the chapter. There are also some relevant additional poems (Readings 4.13–4.17) which are not discussed here but which you might like to read after you have finished the chapter.

The early twentieth century was a period of great movement of African-Americans from the American South to New York, partly because of the need for labour in a city under perpetual construction and, more importantly, because the North was less overtly racist than the South. As Langston Hughes's poem 'Not a Movie' says, 'there ain't no Ku Klux / on a 133rd' (Reading 4.1, ll. 14–15). While discrimination was still a serious social problem and remained so throughout this period, there were no lynchings in New York. Writers like Claude McKay (1889–1948) and Langston Hughes (1902–1967) were part of this diaspora. McKay, a left-wing political activist born in Jamaica, arrived in New York in 1914 hoping to open a restaurant. Hughes came to New York in 1921 to enrol in college but lasted only a year at Columbia University. Both men found low-paid manual work, including waiting tables, before McKay left to travel extensively in Europe. Hughes eventually found employment as part of a crew sailing to Africa, and he too travelled around Europe. Both men eventually returned to the USA. Hughes found the cultural life and general excitement of the New York neighbourhood of Harlem seductive, for in the early decades of the twentieth century it became a vibrant centre for musicians, artists, writers and dancers. This extraordinary burst of creativity became known as the Harlem Renaissance.

In his book *Harlem: Negro Metropolis*, McKay says that the area had been described rather derisorily as:

> a vast circus in which the people seem satisfied with an army of noise makers who swing in the dance halls and sing wildly in peace kingdoms; that they love spectacular parades of drums and uniforms, and prancing on the pavements by day and jiving in the honkey-tonks by night.

(McKay, 1940, p. 15)

This description certainly conveys some of the noise and excitement: his reference to 'spectacular parades' that were 'glittering with gorgeous uniforms' (p. 20) refers to the movement started in Harlem by Marcus Garvey (1887–1940), which quickly spread throughout the USA. Its slogan was 'Africa for Africans' and its aim was exactly that: to free Africa from white dominance.

Claude McKay says that Harlem

> is the queen of black belts, drawing Aframericans together into a vast humming hive. They have swarmed in from the different states, from the islands of the Caribbean and from Africa. And they still are coming in spite of the grim misery that lurks behind the inviting façades. Overcrowded tenements … do not daunt them. Harlem remains the magnet.
>
> Harlem is more than the Negro capital of the nation. It is the Negro capital of the world. And as New York is the most glorious experiment on earth of different races and divers groups of humanity struggling and scrambling to live together, so Harlem is the most interesting sample of black humanity marching along with white humanity.
>
> (McKay, 1940, p. 16)

Here again, McKay's image of a bee hive suggests sound as well as energetic, restless and relentless movement. He doesn't deny poverty, but still confidently declares that New York is 'glorious' in its diversity. So, for example, Langston Hughes's poem 'Second Generation: New York' (Reading 4.2) is about Irish and Polish emigrants, while his 'Harlem Sweeties' (Reading 4.3) is a sustained celebration of variations of colour, indicating the multiple heritages of Harlem's inhabitants.

Because of the importance of the Harlem Renaissance in the 1920s and its significance for the period, the majority of the texts we will study focus on Harlem. But New York was, and remains, a city of extraordinary diversity, so we will also read some poetry and prose that present other views of New York, beginning with arrivals to the city.

First impressions

As Suman Gupta explained in the previous chapter, the film-maker
Fritz Lang's response to New York was ambiguous. It 'made a great
impression on me', he said:

> The first evening, when we arrived, we were still enemy aliens so
> we couldn't leave the ship. It was docked somewhere on the West
> Side of New York. I looked into the streets – the glaring lights and
> the tall buildings – and there I conceived *Metropolis.*
>
> (Lang quoted in Robinson and Bletter, 1975, p. 67)

Lang was excited but not entirely seduced by the vibrant dazzling
display; his film suggests that he looked beneath the superficial glamour
and thought as well about the myriad unseen workers whose toil made
it possible. New York, as we have already begun to see, is full of
contradictions.

Since he was a child, Langston Hughes had been drawn to New York.
'I would go down to the railroad station in Kansas', he recalls,

> and touch the side of Pullman cars that had come through from
> Chicago and say to myself Chicago isn't so far from New York.
> And a person who had really been to New York was more
> wonderful to me than angels.
>
> (Hughes in Bernard, 2001, p. 32)

New York is over seven hundred miles from Chicago, but in the child's
imagination that distance was negligible, and an idea of New York was
powerfully embedded in his mind. Hughes finally arrived there when he
was nineteen. In his autobiography (an extract of which is reproduced
as Reading 4.4), he recalled the excitement like this:

> But, boy! At last! New York was pretty, rising out of the bay in the
> sunset – the thrill of those towers of Manhattan with their million
> golden eyes, growing slowly taller and taller above the green water,
> until they looked as if they could almost touch the sky! Then

Brooklyn Bridge, gigantic in the dusk! Then the necklaces of lights, glowing everywhere around us, as we docked on the Brooklyn side. All this made me feel it was better to come to New York than to any other city in the world.

(Hughes in McLaren, 2002, p. 82)

Countless travellers must have had similar impressions, but even those familiar with the city could be struck by its beauty, like the novelist F. Scott Fitzgerald (1896–1940). For his character Nick Carraway in *The Great Gatsby* (1925), New York seen from the Queensboro Bridge 'rising up across the river in white heaps and sugar lumps' is 'always the city seen for the first time, in its first wild promise of all the mystery and the beauty in the world' (2010 [1925], p. 72). The image of 'sugar lumps' to describe the skyscraper skyline suggests a construction of confectionery, beautiful but fragile and insubstantial, as well as likely to dissolve, while the idea of the city promising 'all the mystery and the beauty in the world' is a romantic one, dependent on the perspective of the bridge.

The poet Hart Crane (1899–1932) takes a similar distanced view in 'To Brooklyn Bridge'. It is the first in a long sequence of poems simply called *The Bridge* (1930).

Activity 1

Read Hart Crane's poem 'To Brooklyn Bridge' (Reading 4.5) now. How is the bridge described, and what is the perspective of the speaker?

Discussion

The opening stanzas are seen from the point of view of a seagull, or of the speaker watching a seagull:

> How many dawns, chill from his rippling rest
> The seagull's wings shall dip and pivot him,
> Shedding white wings of tumult, building high
> Over the chained bay waters Liberty –

(ll. 1–4)

It is the space above the city, the bay and the bridge that is described and defined by the bird's flight here, with subtle references to the image of New York's skyscrapers in the notion of the seagull '*building high* / Over the

Figure 4.1   People gathering by Brooklyn Bridge, 24 May 1933. Photo: ©
Bettmann/Corbis.

chained bay waters Liberty' (my emphasis). There is a suggestion of
tension, though, in the juxtaposition of sea, which is constrained ('chained')
to make a harbour, with the iconic symbol of freedom, the Statue of Liberty
that dominates the view. Freedom and confinement, then, are both present
right at the start, ideas that are developed later in the poem. The seagull's
flight describes clean lines, 'with inviolate curve' (l. 5) echoing the curve of
Brooklyn Bridge and the massive steel cables that suspend it between the
water and sky, as the seagull in flight is also suspended. The cables are
described later as 'choiring strings' (l. 30), suggesting stringed instruments,
perhaps a harp, as well as printed staves, so music, and not just sound,
becomes part of the vision.

The first four stanzas form one long sentence, but by the beginning of
the fourth, the speaker addresses Brooklyn Bridge directly:

> And Thee, across the harbour, silver-paced
> As though the sun took step of thee, yet left

> Some motion ever unspent in thy stride, –
> Implicitly thy freedom staying thee!
>
> (ll. 13–16)

The language of the poem is often deliberately archaic: the use of 'Thee' helps to elevate the tone, and the poem becomes a hymn of praise to the bridge; in this way a religious, or spiritual, aspect is conferred. The bridge is static, but this stanza is about the tension between movement and being fixed in one place: as pylons may appear to march across the landscape, so the bridge is 'silver-paced'. The use of the words 'step', 'motion' and 'stride' lead us back to the idea of freedom and constraint with the last line of the stanza. Brooklyn Bridge exists, after all, to allow people to travel between Brooklyn and Manhattan.

Like Fitzgerald's image of the city, Crane's poem opens with a Romantic solitary vision. The first stanza evokes dawn, conventionally a time of peace and contemplation, but although the poem's overriding theme is of distance from the city, there are moments of quintessentially modern 'reality', like the elevators that 'drop us from our day' in stanza two (l. 8). This alerts us to different, more everyday aspects of New York city life: cinemas, the subway, Wall Street (implying finance and commerce), the 'cloud-flown derricks' (l. 23) evoking a workforce along the wharves however much the cranes soar into the sky, and 'traffic lights that skim' (l. 33) the bridge. The only individualised figure is the 'bedlamite' (l. 18), or lunatic, who falls or leaps to his or her death from the parapet of the bridge, sounding a note of disquiet in this tribute to the aesthetic beauty and technological achievement of Brooklyn Bridge.

Conscious of writing in the early twentieth century and feeling the need to confront modern life and technology in his work, Crane said that 'unless poetry can absorb the machine' then it has 'failed of its full contemporary function' (quoted in Gray, 1990, p. 209). According to Richard Gray, in choosing Brooklyn Bridge as his subject Crane was 'making a deliberate attempt to "absorb the machine": to find a source of creativity in the industrial age' (1990, p. 209). This need to engage with the changing world, the search to find new ways of writing to express and accommodate new experience, particularly urban experience, is one aspect of modernist writing that developed to a high degree during the 1920s. Crane's *The Bridge* is partly a response to T.S. Eliot's (1888–1965) important modernist poem *The Waste Land* (1922), mentioned in the 'Introduction to Part 1'. Eliot's poem expresses his sense of life in London after the First World War as characterised by loss of faith, enervation, sterility and disaffection. Crane acknowledges such aspects of modern life in *The Bridge* but his poem as a whole (we have read only the first part here) attempts to invest the new intensely industrialised city of New York with a sense of spirituality by connecting it with its past, and by celebrating the aspirations and creativity of the new technology. Clearly the poem could not have been written before the early twentieth-century period, but the Romantic associations of dawn and the contemplative solitary figure of the poet work to reinforce the idea that periodisation is not a completely straightforward way of classifying literary texts, and that writers working in a particular literary period are indebted to those who came before them.

Activity 2

With these ideas about period in mind, now read Claude McKay's **sonnet** 'Dawn in New York' reproduced below. Compare form, content and the speaker's point of view to Crane's 'To Brooklyn Bridge' (Reading 4.5):

> The Dawn! The Dawn! The crimson-tinted, comes
> Out of the low still skies, over the hills,
> Manhattan's roofs and spires and cheerless domes!
> The Dawn! My spirit to its spirit thrills.
> Almost the mighty city is asleep,   5
> No pushing crowd, no tramping, tramping feet.
> But here and there a few cars groaning creep
> Along, above, and underneath the street,
> Bearing their strangely-ghostly burdens by,
> The women and the men of garish nights,   10
> Their eyes wine-weakened and their clothes awry,
> Grotesques beneath the strong electric lights.
> The shadows wane. The Dawn comes to New York.
> And I go darkly-rebel to my work.

(McKay in Eastman, 1922, p. 43)

Discussion

'Dawn in New York' has some elements in common with Crane's poem. Each uses the dawn, drawing on Romantic associations of this normally deserted, silent time of day to contrast with the noise and movement of city life; indeed, Crane's seagull may recall – in a more prosaic way – Percy Bysshe Shelley's ode 'To a Skylark' (1820). 'To Brooklyn Bridge' consists of fairly regular quatrains, while 'Dawn in New York' is a sonnet, so neither Crane nor McKay is interested here in experimenting with ways of representing this new, extraordinary city; instead they rely on traditional forms. In each poem the poet is an isolated figure recalling Romantic introspection.

Crane's 'bedlamite' (l. 18) emerging from the subway is another, more extreme, version of McKay's '[t]he women and the men of garish nights' (l. 10), so if the setting and the form of the poem are attempts to reconcile the present with a less metropolitan, pre-industrialised past, casualties of modern living still break through.

The subject matter of both these poems is firmly located in the twentieth century, but each deliberately draws on and effectively 'updates' earlier poems. 'To Brooklyn Bridge' has Walt Whitman's 'Crossing Brooklyn Ferry' (1856) as a precursor – until the bridge was built between 1869 and 1883 the ferry was the only means of crossing between Manhattan and Brooklyn. Similarly McKay's 'Dawn in New York' does not just draw on general Romantic associations from the past, but deliberately recalls the Romantic poet William Wordsworth's (1770–1850) sonnet 'Upon Westminster Bridge, September 3, 1802', which, like McKay's, has a dawn setting. McKay deliberately points up the contrast between 'then' and 'now'.

Activity 3

Read Wordsworth's 'Upon Westminster Bridge', reproduced below, and compare it with McKay's 'Dawn in New York'.

> Earth has not anything to show more fair:
> Dull would he be of soul who could pass by
> A sight so touching in its majesty:
> This City now doth, like a garment, wear
> The beauty of the morning; silent, bare,   5
> Ships, towers, domes, theatres, and temples lie
> Open unto the fields, and to the sky;
> All bright and glittering in the smokeless air.
> Never did sun more beautifully steep
> In his first splendour, valley, rock, or hill;   10
> Ne'er saw I, never felt, a calm so deep!

The river glideth at his own sweet will:
Dear God! the very houses seem asleep;
And all that mighty heart is lying still!

(Wordsworth in De Selincourt, 1936, p. 214)

Discussion

McKay's fifth line deliberately echoes Wordsworth's final lines, 'Dear God! the very houses seem asleep; / And all that mighty heart is lying still!' (ll. 13–14). Two hundred years later, no matter what the hour, New York is only ever 'Almost' asleep, largely owing to the installation of electric light that effectively banishes the night and irrevocably changes working and sleeping patterns. While the daytime crowds are absent, in spite of the repeated insistence on 'The Dawn', clear divisions of time are no longer observed: revellers from the night before with 'eyes wine-weakened and their clothes awry' (l. 11) are finally on their way home while the speaker is reluctantly setting off for a day's work. The tone is altogether different from Wordsworth's elevated Romantic vision of deserted London. In New York, in the twentieth century, although the speaker's spirit 'thrills' (l. 4) in response to the dawn, the decadence implied by the 'garish nights' (l. 10) and the competition between the 'crimson-tinted' (l. 1) dawn and the 'strong electric lights' (l. 12) suggests that there is no possibility of peace. The speaker's position in each poem is different too: Wordsworth's has the luxury of quiet, detached contemplation of a city with sleeping inhabitants, while McKay's, as we learn in the last lines, though reluctant, is nevertheless actively involved in the movement of the city, 'darkly-rebel' on his way to work.

To sum up, both Crane and McKay are conscious of their position in the modern twentieth-century world, while each in slightly different ways draws on tradition, drawing contrasts with the past in order to express their sense of this modernity. Crane, in particular, celebrates technology in describing Brooklyn Bridge, and were you to read 'The Bridge' in its entirety, you would see that he uses a variety of different poetic forms – as T.S. Eliot does in *The Waste Land*. McKay's representation of the city at dawn is more qualified; but he deliberately chooses a conventional sonnet form – juxtaposing the present with the past by drawing on earlier poets in order to establish a sense of difference, expressing what life is like *now*. In this way it is possible to see that what we may think of as new and discrete periods rely on earlier ones.

In McKay's poem 'When Dawn Comes to the City' (Reading 4.6) the speaker's present is contrasted sharply with the rural island heritage he has left behind. He draws on the **pastoral** tradition in Western literature which Sara Haslam discusses in the 'Introduction to Part 1', with its binary opposition between country and city where the latter is considered corrupt, or at the very least inferior to rural life. In this poem, New York has lost any Romantic gloss a distant perspective might have conferred and instead the 'tired cars go grumbling by' (l. 1) under 'the same dull stars' (l. 4):

> Out of the tenements, cold as stone,
>   Dark figures start for work;
> I watch them sadly shuffle on,
>   'Tis dawn, dawn in New York.

(ll. 5–8)

Those cold tenements are a far cry from the Romantic and idealised 'mystery and beauty' of F. Scott Fizgerald's 'white heaps and sugar lumps' rising from the river. Here the city has no energy or excitement; instead it stands in sharp contrast to the richness of the 'island of the sea'. If you look at the pattern of the stanzas on the page, you will notice that the verse form expands – the lines lengthen – as the Caribbean island is described, only to contract again when the narrow, circumscribed existence in New York is compared nostalgically to the possibilities offered by the island. 'Subway Wind' (Reading 4.7) and 'The Tropics in New York' (Reading 4.8) demonstrate a similar sense of loss. McKay's experience of living and working in the city is very different, then, from the excited anticipation Langston Hughes had as a child, or the brilliant visual recollection of his eventual arrival, or the various distanced perceptions of the city that we encountered earlier.

Hughes's sense of excitement endured on his first day (the New York City subway had opened for the first time in 1904). In his autobiography (reproduced in Reading 4.4) he says:

> I can never put on paper the thrill of that underground ride to Harlem. I had never been in a subway before and it fascinated me – the noise, the speed, the green lights ahead. At every station I kept watching for the sign: 135TH STREET. When I saw it, I held my breath. I came out onto the platform with two heavy bags and

looked around. It was still early morning and people were going to work. Hundreds of colored people! I wanted to shake hands with them, speak to them. I hadn't seen any colored people for so long – that is, any Negro colored people.

(p. 142)

The focus has changed from a panoramic perspective of the city seen from the sea, to a particular location. This is the city close up. Hughes is fascinated – not bewildered, confused or intimidated – by his first subway journey, and arriving at 135th Street he feels a sense of kinship with the predominantly black population, to the extent of wanting to greet individuals. His description encapsulates some of the contradictions of city life: it is a space for social encounter but also of social division; only on 135th Street does Hughes first notice 'hundreds of colored people!' His previously unarticulated sense of difference is subsumed in his feeling of being among people who look like him, but his desire to greet these 'hundreds' of unknown strangers also betrays his own strangeness in the city.

There are two important points to draw from this. First, as the perspective of the texts we have read so far moves from distance to close up, the changes suggest that far from appearing as one city, New York becomes more like many cities compressed together. Robert Park, for example, says that:

processes of segregation establish moral distances which make the city a mosaic of little worlds which touch but do not interpenetrate. This makes it possible for individuals to pass quickly and easily from one moral milieu to another, and encourages the fascinating but dangerous experiment of living at the same time in several contiguous, but otherwise highly separated, worlds.

(Park quoted in Tonkiss, 2005, p. 14)

The way in which Hughes seeks out 135th Street not only as exciting, but also, perhaps, as a community where he will feel at home, implies that there are areas of the city where he would not be welcome; it raises issues of segregation. If, for example, Harlem in the 1920s and 1930s was largely associated with the black population, the Bronx in the 1940s was mainly home to American Jews. That leads into my second point: city life provides anonymity, isolation and, compared to rural places where many of New York's migrants like Hughes and McKay came from, a loss of community. However, by clustering together in new urban environments, parts of the city become defined by the ethnic origins of their inhabitants and new communities arise. As Fran Tonkiss suggests:

> Ethnicity and class provided the twin analytical frames for an emerging sociology of community, and did so by describing both distinct social groups and segregated spaces in the city. Being part of a community, on these terms, could be seen as a badge of social disadvantage or of ethnic difference … bringing together notions of cultural ties, social networks and local spaces.
>
> (Tonkiss, 2005, p. 9)

We will return to these contradictions as we consider other texts in this chapter.

The city at night

New York has long been known as 'the city that never sleeps'; its blaze of artificial light challenged the natural order of night and day and transformed urban life in terms of work and leisure. The texts that we will read in this section – and in the one that follows which focuses on music – suggest that night life is vital, restless and relentless.

Activity 4

Now read Langston Hughes's 'Pushcart Man' (Reading 4.9). How does it compare to the short stories you read in *Dubliners*?

Discussion

'Pushcart Man' presents a snapshot of life on Eighth Avenue in Harlem on a Saturday night. It consists of reported snatches of apparently overheard dialogue with minimal narrative intervention, rather than conforming to a more traditional form of short story where we might expect to find fewer characters, but more characterisation and more sense of a plot. Although Joyce's short stories are very different from 'Pushcart Man' in the ways they express a character's inner self and feelings, building to a moment of understanding (or epiphany), like Hughes's story they are very much products of the early twentieth century. Each writer eschews narrative closure or resolution, which would have been an expectation in conventional nineteenth-century short stories, focusing instead on conveying impressions.

The third-person narrator sets the scene in the first paragraph of 'Pushcart Man' where 'the usual' series of 'squalls and brawls' are reported in short, rather abrupt sentences (p. 149). The only comment the narrator makes is 'Saturday night jumped' (p. 149): he makes no moral judgements about these scenes. This again is characteristic of modernist texts and is one way in which they tend to differ from earlier writing. No one in the story is contented. The 'Sanctified Sister' – a nun – uses formal ritualised language from the New Testament, when she says 'Forgive them Father, for they know not what they do' as she encounters a 'group of sinners'. But a 'young punk' contradicts her: they do know what they are doing, they just 'don't give a damn!' (p. 149). Religion, then, has no moral force here. The nun objects to such language, and does so again when she overhears a quarrel between a 'dark young fellow' and a 'light young girl' (p. 149), but no one pays her any attention.

The scene is packed with action and incident. Any one of the vignettes suggests a potential story which remains untold – why, for instance, is it so important that the studious young man gets hold of a copy of *The Times* rather than the *Daily News* or *Mirror* (p. 149)? There are so many individuals and so much discontent, and yet the overall impression is less one of fear or danger than of life and energy. If religion has no influence, and the portly matron's directives are ignored by the children, then the cop still has enough presence and status to break up a fight.

The picture represented by this short prose piece is of a community where life is lived on the streets, and continues on into the night. Children should be at home in bed at this hour, not watching fights, but 'There ain't nobody at my house' (p. 150) to go home to. There is no self-pity here, just statement of fact: 'we don't have to go home' (p. 150). Instead, in the heat of the middle of the night the children head off to 143rd Street where they can sit on blocks of ice to cool off.

Distinctively modern writing

We have already begun to consider how this short fiction differs from earlier writing, but now let us try to identify what it is that marks 'Pushcart Man' out as distinctively belonging to the beginning of the twentieth century, starting by considering the figures that people the narrative. They are caricatures rather than characters, sketched in and undeveloped, but they wouldn't be out of place in a crowd scene in one of Dickens's nineteenth-century novels, and they might also recall Wordsworth's description of 'the crowded Strand' in London in Book 7 of his long poem *The Prelude*, where he describes 'Stalls, barrows, porters' and

> midway in the street
> The scavenger, who begs with hat in hand,
> The labouring hackney coaches, the rash speed
> Of coaches travelling far, and whirled on with horn
> Loud blowing ...
> Here there and everywhere a weary throng

> (Wordsworth, 1976 [1805–6], Book 7, ll. 163–7, 171)

For Wordsworth and for Dickens, the city was both a fascinating and a fearful place where anonymity is sought and where crime thrives under cover of darkness. There is a sense in which Hughes is writing in the same tradition, especially as at the time Harlem was the riskier part of New York, not as well lit as other neighbourhoods (as we shall see). Wordsworth was writing a poem in blank verse, whereas Hughes's street scenes are presented in prose – although you might want to consider whether 'poetic prose' is a better descriptive term for the piece than 'short story'. Once again, however, you will notice the difficulties of classifying literary periods in terms of how they deal with similar subject matter.

Yet despite the links between Hughes's representation of the city and those of earlier writers, the techniques he employs in 'Pushcart Man' can be seen as distinctively modern ones. For example, he relies on dialogue with minimal narrative intervention, using the briefest of phrases (a 'passing girl paused', for example), while speech is attributed to 'a guy leaning on a mailbox' (p. 149). A sense of energy is created through the speedy exchanges of dialogue, the rapid change of focus from one group of characters to the next, and the swift succession of incidents. The narrative is fragmented, discontinuous, representing modern life, while a sense of structure comes not from plot, but from patterning. You might think back to the *Dubliners* stories you have studied and find some echoes there in Joyce's use of repeated words, images, colours and phrases, providing aesthetic coherence for each individual story, as well as giving shape to his collection as a whole.

Along with the other characters who appear (with the exception of Mary), the Pushcart Man is individualised only by his occupation: he doesn't have a name. But he appears in the opening sentence and his words conclude the piece. Variations of his cryptic cry 'If you can't get potatoes, buy tomatoes' punctuate the piece, and this repetition – sometimes referred to as a **motif** – gives readers a focus and provides the narrative with a structure. By the end of the piece we have 'trucked up Eighth Avenue in Harlem' (the destination mentioned in the opening paragraph) with him, and following his journey in this way emphasises the restlessness of this endlessly moving city. In common with other writers of the period Hughes has adapted the short story form: each of the techniques he employs serves his first consideration, which is to convey impressions to his readers rather than to develop a plot.

Hughes writes about poverty and inequalities, but his poems are also often full of energy and vitality: sounds, sights, religion, the consolations of gambling, boxing, music, love and seduction, aspirations, hopes and dreams. The characters in his poems inhabit bars and clubs, drink and take drugs; there are places where it is safe to be and places in the city where they do not belong. 'Drama for Winter Night (Fifth Avenue)' (Reading 4.10), for example, depends on readers knowing that Fifth Avenue symbolises wealth and status; by the 1920s it was known as the most expensive street in the world. 'Drama for Winter Night (Fifth Avenue)', then, points up the sharp divisions between those who can afford to be there and those who cannot, and the impossibility of crossing the geographical divisions that mark the boundaries of wealth and status.

This chapter began with a description of the impact electric light had on New York, but it is also important to know that illuminated advertising signs did not reach as far as Harlem. According to W.C. Sharpe, Americans regarded lighting as 'a commercial commodity produced by and for the benefit of commercial enterprise, and lit each locality in direct proportion to the profits it could generate' (2008, p. 6). For this reason it was simply 'darker in Harlem than anywhere else in New York. Indoors and out, Harlem relied on gas lamps as late as the

1920s' (p. 177). The entrances to clubs and venues like the Lafayette Vaudeville theatre in Harlem certainly were illuminated, but the impact was nothing like 'The Great White Way'.

In 1938 Palmer Hayden (1890–1973) painted *Midsummer Night in Harlem* (see Figure 4.2), which depicts a very different version of the district's population from Hughes's in 'Pushcart Man'. The tenement steps are crowded with men, women and children, while others look down from the windows of the building. There are no white faces to be seen. A small boy sits on the pavement by a fire hydrant, but even he is respectably dressed, while a car on the left-hand side of the painting suggests a level of affluence. The light source comes from a full moon, drawing attention to the church in the background, and even at this time of night – it must be late for the night sky to be dark on midsummer eve – members of the congregation are only just leaving. Hayden's picture conveys a sense of community with people peacefully enjoying each other's company. There are no brawls, bars, clubs or violence here.

Figure 4.2   Palmer Hayden, *Midsummer Night in Harlem*, 1938. Photo: US National Archives and Records Administration.

Figure 4.3   William H. Johnson, *Moon Over Harlem*, 1944, oil on plywood, 73 × 91 cm. Smithsonian American Art Museum, Washington, 1967.59.577. Photo: © Art Resource/Scala, Florence.

Six years later, William H. Johnson (1901–1970) painted *Moon Over Harlem* (see Figure 4.3) to commemorate the riots that took place there the year before. It depicts a very different image from Hayden's: the romantic potential hinted at in the title is intended to be an ironic comment. Here, the moon is blood red, and the subject is street violence: bottles roll on the ground while three of the characters are bleeding. There are varieties in skin tone, but significantly the arresting police officers are not white. The label in the Smithsonian Museum where Johnson's painting hangs explains that the riots started

> when a confrontation between a white police officer, a black woman, and a black soldier resulted in a melee of fighting and burning that left several killed and hundreds wounded. William H. Johnson based the pairs of figures at the left and right margins on photographs of rioters arrested by white officers. But Johnson painted the police as black men … as if the artist wanted to

suggest that the people of Harlem were brutalizing themselves through their own behavior.

(Smithsonian label text)

Like McKay and Hughes, both Palmer and Johnson were African-Americans born elsewhere: Hayden in Virginia in 1890; Johnson in South Carolina in 1901. They arrived in New York in 1919 and 1918 respectively, not least because it was the thriving centre for black culture.

Music and the night

In an essay entitled 'The Negro Artist and the Racial Mountain', Hughes said that as far as he was concerned jazz was

> one of the inherent expressions of Negro life in America; the eternal tom-tom beating in the Negro soul – the tom-tom of revolt against weariness in a white world, a world of subway trains, and work, work, work; the tom-tom of joy and laughter, and pain, swallowed in a smile.

(Hughes quoted in Wagner, 1973, p. 402)

Given that so many of New York's black population were employed in the service industries, in soul-destroying manual labour often at wages lower than their white counterparts, music could provide a means of release. If daytime meant working life, the night belonged to them, and music – especially jazz – could celebrate this. Hughes also said 'jazz is a heartbeat – its heartbeat is yours' (quoted in Wagner, 1973, p. 403); carrying this into his poems and freeing himself from the constraints of traditional poetic forms, he forges new ones, and new rhythms crafted to express Harlem life.

Activity 5

With the rhythm of heartbeats in mind, read 'Juke Box Love Song' below, and think about how its effects are achieved.

I could take the Harlem night
and wrap around you,
Take the neon lights and make a crown,
Take the Lenox Avenue busses,
Taxis, subways,   5
And for your love song tone their rumble down.
Take Harlem's heartbeat,
Make a drumbeat,
Put it on a record, let it whirl,
And while we listen to it play,   10
Dance with you till day –
Dance with you, my sweet brown Harlem girl.

(Hughes in Rampersad, 1994, p. 393)

Discussion

The poem is about making a love song from the sounds of Harlem. We
have the sense that life goes on throughout the night: the noise of buses,
taxis and subways never ceases and this relentless 'rumble' (l. 6)
becomes Harlem's distinctive heartbeat, a rhythm that could become a
'drumbeat' (l. 8) as the sounds are transformed into the song. Line
lengths are not regular; the three longest lines are almost (but not quite)
iambic pentameters. 'Harlem night', the 'sweet brown Harlem girl' and
'Harlem's heartbeat' occur in the first, last and more or less middle lines
of the poem, lending it an individual structure that focuses closely on the
sense of place: very different from McKay's formal sonnets that we read
earlier in this chapter. There are rhymes, but they are not regularly
placed, while line beginnings are as important as line endings: the
repeated imperative 'Take' eventually rhymes with 'Make' (l. 8), for
example, while the record whirling on the gramophone's turntable mimics
the speaker's dance with the girl. Significantly the dance will only last 'till
day' (l. 11) – music and dancing are for the night.

'Lenox Avenue' also begins with a reference to music, but the tone is
quite different from 'Juke Box Love Song' in spite of the fact that both
poems are made from similar material. The critic Onwuchekwa Jemie
quotes from the poem when he says that:

> In tune as he [Hughes] was with the currents of life around him, it
> is not surprising that he came to regard this music as a paradigm
> of the black experience and a metaphor for human life in general.

'The rhythm of life / Is a jazz rhythm,' he declared in 1926. Conversely a poem in jazz rhythm has the rhythm of life; to capture the rhythm of jazz is to capture (as an aspect of, a slice of) life. And the rhythm of life: long, incantative, endless like the jazz, with its riffs and breaks and repetitions, with love and joy and pain interchanging, alternating in 'Overtones, / Undertones, / To the rumble of street cars, / To the swish of rain' – the hard fierce beat of street cars and rain an appropriate urban metaphor for the movements and vibrations and cycles of which human life is composed.

(Jemie quoted in Mullen, 1986, pp. 109–10)

Activity 6

Now read 'Lenox Avenue: Midnight' (1926) reproduced below. What is the tone of the poem and what is the effect of the specific location mentioned in the title? You need to know that Lenox Avenue is the part of Sixth Avenue that runs through Harlem.

The Rhythm of life
Is a jazz rhythm,
Honey.
The gods are laughing at us.

The broken heart of love,   5
The weary, weary heart of pain, –
    Overtones,
    Undertones,
To the rumble of street cars,
To the swish of rain.   10

Lenox Avenue,
Honey.
Midnight,
And the gods are laughing at us.

(Hughes in Rampersad, 1994, p. 92)

Discussion

Time and place are equally potent; in fact, even if you didn't know that Lenox Avenue is in Harlem you would probably infer that (at least as far as this poem is concerned) it signifies a run-down area. There is a general sense of weariness in the poem's sounds and imagery: midnight here is bleak. The use of language – the repetition of 'weary' (l. 6), the 'broken heart' (l. 5), the 'pain' (l. 6) – all contribute to a sense of being down and out. The background noise of traffic, the 'rumble of street cars' (l. 9) and 'swish of rain' (l. 10) lend an exhausted tone to the poem, especially if we take the laughter of the gods literally, setting the sound of unfeeling merriment against the general sense of enervation. That line, 'And the gods are laughing at us' (l. 14) recalls Gloucester's words in Shakespeare's tragedy *King Lear*: 'As flies to wanton boys are we to th' gods, / They kill us for their sport' (2008 [1605], Act 4, Scene 1, ll. 36–7); or Thomas Hardy's 'President of the Immortals' in *Tess of the d'Urbervilles* who had 'ended his sport with Tess', abandoning her to her execution (Hardy, 1998 [1891], p. 397). Whether you were aware of these associations or not, the idea of one's unhappiness merely providing entertainment for others is not pleasant. It also suggests that there is no possibility of self-determination, no way out. Set against this, however, in spite of the 'broken heart of love' (l. 5), is an implicit relationship with 'Honey' – the person to whom the poem is addressed – and Honey is a sweet, warm name, repeated twice in the poem suggesting that there are some consolations to be found.

Harlem comes into its own at night-time, and for this reason it becomes a place for visitors as well as the people who live there:

> Guidebooks advised visitors to go to Harlem late, after the unadventurous whites downtown had gone to bed. The lateness of the hour added to the sense that one was venturing to the heart of darkness, the city of night where all things forbidden during the day were available in those few hours stolen from conventional life.
>
> (Erenberg, 1981, pp. 255–6)

Visitors dramatically change the dynamics: instead of being a place where people live and work, Harlem becomes a tourist attraction. Outsiders going with the express intent of being thrilled and possibly shocked turn it into a performance, very different from a Harlem resident writing about the place. Erenberg's description above implies all of this, together with the idea of transgression, something Hughes's poem 'Harlem Night Club' (Reading 4.11) addresses with 'Dark brown girls / In blond men's arms' (ll. 10–11). McKay's sonnet 'The Harlem

Dancer' (1917), however, specifically raises the issue of the role of the onlooker.

> Applauding youths laughed with young prostitutes
> And watched her perfect, half-clothed body sway;
> Her voice was like the sound of blended flutes
> Blown by black players upon a picnic day.
> She sang and danced on gracefully and calm,   5
> The light gauze hanging loose about her form;
> To me she seemed a proudly-swaying palm
> Grown lovelier for passing through a storm.
> Upon her swarthy neck black shiny curls
> Luxuriant fell; and tossing coins in praise,   10
> The wine-flushed, bold-eyed boys, and even the girls,
> Devoured her shape with eager, passionate gaze;
> But looking at her falsely-smiling face,
> I knew her self was not in that strange place.

> (McKay in Eastman, 1922, p. 42)

McKay's speaker watches the dancer's audience, as well as the dancer. In this way he distances and separates himself from the crowd of 'Applauding youths' (l. 1), the 'wine-flushed, bold-eyed boys, and even the girls' (l. 11) who devour the dancer's 'perfect, half-clothed body' (l. 2). The suggestion is that to dance in this way is degrading, in spite of the tension created by the speaker's obvious pleasure in her voice and movement. The final couplet endorses his superior perception as he 'knew' that the dancer must mentally remove herself from her situation in order to perform. Suman Gupta's discussion of the 'male gaze' in *Metropolis* in Chapter 3 makes for interesting comparisons here.

The speaker's perspective, then, also functions to separate the dancer from those around who watch her. If 'her self was not in that strange place' (l. 14), where is her identity located? The sonnet only answers this implicitly, and it has more to do with the speaker than with the dancer. In the last two lines of the octet (the first eight lines of a sonnet), 'To me she seemed a proudly-swelling palm / Grown lovelier for passing through a storm', he places her in the same kind of Caribbean island setting described in 'When Dawn Comes to the City' (which you read earlier in this chapter). He imagines that she has come from such a place, as McKay himself came from Jamaica. She is a displaced person who does not belong in these surroundings. The image of the palm tree, lovelier for enduring a storm, suggests trials that ultimately have made her stronger. In spite of its title, McKay's sonnet is more about the speaker than the dancer, for we have no access to her private thoughts.

The end of the period

This chapter began with preconceived ideas about New York, accounts of arrivals, and the city seen from a distance. Our discussion has brought us back to the idea of different kinds of arrivals, of tourists and of emigrants, people who arrive in the city for different reasons: those who come to marvel, and those who need to settle down and make a living.

Our last text continues and develops this idea. It is an extract from the semi-autobiographical novel *The Town and the City* by Jack Kerouac (1922–1969), which was published in 1950. We finish as we began, then, with another account of an arrival, this time from the very end of the period covered in this part of the book.

Activity 7

Now read the extract from *The Town and the City* (Reading 4.12). How can the narrative perspective be described, and what advantages does it confer?

Discussion

The third-person narrator begins by considering ways of arriving in New York, and in the third paragraph claims that coming by bus from Connecticut is best. Peter Martin (a fictional representation of Kerouac himself) makes this journey 'in the spring of 1944' (p. 153) but has done this many times in the past, so tries to imagine travelling to the city for the first time, not by remembering his own experience, but by imagining someone else's. This complicates the narrative perspective: Peter Martin imagines that the old lady sitting next to him on the bus is making this trip for the first time. She looks like a 'farmer's wife' (p. 153); in other words, while the spectacle of New York is extraordinary to anyone who has never seen it before, to this rural outsider it will seem even more so. Kerouac conveys this by using **focalisation** and free indirect style to increase a sense of immediacy. So, for example, at one point the old lady's thoughts are presented within speech marks '"Say, where the hell is it?"', whereas later the narrative moves into her consciousness without the intervention of either speech marks or a narrator's tag such as 'she thought': we simply have unmediated 'Where? What?' or 'It was Harlem, that's what it was!' (p. 155) as part of the seamless flow of the narrative. In this way an extreme sense of wonder and sometimes bewilderment is conveyed to readers.

When the bus goes through the Bronx, Peter watches

> greedily the grin of fascination on the old lady's face ... What was she thinking? Of the fabulous young Jew, Bronx-brooding and Bronx-fierce, who had written the play with that springtime yet Bronx-slain title, *Awake and Sing!*? ... Why the grin of fascination and delight on her face? ... with her big piano legs and her comfortable fat way of sitting back deep in the seat and possessing it whole, and her smile of delight because this was the Bronx and she was going through the Bronx at last.
>
> (p. 154)

'Bronx' is repeated five times in that short passage, and on three occasions it is turned into a compound adjective – 'Bronx-brooding', 'Bronx-fierce' and 'Bronx-slain' – conveying a sense of the power of Clifford Odets (1906–1963) and his play *Awake and Sing* (1935), at the same time implying that the power of this playwright and his social-protest drama is derived from the very place itself. The narrative focuses on imagining the newcomer's thoughts: she can assimilate this strange environment by naming it, 'possessing it whole' as she possesses her seat on the bus; her satisfaction conveyed not just by the 'comfortable fat way' in which she sits back, but by naming and repeating 'the Bronx'. Repetition confers the illusion that she knows it.

But one of the implicit questions that this extract actually poses is whether it is ever possible really to know a city? The paragraph quoted above suggests that we may recognise a place first through representations – photographs, a film, a book, or in the case of Kerouac's old lady, a play. The extract as a whole is punctuated by her movement 'sitting back deep in her seat and possessing it whole' as they drive through the Bronx, then leaning forward 'with a frown of perplexity', thinking 'Say, where the hell is it?' as she realises that she has yet to reach New York. Harlem, a 'crowded blazing carnival', is characterised with more individuality than the Bronx and has her leaning forward in her seat again,

> staring slack-jawed at everything that passed and blurred swiftly by her window. She even looked away for a moment to wipe her glasses, to stare appealingly at Peter, and then hunched her great bulk forward to feast her eyes on the dense blazing scenes that grew and grew in size as they plunged on.
>
> (pp. 155–6)

Here she has no comfortable frame of reference to rely on. The act of looking away to wipe her glasses suggests that she cannot quite believe the evidence of her own eyes, and her appeal to Peter is a mute request for him to explain what she sees with amazement, but cannot fully understand.

The extract poses related questions: where does the city begin, and where does it end? How do travellers know when they have arrived? What exactly does the city consist of? Neither the Bronx nor Harlem constitutes the essence of New York. The question 'But where were the shining towers of Manhattan?' (p. 156) changes after arrival in Times Square to 'And where were the sparkling towers of Manhattan now?' (p. 157). The passage provides its own answer about the unknowability of the city, for the towers cannot be seen 'when one was buried in them', while how they could possibly have been missed 'from afar' (p. 157) remains a mystery. In a similarly contradictory way, while an 'uncountable nation' of families lived on the bus route '"nowhere near New York"', paradoxically and 'indisputably' those same families are at the same time 'denizens and partisans of the huge unknown thing called New York' (p. 154). In other words, the city escapes comprehension even as the travellers contemplate its 'unbelieveable hugeness' (p. 156).

The word 'light' is repeated at least fifteen times, amplified by repetitions of related words: 'dazzling', 'glowing', 'neon', 'lurid', 'flash' and 'flashing', 'blaze' and 'blazing'. None of these lights illuminates an interior: the life of New York takes place out of doors. Only through accumulation of detail like this, coupled with relentless repetition, can the city be described.

Activity 8

In the extract from Kerouac (Reading 4.12), when New York is first mentioned, Manhattan is described as its 'vital and dramatic heart'. But the city is built on a grid system, a mechanical plan that suggests the opposite of this organic image. How are the contrasting ideas of organic and mechanistic presented? Concentrate on analysing the end of the extract, from 'And in one brief fleeting blink …' (p. 156) to '… missed them from afar?' (p. 157).

Discussion

Ninth Avenue is 'straight as an arrow' and its cross-streets produce 'hundreds of thousands, perhaps a million street corners', all of which are 'perfectly square and measured'. But these geometric spaces are 'thronged and trafficked and peopled and furious'. As the bus speeds down 59th Street, humanity takes on biblical proportions: 'a sea of heads' and people 'in *multitudes*', Kerouac's italics here emphasising massed humanity thronging the city and blurring geometric constructions. The vastness of the city is daunting in its 'appalling hugeness'. The vision of 'One thousand yellow taxicabs speeding in the deep canyon-side' is repeated, so the inhuman emptiness of desert canyons in the Wild West serves to convey the magnitude of the absolute opposite – the man-made city, which is rapidly becoming a nightmare experience. Skyscrapers, people and traffic alike come together in 'the vast straggles and confusions and uproar, again and again at each block'. Together, these are the components that make up New York.

Conclusion

From the excitement of arriving in the city and the potential that it might offer, we have arrived at a vision of New York that borders on the inhuman. The next section of Kerouac's *The Town and the City* makes the movement from anticipation to a more qualified response quite clear:

> The sight of New York now, the way it unfolded itself in a horror of endless streets and incomprehensible sprawl and distance, was as full of dark mystery and ghostly sorrow as the world itself – the world as it had become to him since the beginning of the war, or

since some unnoticed time when he had begun to look around and say to himself: 'It is not known, it is not known!'

(Kerouac, 2000 [1950], p. 359)

New York has become a **metaphor** for 'the world' after the Second World War. The blazing lights, which are such a dominant image in the extract, have metaphorically gone out – instead the city is full of dark 'endless streets'. Further, the word 'horror' is clearly articulated. The movement of the previous passage from pleasurable anticipation to bewilderment is confirmed here. The city, like the narrator's sense of the world itself, is, and will remain, 'incomprehensible' and 'unknown'. The bus passenger is both part of, and separate from, the New York scenes that excite, amaze and confuse her. However, like the audience who watch McKay's Harlem dancer, she has by her very presence become part of the mass of humanity that constitutes New York.

References

Bernard, E. (ed.) (2001) *Remember Me to Harlem: The Letters of Langston Hughes and Carl Van Vechten 1925–1964*, New York, Alfred Knopf.

De Selincourt, E. (ed.) (1936) *Wordsworth: Poetical Works*, Oxford, Oxford University Press.

Eastman, M. (1922) *Harlem Shadows: The Poems of Claude McKay*, New York, Harcourt, Brace and Company.

Erenberg, L.A. (1981) *Steppin' Out: New York Nightlife and the Transformation of American Culture*, London, Greenwood Press.

Fitzgerald, F.S. (2010 [1925]) *The Great Gatsby*, London, Penguin Classics.

Gray, R. (1990) *American Poetry of the Twentieth Century*, Harlow, Longman.

Hardy, T. (1998 [1891]) *Tess of the d'Urbervilles*, London, Penguin.

Harper, A.S. (1966) *Langston Hughes Short Stories*, New York, Hill and Wang.

Hughes, L. (2002) *Autobiography: The Big Sea*, Columbia, MO, University of Missouri Press.

Kerouac, J. (2000 [1950]) *The Town and the City*, London, Penguin.

Keun, O. (1939) *I Think Aloud in America*, London, Longmans, Green and Co.

McKay, C. (1940) *Harlem: Negro Metropolis*, New York, Harcourt Brace Jovanovich.

Mullen, E.J. (ed.) (1986) *Critical Essays on Langston Hughes*, Boston, MA, G.K. Hall.

Rampersad, A. (ed.) (1994) *The Collected Poems of Langston Hughes*, New York, Random House.

Robinson, C. and Bletter, R.H. (1975) *Skyscraper Style: Art Deco New York*, Oxford, Oxford University Press.

Shakespeare, W. (2008 [1605]) *King Lear* in Greenblatt, S. (ed.) *The Norton Shakespeare*, 2nd edn, New York, W. W. Norton.

Sharpe, W.C. (2008) *New York Nocturne: The City After Dark in Literature, Painting, and Photography, 1850–1950*, Princeton, NJ and Oxford, Princeton University Press.

Tonkiss, F. (2005) *Space, the City and Social Theory: Social Relations and Urban Forms*, Cambridge, Polity Press.

Wagner, J. (1973) *Black Poets of the United States: From Paul Laurence Dunbar to Langston Hughes*, Urbana, IL, University of Illinois Press.

Wordsworth, W. (1976 [1805–6]) *The Prelude: A Parallel Text* (ed. J.C. Maxwell), Harmondsworth, Penguin.

Further reading

Lehan, R. (1988) *The City in Literature*, Berkeley and Los Angeles, CA, University of California Press.

Muyumba, W.M. (2009) *The Shadow and The Act: Black Intellectual Practice, Jazz Improvisation, and Philosophical Pragmatism*, Chicago, IL, University of Chicago Press.

Conclusion to Part 1

Sue Asbee

If, as Malcolm Bradbury and James McFarlane have said, modernism was 'less a style than a search for a style', the imperative behind that search was the conviction that the world had changed (1986, p. 29). If any kind of creative endeavour – whether from writers, artists, film-makers, architects or musicians and composers – was going to engage with that world, new ways of expressing it must be found. So although you will be unlikely ever to hear Jack Kerouac described as modernist, he certainly inherited a quest to find the most appropriate means of expression in his writing, thirty odd years after what we think of as 'high' modernism in the 1920s and early 1930s.

We have studied a variety of representations of real and imaginary cities in this first part of *The Twentieth Century.* Fritz Lang's *Metropolis,* partly inspired by his experience of New York, offers some fairly straightforward comparisons and connections with the poetry and prose you read in Chapter 4, but the gap between James Joyce's *Dubliners* and Kerouac's *The Town and the City* seems much wider for several reasons. Joyce's stories were first published in 1914, but written a few years earlier than that, whereas Kerouac's novel came out in 1950 – right at the end of the period covered in this part of the book. Joyce deliberately crafted and weighed each word he used, while Kerouac advocated (even if he did not always follow) the idea that one's first thought was the best one. It is this spontaneous approach to his description of the journey into New York that generates excitement. Joyce on the other hand conveys, for the most part, a sense of a city ruled by 'the conventions which regulate the civic life' ('A Painful Case', p. 105). Each writer, however, also makes extensive use of free indirect style filtered through the narrator and in this way provides subjective, personal views of the cities they describe. (Free indirect style has been a technique of prose fiction for many centuries, but writers like Jane Austen (1775–1817) used it less extensively and in addition to more conventional third-person narrative strategies, than Joyce and Kerouac do here.) Both also make equally extensive use of repetition: the words 'cold' and 'lonely' echo through 'A Painful Case', characterising one man's experience of Dublin in the same way that light explodes the darkness of Kerouac's New York.

The cities we have studied are represented by different pulsating rhythms, each of which is attuned to the past, present or future, thus evoking their particular attention to questions of period. From Joyce's measured prose, reaching a hypnotic apotheosis in the last paragraphs of 'The Dead', to the repetitive movement of Lang's mass of humanity, machines and clocks, and Langston Hughes's jazz rhythms, we learn that cities and their inhabitants never rest but are perpetually in motion.

Writing about the London of the 1920s and 1930s, Francesca Frigerio says:

> The modern metropolis is ... the very 'text' where modernity is inscribed and with which the writer must decipher the kaleidoscope of images that confronts him at every turn.
>
> (Frigerio quoted in Phillips, 2004, p. 29)

As Suman Gupta pointed out in Chapter 3, Fritz Lang saw the streets of New York as shafts of light 'like a testimony to happy life' (p. 78), but elsewhere felt that the city was 'the crossroads of multiple and confused human forces, blinded ... and living in perpetual anxiety' (Berg, 2003 [1966], pp. 68–9). Cities, as we have seen, suggest a mass of contradictions: they may hold out the promise of anonymity, but equally offer the excitement and possibilities of social encounter; communities are formed, but may also imply segregation and division. Whereas poets and novelists from earlier periods were more likely to attempt to explain and guide readers' understandings, the artists who produced these multiple versions of twentieth-century cities expected their readers and viewers to work at making their own sense of the bewildering kaleidoscopes of images found in their work.

References

Berg, G. (2003 [1966]) 'The Viennese night: a Fritz Lang confession, parts one and two' in Grant, B.K. (ed.) *Fritz Lang Interviews*, Jackson, University Press of Mississippi, pp. 50–76.

Bradbury, M. and McFarlane, J. (eds) (1986) *Modernism 1890–1930*, Harmondsworth, Penguin.

Phillips, L. (ed.) (2004) *The Swarming Streets: Twentieth-Century Literary Representations of London*, Amsterdam and New York, Rodopi.

Readings for Part 1

Contents

Reading 4.1 Langston Hughes, 'Not a Movie'

Source: Arnold Rampersad (ed.) (1994) *The Collected Poems of Langston Hughes*, **New York, Vintage, p. 396.**

Well, they rocked him with road-apples
because he tried to vote
and whipped his head with clubs
and he crawled on his knees to his house
and he got the midnight train   5
and he crossed that Dixie line
now he's livin'
on a 133rd.

He didn't stop in Washington
and he didn't stop in Baltimore   10
neither in Newark on the way.
Six knots was on his head
but, thank God, he wasn't dead!
And there ain't no Ku Klux
on a 133rd.   15

Reading 4.2 Langston Hughes, 'Second Generation: New York'

Source: Arnold Rampersad (ed.) (1994) *The Collected Poems of Langston Hughes*, New York, Vintage, pp. 351–2.

Mama
Remembers the four-leaf clover
And the bright blue Irish sky.

I
Remember the East River Parkway   5
And the tug boats passing by.

I
Remember Third Avenue
And the el trains overhead,
And our one window sill geranium   10
Blooming red.

Mama
Remembers Ireland.
All I remember is here –
And it's dear!   15

Papa
Remembers Poland,
Sleighs in the wintertime,
Tall snow-covered fir trees,
And faces frosty with rime.   20

Papa
Remembers pogroms
And the ghetto's ugly days.
I remember Vocational High,
Park concerts,   25
Theatre Guild plays.

Papa
Remembers Poland.
All I remember is here –
    This house,   30
    This street,
    This city –
And they're dear!

Reading 4.3 Langston Hughes, 'Harlem Sweeties'

Source: Arnold Rampersad (ed.) (1994) *The Collected Poems of Langston Hughes,* **New York, Vintage, pp. 245–6.**

Have you dug the spill
Of Sugar Hill?
Cast your gims
On this sepia thrill:
Brown sugar lassie,   5
Caramel treat,
Honey-gold baby
Sweet enough to eat.
Peach-skinned girlie,
Coffee and cream,   10
Chocolate darling
Out of a dream.
Walnut tinted
Or cocoa brown,
Pomegranate lipped   15
Pride of the town.
Rich cream colored
To plum-tinted black,
Feminine sweetness
In Harlem's no lack.   20
Glow of the quince
To blush of the rose.
Persimmon bronze
To cinnamon toes.
Blackberry cordial,   25
Virginia Dare wine –
All those sweet colors
Flavor Harlem of mine!
Walnut or cocoa,
Let me repeat: 30
Caramel, brown sugar,
A chocolate treat.
Molasses taffy,
Coffee and cream,

Licorice, clove, cinnamon   35
To a honey-brown dream.
Ginger, wine-gold,
Persimmon, blackberry,
All through the spectrum
Harlem girls vary –   40
So if you want to know beauty's
Rainbow-sweet thrill,
Stroll down luscious,
Delicious, *fine* Sugar Hill.

Reading 4.4 Langston Hughes, 'Manhattan Island' and 'Dormitory'

Source: Joseph McLaren (ed.) (2002) *The Collected Works of Langston Hughes*, **volume 13,** *Autobiography: The Big Sea*, **Columbia and London, University of Missouri Press, pp. 82–3.**

Manhattan Island

I was glad to leave Mexico. My father came with me as far as the capital and when the train pulled out of Buena Vista station for Vera Cruz one day in September, 1921, I said: *'Gracias a dios!'*

The next day for the first time in my life I saw the ocean – the Gulf of Mexico, with its smell of seaweed and salt water, its wharves, and big boats. But Vera Cruz in September was the hottest city I have ever known and the mosquitoes were legion. You sweltered in a bed made airless by double mosquito netting, in a room that hummed like a beehive. And when you got on the boat for New York, you were *mighty* glad.

In Merida there was quarantine. In Havana there was quarantine. Folks were sick. We couldn't go ashore.

But, boy! At last! New York was pretty, rising out of the bay in the sunset – the thrill of those towers of Manhattan with their million golden eyes, growing slowly taller and taller above the green water, until they looked as if they could almost touch the sky! Then Brooklyn Bridge, gigantic in the dusk! Then the necklaces of lights, glowing everywhere around us, as we docked on the Brooklyn side. All this made me feel it was better to come to New York than to any other city in the world.

I didn't know how to get to Harlem or where to stay after I got there, so I went that night with two Mexican friends I'd met on the boat, to a hotel off Times Square. One was a young mechanic, coming to take a course at an automobile school in Detroit and he kept saying, as the taxi carried us up town: 'But where are all the poor people? *Caramba!* Every one is dressed up here! Everybody wears shoes!' The other friend was an old man, coming to live with his son's family in Jersey. He kept saying: 'Where is the grass? Where will I keep my chickens? *Puta madre!* Is there no grass?' He had brought along a crate of game cocks, which he refused to surrender even to the bell boy in the crowded lobby of the hotel.

It was a gyp-joint hotel, between Broadway and Sixth. The clerk declared all their rooms came in suites, and he rented us a suite at nine dollars a day, each. We didn't want a suite. And we didn't want to pay nine dollars, but we didn't know where else to go that night, so we paid it, and each of us slept in an enormous bed, in an apartment that looked out onto a noisy street off the Great White Way.

Toward morning, the old man's chickens began to crow and woke me up, so we had breakfast early, shook hands, promised to write each other, and went our separate ways. I took the subway to Harlem and never saw either of them again.

Dormitory

Like the bullfights, I can never put on paper the thrill of that underground ride to Harlem. I had never been in a subway before and it fascinated me – the noise, the speed, the green lights ahead. At every station I kept watching for the sign: 135TH STREET. When I saw it, I held my breath. I came out onto the platform with two heavy bags and looked around. It was still early morning and people were going to work. Hundreds of colored people! I wanted to shake hands with them, speak to them. I hadn't seen any colored people for so long – that is, any Negro colored people.

[…]

Reading 4.5 Hart Crane, 'To Brooklyn Bridge'

Source: Frank Waldo and Thomas A. Vogler (eds) (1970) *Hart Crane: The Bridge*, **New York, Liveright, p. 1.**

How many dawns, chill from his rippling rest
The seagull's wings shall dip and pivot him,
Shedding white rings of tumult, building high
Over the chained bay waters Liberty –

Then, with inviolate curve, forsake our eyes   5
As apparitional as sails that cross
Some page of figures to be filed away;
– Till elevators drop us from our day …

I think of cinemas, panoramic sleights
With multitudes bent toward some flashing scene   10
Never disclosed, but hastened to again,
Foretold to other eyes on the same screen;

And Thee, across the harbour, silver-paced
As though the sun took step of thee, yet left
Some motion ever unspent in thy stride, –   15
Implicitly thy freedom staying thee!

Out of some subway scuttle, cell or loft
A bedlamite speeds to thy parapets,
Tilting there momently, shrill shirt ballooning,
A jest falls from the speechless caravan.   20

Down Wall, from girder into street noon leaks,
A rip-tooth of the sky's acetylene;
All afternoon the cloud-flown derricks turn …
Thy cables breathe the North Atlantic still.

And obscure as that heaven of the Jews,   25
Thy guerdon … Accolade thou dost bestow
Of anonymity time cannot raise:
Vibrant reprieve and pardon thou dost show.

O harp and altar, of the fury fused,
(How could mere toil align thy choiring strings!)   30
Terrific threshold of the prophet's pledge,
Prayer of pariah, and the lover's cry, –

Again the traffic lights that skim thy swift
Unfractioned idiom, immaculate sigh of stars,
Beading thy path – condense eternity: 35
And we have seen night lifted in thine arms.

Under thy shadow by the piers I waited;
Only in darkness is thy shadow clear.
The City's fiery parcels all undone,
Already snow submerges an iron year ...   40

O Sleepless as the river under thee,
Vaulting the sea, the prairies' dreaming sod,
Unto us lowliest sometime sweep, descend
And of the curveship lend a myth to God.

Reading 4.6 Claude McKay, 'When Dawn Comes to the City'

Source: Max Eastman (ed.) (1922) *Harlem Shadows: The Poems of Claude McKay,* **New York, Harcourt, Brace and Company, p. 60.**

The tired cars go grumbling by,
   The moaning, groaning cars,
And the old milk-carts go rumbling by
   Under the same dull stars.
Out of the tenements, cold as stone,   5
   Dark figures start for work;
I watch them sadly shuffle on,
   'Tis dawn, dawn in New York.

But I would be on the island of the sea,
In the heart of the island of the sea,   10
Where the cocks are crowing, crowing, crowing,
And the hens are cackling in the rose-apple tree,
Where the old draft-horse is neighing, neighing, neighing
   Out on the brown dew-silvered lawn,
And the tethered cow is lowing, lowing, lowing,   15
And dear old Ned is braying, braying, braying,
And the shaggy Nannie goat is calling, calling, calling
   From her little trampled corner of the long wide lea
That stretches to the waters of the hill-stream falling
   Sheer upon the flat rocks joyously!   20
   There, oh there! on the island of the sea,
     There I would be at dawn.

The tired cars go grumbling by,
   The crazy, lazy cars,
And the same milk-carts go rumbling by   25
   Under the dying stars.
A lonely newsboy hurries by,
   Humming a recent ditty;
   Red streaks strike through the gray of the sky,
     The dawn comes to the city.   30

But I would be on the island of the sea,
In the heart of the island of the sea,
Where the cocks are crowing, crowing, crowing,
And the hens are cackling in the rose-apple tree,
Where the old draft-horse is neighing, neighing, neighing   35
   Out on the brown dew-silvered lawn,

And the tethered cow is lowing, lowing, lowing,
And dear old Ned is braying, braying, braying,
And the shaggy Nannie goat is calling, calling, calling
   From her little trampled corner of the long wide lea   40
That stretches to the waters of the hill-stream falling
     Sheer upon the flat rocks joyously!
    There, oh there! on the island of the sea
      There I would be at dawn.

Reading 4.7 Claude McKay, 'Subway Wind'

Source: Max Eastman (ed.) (1922) *Harlem Shadows: The Poems of Claude McKay,* **New York, Harcourt, Brace and Company, p. 54.**

Far down, down through the city's great, gaunt gut
    The gray train rushing bears the weary wind;
In the packed cars the fans the crowd's breath cut,
    Leaving the sick and heavy air behind.
And pale-cheeked children seek the upper door   5
    To give their summer jackets to the breeze;
Their laugh is swallowed in the deafening roar
    Of captive wind that moans for fields and seas;
Seas cooling warm where native schooners drift
    Through sleepy waters, while gulls wheel and sweep,   10
Waiting for windy waves the keels to lift
    Lightly among the islands of the deep;
Islands of lofty palm trees blooming white
    That lend their perfume to the tropic sea,
Where fields lie idle in the dew drenched night,   15
    And the Trades float above them fresh and free.

Reading 4.8 Claude McKay, 'The Tropics in New York'

Source: Max Eastman (ed.) (1922) *Harlem Shadows: The Poems of Claude McKay,* **New York, Harcourt, Brace and Company, p. 8.**

Bananas ripe and green, and ginger-root
   Cocoa in pods and alligator pears,
And tangerines and mangoes and grape fruit,
   Fit for the highest prize at parish fairs,

Set in the window, bringing memories   5
   Of fruit-trees laden by low-singing rills,
And dewy dawns, and mystical blue skies
   In benediction over nun-like hills.

My eyes drew dim, and I could no more gaze;
   A wave of longing through my body swept,   10
And, hungry for the old, familiar ways,
   I turned aside and bowed my head and wept.

Reading 4.9 Langston Hughes, 'Pushcart Man'

Source: Akiba Sullivan Harper (ed.) (1996) *Short Stories: Langston Hughes*, **New York, Hill and Wang, pp. 214–6.**

The usual Saturday night squalls and brawls were taking place as the Pushcart Man trucked up Eighth Avenue in Harlem. A couple walking straggle-legged got into a fight. A woman came to take her husband home from the corner saloon but he didn't want to go. A man said he had paid for the last round of drinks. The bartender said he hadn't. The squad car came by. A midget stabbed a full-grown man. Saturday night jumped.

'Forgive them, Father, for they know not what they do,' said a Sanctified Sister passing through a group of sinners.

'Yes, they do know what they do,' said a young punk, 'but they don't give a damn!'

'Son, you oughtn't to use such language!'

'If you can't get potatoes, buy tomatoes,' yelled the Pushcart Man. 'Last call! Pushing this cart on home!'

'Have you got the *Times*?' asked a studious young man at a newsstand where everybody was buying the *Daily News*.

'I got the *News* or *Mirror*,' said the vendor.

'No,' said the young man, 'I want the *Times*.'

'You can't call my mother names and live with me,' said a dark young fellow to a light young girl.

'I did not call your mother a name,' said the girl. 'I called *you* one.'

'You called *me* a son of a –'

'Such language!' said the Sanctified Sister.

'He just ain't no good,' explained the girl. 'Spent half his money already and ain't brought home a thing to eat for Sunday.'

'Help the blind, please,' begged a kid cup-shaker pushing a blind man ahead of him.

'That man ain't no more blind than me,' declared a fellow in a plaid sport shirt.

'I once knew a blind man who made more money begging than I did working,' said a guy leaning on a mailbox.

'You didn't work very hard,' said the Sport Shirt. 'I never knowed you to keep a job more than two weeks straight. Hey, Mary, where you going?'

'Down to the store to get a pint of ice cream.' A passing girl paused. 'My mama's prostrate with the heat.'

An old gentleman whose eyes followed a fat dame in slacks muttered, 'Her backside looks like a keg of ale.'

'It's a shame,' affirmed a middle-aged shopper on her way in the chicken store, 'slacks and no figure.'

'If you don't like pomatoes, buy totatoes!' cried the Pushcart Man.

'This bakery sure do make nice cakes,' said a little woman to nobody in particular, 'but they's so high.'

'Don't hit me!' yelled a man facing danger, in the form of two fists. 'Stop backing up!'

'Then stop coming forward – else I'll hurt you.' He was cornered. A crowd gathered.

'You children go on home,' chided a portly matron to a flock of youngsters. 'Fights ain't for children.'

'You ain't none of my mama.'

'I'm glad I ain't.'

'And we don't have to go home.'

'You-all ought to be in bed long ago! Here it is midnight!'

'There ain't nobody at my house.'

'You'd be home if I was any relation to you,' said the portly lady.

'I'm glad you ain't.'

'Hit me! Just go on and hit me – and I'll cut you every way there is,' said the man.

'I ain't gonna fight you with my bare fists 'cause you ain't worth it.'

'Break it up! Break it up! Break it up!' barked the cop. They broke it up.

'Let's go play in 143rd Street,' said a little bowlegged boy. 'There's blocks of ice down there we can sit on and cool off.'

'If you don't get potatoes, buy tomatoes,' cried the Pushcart Man.

A child accidentally dropped a pint of milk on the curb as he passed. The child began to cry.

'When you get older,' the Pushcart Man consoled the child, 'you'll be glad it wasn't Carstairs you broke. Here's a dime. Buy some more milk. I got tomatoes, potatoes,' cried the pushcart vendor. 'Come and get 'em – 'cause I'm trucking home.'

Reading 4.10 Langston Hughes, 'Drama for Winter Night (Fifth Avenue)'

Source: Arnold Rampersad (ed.) (1994) *The Collected Poems of Langston Hughes*, New York, Vintage, p. 47.

You can't sleep here,
My good man,
You can't sleep here.
This is the house of God.

The usher opens the church door and he goes out.   5

You can't sleep in this car, old top,
Not here.
If Jones found you
He'd give you to the cops.
Get-the-hell out now,   10
This ain't home.
You can't stay here.

The chauffeur opens the door and he gets out.

Lord! You can't let a man lie
In the streets like this.   15
Find an officer quick.
Send for an ambulance.
Maybe he is sick but
He can't die on this corner,
Not here!   20
He can't die here.

Death opens a door.

Oh, God,
Lemme git by St. Peter.
Lemme sit down on the steps of your throne.   25
Lemme rest somewhere.
What did yuh say, God?
What did yuh say?
You can't sleep here. ...
Bums can't stay. ...   30

The man's raving.
Get him to the hospital quick.
He's attracting a crowd.
He can't die on this corner.
No, no, not here.   35

Reading 4.11 Langston Hughes, 'Harlem Night Club'

Source: Arnold Rampersad (ed.) (1994) *The Collected Poems of Langston Hughes*, **New York, Vintage, p. 90.**

Sleek black boys in a cabaret.
Jazz-band, jazz-band, –
Play, plAY, PLAY!
Tomorrow … who knows?
Dance today!   5

White girls' eyes
Call gay black boys.
Black boys' lips
Grin jungle joys.

Dark brown girls   10
In blond men's arms.
Jazz-band, jazz-band, –
Sing Eve's charms!

White ones, brown ones,
What do you know   15
About tomorrow
Where all paths go?

Jazz-boys, jazz-boys, –
Play, plAY, PLAY!
Tomorrow … all is darkness.   20
Joy today!

Reading 4.12 Jack Kerouac, *The Town and the City*

Source: Jack Kerouac (2000 [1950]) *The Town and the City,*
London, Penguin, pp. 354–8.

There are a lot of ways of traveling into New York, into the vital and dramatic heart of it – Manhattan – but only one way thoroughly reveals the magnitude, the beauty, and the wonder of the great city. This way is never taken by the spokesmen and representatives and leaders of the world, who come in airplanes and in trains. The best approach is by bus – the bus from Connecticut that comes down through the Bronx, along Grand Concourse, over to Eighth Avenue, and down Ninth Avenue to the Times Square carnival of light.

Busses coming from New Jersey or down the Hudson River drives do not penetrate by degrees into the city's heart, but suddenly emerge, either out of a tunnel or over a bridge, or out of forested parkways. But when the bus coming down from Connecticut begins to pass through places like Portchester and New Rochelle, the realization slowly occurs that these are not towns properly, but far-flung yet firmly connected doorsteps and suburbs of the great huge thing that is New York. And gradually these places are no longer vague towns, they are continuous and unending suburban sprawls. A tremendous feeling comes from this simple and terrifying fact: what vastness is this that feeds the heart in the throbbing center? How big can the city actually be? What in the world is it going to be like?

Peter Martin was traveling on this bus one rainy night in the spring of 1944, coming back from a nostalgic and sad visit to Galloway. Nothing had happened there. He had expected something intensely meaningful, dark, immense, and wonderful. Out of the sadness of his heart, he began to imagine that he had never been to New York and that he was coming into it for the first time in his life. He even selected an old woman who looked like a farmer's wife, who was riding in the same seat with him with a grin of awe and delight, as proof human and simple that coming into New York for the first time in one's life was an event of the most wonderful importance. He watched her greedily.

They came down through Mamaroneck and all the bright places, and in the soft rainy darkness of April, they began to see apartment houses, huge ones, window-glowing in the night all around. Sometimes they saw these apartment houses where there was no town to connect them to anything. They just simply appeared, fifteen stories high with a thousand shining windows, innumerable cars parked in front, and dentists' offices and doctors' offices busy with lights. The bus would roll on and pass occasional dark parks, sometimes a field, sometimes even a farmhouse, and suddenly a roadside inn with pink neon, white gravel and parked cars, and then again the huge glowing apartment houses bulking up in the night, some of them built like forts on cliffs of rock.

Though there were more and more of these apartment houses and the distant spread of incomprehensible lights in the night rain – still they were 'not anywhere near New York,' according to the bus-riders who knew, they were 'only in Larchmont' or 'only in New Rochelle,' and so on. Instead of the dazzling view of Manhattan towers in the night, there were just these same innumerable huge apartment houses standing high in the darkness with their thousands of windows, their thousands of parked cars, their unending drab shrubbery-vases in gravel courtyards.

Then bridges … incomprehensible bridges glistening in the rain, underpasses and overpasses, ups and downs along the crowded road, and still no dazzling Manhattan towers. Still the apartment houses – the Broadmoor, and the Cliffview, and the River Towers – but not the slightest sign of the tremendous Metropolis. The traveler in the bus grew more and more awed at the thought of the sheer numbers of people living in all the apartment houses that stretched back for miles, the uncountable nation of families that dwelled here 'nowhere near New York,' yet indisputably denizens and partisans of the huge unknown thing called New York.

Finally the apartment houses became so numerous and so vastly spread out in all directions that it became evident that something was coming up at last. What was this? 'This is the Bronx.' Peter watched greedily the grin of fascination on the old lady's face beside him. What was she thinking? Of the fabulous young Jew, Bronx-brooding and Bronx-fierce, who had written the play with that springtime yet Bronx-slain title, *Awake and Sing!*? Was she thinking about that? Why the grin of fascination and delight on her face? With her parcel of wrapped newspapers that passed for a traveling bag, with her big piano legs and her comfortable fat way of sitting back deep in the seat and possessing it whole, and her smile of delight because this was the Bronx and she was going through the Bronx at last. What was she seeing with her eyes and with her soul?

Now the bus crossed more bridges and suddenly the apartment houses loomed everywhere immediately above, and the streets were suddenly zooming by in explosions of light and traffic and thronging crowds. 'We have just passed a shopping center.' Some of the streets were darker than others, they merely glistened forlornly in the misty rain, cars were parked densely on each curb in the canyons between the apartment houses, a few people moved along the sidewalks, but the lights were not dazzling and many.

Then suddenly, between the apartment houses, strange tenements began to appear, darker, red-bricked, with lights in the windows that were somehow brown and dull instead of glittering bright. Then, in a flash, a great broad street exploded into view strung incredibly for a mile with lights and cars and trolleys and people, and this too disappeared, but only for a moment, as another thronging blazing street zoomed into view and passed flashing. 'This is New York! O this is New York!' they thought gleefully, and Peter's old woman leaned back comfortably and began to grin a little more complacently, knowingly, with a shrewd old pleasure and joy.

But nothing changed: the tenements and the blazing crowded streets continued on and on, and this was certainly not New York. 'We're still in the Bronx.' So, all right, it was still the Bronx. The travelers leaned forward once more, the old lady leaned forward with a frown of perplexity, and they all searched outside through the beady panes for their New York that was not there. 'Say, where the hell is it?' thought the old lady in secret.

The bus rolled on and finally began crossing great dark networks of bridges. They could see abutments and steel girders, black limbs of bridges swooping in the night, in the rain, backgrounded by a thousand scattered nonunderstandable lights, just so many swooping scaffolds and pinpoints of light everywhere. Where? What?

Then they were off the bridges and on solid ground again, and rolling fast. More dark tenements, a crowded blazing carnival scene at each corner, cars and trolleys and movie marquees, more and more of them except – well, by God – look! a million Negroes in the streets, all the Negroes in the world – fabulous and fantastic and thronging in the lights! – and what lights now! what lights! Every corner a blaze of lights and a blur of voices and klaxons and screeching trolley wheels. And one more thing! – now all the corners were absolutely square, the streets zoomed by in regular measured beats, everything was constructed in perfect squares, and such teeming tenemented carnival squares each one! It was Harlem, that's what it was! 'Say – this is Harlem!' The old lady, no longer placid and grinning, leaned forward in her seat staring slack-jawed at everything that passed and blurred swiftly by her window.

She even looked away for a moment to wipe her glasses, to stare appealingly at Peter, and then hunched her great bulk forward to feast her eyes on the dense blazing scenes that grew and grew in size as they plunged on.

But where were the shining towers of Manhattan?

The passengers waited as the bus lurched around a corner at a park, on a broad square lurid with marquee lights, and went roaring along the trees and by tenements on the other side. What was this? One could sense it for sure, something tremendous was coming up!

And in one brief fleeting blink of the eye, as the bus roared through the green light at 110th Street, they saw the magnificent space of Central Park West stretching almost three miles down to the glittering towers of Columbus Circle. In one instant they had seen it all! They had seen not only the tremendous 'penthouses' of New York ranged along a great park boulevard, but they had seen the careful straight-distanced magnificence of Central Park and its stone walls and broad promenading pavement, they had seen a vision of one thousand yellow taxicabs speeding in the deep canyon-side by glittering penthouse fronts. This was it!

They had seen only the smoothness and swankness. Now they were going to see the unbelievable hugeness. For, as they sped down Ninth Avenue by store fronts and fruit markets and crowded tenements, as they saw the hordes of people moving about in the lights, they realized somehow that this street, as many others in New York, was as straight as an arrow, and broad and long enough to lose itself in vistas even on a clear day, and just as crowded as this on every inch of its miles.

And then they saw the cross-streets flashing by, When they saw how *these* streets, which numbered in the two hundreds, crossed seemingly endless avenues and were losing themselves over the curve of the island's rock to the east, they had a vision of hundreds of thousands, perhaps a million streetcorners in all of New York, perfectly square and measured, and each one, as well as the intervening space between corners, thronged and trafficked and peopled and furious.
How could it be?

But the appalling hugeness had not revealed itself entirely. As they sped downtown past 59th Street, they began to see people in *multitudes*, they began to see a sea of heads weaving underneath lights unlike the lights they had already seen. These lights were a blazing daytime in themselves, a magical universe of lights sparkling and throbbing with the intensity of a flash explosion. They were white like the hard white light of a blowtorch, they were the Great White Way itself. And all the

cross-streets were now canyons, each exploded high in the night with
white light, and below were the multitudes of New York, the sea of
heads, the whirlpools of traffic, the vast straggles and confusions and
uproar, again and again at each block.

Was this the end of New York?

'Oh, no, this is Times Square, where we get off. But there's
downtown, oh, about six miles more downtown, down to Wall Street
and the financial district and the waterfront and the bridges – and then
Brooklyn, you see.'

And where were the sparkling towers of Manhattan now? How
could they be seen when one was buried in them, how could one have
possibly missed them from afar?

Reading 4.13 Langston Hughes, 'The Weary Blues'

Source: Arnold Rampersad (ed.) (1994) *The Collected Poems of Langston Hughes*, **New York, Vintage, p. 50**

Droning a drowsy syncopated tune,
Rocking back and forth to a mellow croon,
   I heard a Negro play.
Down on Lenox Avenue the other night
By the pale dull pallor of an old gas light   5
   He did a lazy sway. ...
   He did a lazy sway. ...
To the tune o' those Weary Blues.
With his ebony hands on each ivory key
He made that poor piano moan with melody.   10
   O Blues!
Swaying to and fro on his rickety stool
He played that sad raggy tune like a musical fool.
   Sweet Blues!
Coming from a black man's soul.   15
   O Blues!
In a deep song voice with a melancholy tone
I heard that Negro sing, that old piano moan –
   'Ain't got nobody in all this world,
     Ain't got nobody but ma self.   20
     I's gwine to quit ma frownin'
     And put ma troubles on the shelf.'

Thump, thump, thump, went his foot on the floor.
He played a few chords then he sang some more –
   'I got the Weary Blues   25
     And I can't be satisfied.
     Got the Weary Blues
     And can't be satisfied –
     I ain't happy no mo'
     And I wish that I had died.'   30
And far into the night he crooned that tune.
The stars went out and so did the moon.
The singer stopped playing and went to bed
While the Weary Blues echoed through his head.
He slept like a rock or a man that's dead.   35

Reading 4.14 Langston Hughes, 'Subway Rush Hour'

Source: Arnold Rampersad (ed.) (1994) *The Collected Poems of Langston Hughes*, **New York, Vintage, p. 423.**

Mingled
breath and smell
so close
mingled
black and white   5
so near
no room for fear.

Reading 4.15 Langston Hughes, 'Good Morning'

Source: Arnold Rampersad (ed.) (1994) *The Collected Poems of Langston Hughes,* **New York, Vintage, pp. 426–7.**

Good morning, daddy!
I was born here, he said,
watched Harlem grow
until colored folks spread
from river to river   5
across the middle of Manhattan
out of Penn Station
dark tenth of a nation,
planes from Puerto Rico,
and holds of boats, chico,   10
up from Cuba Haiti Jamaica,
in buses marked New York
from Georgia Florida Louisiana
to Harlem Brooklyn the Bronx
but most of all to Harlem   15
dusky sash across Manhattan
I've seen them come dark
    wondering
    wide-eyed
    dreaming   20
out of Penn Station –
but the trains are late.
The gates open –
    Yet there're bars
    at each gate.   25

    What happens
    to a dream deferred?
Daddy, ain't you heard?

Reading 4.16 Langston Hughes, 'Harlem Dance Hall'

Source: Arnold Rampersad (ed.) (1994) *The Collected Poems of Langston Hughes*, **New York, Vintage, p. 339.**

It had no dignity before.
But when the band began to play,
Suddenly the earth was there,
    And flowers,
    Trees,   5
    And air,
And like a wave the floor –
That had no dignity before!

Reading 4.17 Langston Hughes, 'Trumpet Player'

Source: Arnold Rampersad (ed.) (1994) *The Collected Poems of Langston Hughes*, New York, Vintage, pp. 338–9.

```
The Negro
With the trumpet at his lips
Has dark moons of weariness
Beneath his eyes
Where the smoldering memory                    5
Of slave ships
Blazed to the crack of whips
About his thighs.

The Negro
With the trumpet at his lips                   10
Has a head of vibrant hair
Tamed down,
Patent-leathered now
Until it gleams
Like jet –                                     15
Were jet a crown.

The music
From the trumpet at his lips
Is honey
Mixed with liquid fire.                         20
The rhythm
From the trumpet at his lips
Is ecstasy
Distilled from old desire –

Desire                                          25
That is longing for the moon
Where the moonlight's but a spotlight
In his eyes,
Desire
That is longing for the sea                     30
Where the sea's a bar-glass
Sucker size.
```

The Negro
With the trumpet at his lips
Whose jacket   35
Has a *fine* one-button roll,
Does not know
Upon what riff the music slips
It hypodermic needle
To his soul —   40

But softly
As the tune comes from his throat
Trouble
Mellow to a golden note.

Part 2
Migration and memory

Introduction to Part 2

Sue Asbee

Welcome to 'Migration and memory', the second part of *The Twentieth Century*. In this part of the book, we will be exploring the themes of migration and memory in a selection of texts from the second half of the twentieth century. Our focus on migration is particularly appropriate for a period which witnessed large-scale movements of people across the globe, aided in their desire to relocate by the unprecedented ease and speed of travel. Migration is intimately linked with the act of memory of the homeland that has been left behind, and this second theme operates in powerfully different ways: personally and individually, as well as collectively and culturally. To explore these ideas we begin by studying Sam Selvon's (1923–1994) *The Lonely Londoners* (1956), a novel that describes collective experiences of Caribbeans emigrating to Britain after the momentous arrival of the *Empire Windrush* at Tilbury in 1948. In this chapter we will also look at some of James Berry's (b. 1924) poems from the collection *Windrush Songs* (2007). In the next chapter we study poems from *Questions of Travel* (1965) by Elizabeth Bishop (1911–1979), whose migratory journeys from Nova Scotia to Boston, Brazil and beyond were – by comparison with the Caribbean experience – individual and solitary. Brian Friel's (b. 1929) play *Dancing at Lughnasa* (1990) concerning a missionary priest returned to Ireland after a long sojourn in Africa follows, while the last work we will study is W.G. Sebald's (1944–2001) *The Emigrants*, first published in Germany in 1992, and translated into English in 1996. In different ways, each of these texts is concerned with memory and migration and ways of reconciling the present with the past.

While migration and memory are the themes of this part, the idea of 'literatures' is the overriding concept that we are concerned with. The word 'literature' does not represent a single or straightforward idea, and using the plural form 'literatures' is one easy way of expressing this fact. In this introduction, then, I am deliberately complicating and opening up notions of what 'literature' might signify, or has signified through time. It is a word which has changed its meaning over the centuries, as consulting the *Oxford English Dictionary* will show. An early meaning is listed there as 'Acquaintance with "letters" or books; polite or humane learning'; whereas an example from 1880 is given as 'In many things he was grotesquely ignorant; he was a man of very small literature'. The third meaning that the *OED* lists is more useful for our purposes:

> Literary productions as a whole; the body of writings produced in a particular country or period, or in the world in general. Now also in a more restricted sense, applied to writing which has claim to consideration on the ground of beauty of form or emotional effect.

This broader definition widens the geographical perspective to include writing from different nations as well as particular periods. But it also uses the word 'restricted' to describe what we might think of as 'fine' writing, emphasising aesthetic qualities. The definition flags up an important meaning, but in this part of the book we are also interested in the process of change, in terms of acknowledging new voices, and new ways of writing, as literature too.

While publishers make decisions about which writing goes into print and thus reaches bookshops and the reading public, teachers make decisions about the texts they deem worthy of study in schools, colleges and universities. Such privileging results in what is known as 'the **canon**', a term that originally referred to decisions made about which religious books were authentic and should therefore become part of the authorised version of the Bible. Used in a much broader sense, the term 'canon' refers to books, music and art considered (you might ask 'by whom?') to be of most importance in shaping Western culture. Literature in this sense, then, is narrow and exclusive. But by thinking of *literatures*, we can open up the narrow range of 'great writers' (like Shakespeare or Wordsworth) and become more inclusive, recognising that there is value and interest in different kinds of writing from different places. Instead of studying English literature, which would have been the norm in most academic institutions in the UK in the first half of the twentieth century, we now study literatures written in English from across the globe, as well as works that have been translated into English – like Sebald's *The Emigrants*.

Turning to the theme of migration, it is a truism that throughout history there have been movements of peoples across the world. In the Old Testament story Moses led the Israelites out of Egypt to the Promised Land. The Greek word 'diaspora' describes this kind of exodus, the movement of a mass of people with a common cultural heritage and a common purpose, which, in the case of the Israelites, was the desire to escape from slavery. That is only one of many reasons for leaving one's birthplace: economic, political, social or familial conditions may be behind decisions to uproot and settle elsewhere. History recounts innumerable stories of those forced to flee, perhaps seeking political asylum, or freedom from oppression or poverty; there are those who believe that by migrating they can improve their own lives, that they can bring enlightenment to the lives of indigenous populations, or perhaps more cynically exploit local natural resources to their own advantage. Then there are those who simply travel. In the texts you will study in this part of the book you will encounter a variety of responses to migration and emigration. One thing is quite clear: migration engenders diverse kinds of writing as cultures collide, and for writers and artists intent on recalling and recording their experiences, the results are exciting and dynamic. New voices emerge, and new idioms and dialects allow us to see what may be a familiar location through the eyes of others.

Figure 1   Sonia Boyce, *Talking Presence*, 1988, mixed media on photographic paper. Photo: © Sonia Boyce.

Almost by definition, any new start will be measured by what has gone before – personally as well as in terms of literary tradition – so the idea of migration is linked with 'memory' throughout this part of the book. In his essay 'Imaginary Homelands' (1981) Salman Rushdie discusses the importance, as well as the reliability, of memory. 'It may be', he says,

> that writers in my position, exiles or emigrants or expatriates, are haunted by some sense of loss, some urge to reclaim, to look back … But if we do look back, we must also do so in the knowledge – which gives rise to profound uncertainties – that our physical alienation from India almost inevitably means that we will not be capable of reclaiming precisely the thing that was lost; that we will, in short, create fictions, not actual cities or villages, but invisible ones, imaginary homelands, Indias of the mind.
>
> (Rushdie, 1981, p. 10)

While Rushdie specifically refers to India, the country of his birth, in this extract, what he says has a wider application which in one way or another touches each of our texts, and also reaches back to the New York writers of Chapter 4, none of whom were native to that city. Claude McKay, for example, compares his New York present unfavourably to his Jamaican past, but never returned there. In his memory and imagination Jamaica became a 'homeland of his mind'.

If McKay felt a sense of alienation in New York, Rushdie uses 'alienation' in a different sense, to describe his sense of being removed – emotionally as well as geographically – from his native India, not his new status in London. In this way he implies an equally common experience of emigrants, culturally disoriented and unsure of their place in their new world, yet knowing that the home they left will not have remained unchanged in their absence; that it is not possible to return unequivocally to their past or, perhaps, even remember it accurately. Rushdie goes on to say that 'my India' was

> a version and no more than one version of the hundreds of millions of possible versions … I knew that my India may only have been one to which I (who am no longer what I was, and who

by quitting Bombay never became what perhaps I was meant to
be) was, let us say, willing to admit I belonged.

(Rushdie, 1981, p. 10)

Memory is not the same thing as history, and no two people will
remember the same events in the same way, but Rushdie argues that
writers – and I would expand this to include emigrants in general –
who are 'out-of-country and even out-of-language' experience the
feeling of a lost past more intensely. 'It is made more concrete' he says,
'by the physical fact of discontinuity, of his present being in a different
place from his past, of his being "everywhere"' (Rushdie, 1981, p. 12).

If a sense of identity is dependent on memory, our names are also
important in declaring – indeed asserting – who we are. Any official
document requires a name, and borders cannot be crossed without a
passport. But names are no more fixed than places of origin, and for
various reasons many emigrants' names are changed. The slave Olaudah
Equiano's (1745–1797) experience was not uncommon: born in Nigeria
and sold to white slave traders, he was Jacob to his master in Virginia,
'but on board the African ship I was called Michael'; sold on again, on
his voyage to England the captain renames him Gustavus Vasa 'and
when I refused to answer to my new name … it gained me many a
cuff' (quoted in Phillips, 1997, pp. 11–12). Here, name changes are
imposed upon the individual; the act is a means of rebranding, asserting
superiority and possession, refusing to engage with a particular
individual as a human being, denying the importance of his heritage and
culture. Things are different in Sebald's *The Emigrants* where one
character changes his name on a tide of academic confidence, as 'a kind
of second confirmation' (p. 20). But in Anglicising his Germanic name
from Hersch Seweryn, the semi-autobiographical fictional character
Henry Selwyn also conceals his 'true background' (p. 21), forging a new
identity in the interests of adapting to a new country and new
circumstances. Names in Selvon's *The Lonely Londoners* are bestowed
differently. Nicknames may be affectionate but still say something
significant: Henry Oliver becomes Sir Galahad, a reference to the
Arthurian legend, in itself a comment on the British education system
imposed on the colonies – as well as to Galahad's romantic, optimistic
idea of England.

This part of the book explores how experiences of migration and
memory are recounted in different genres of writing, and how in each

case the search for literary forms adequate to give expression to very different experiences of migration and memory leads to a testing, and even extension of, inherited meanings of 'literature'. So, for example, Selvon's novel deals with the consequences for a cohort of Caribbean immigrants of answering the British government's recruitment drive after the Second World War. Their efforts to find homes and work, and the difficulties of surviving on low wages are partly ameliorated by opportunities for (often nostalgic) 'oldtalk', reinforcing the sense of a shared past, a necessary touchstone as the characters enter their new futures. In this way, in what is effectively a legacy of colonialism, new British voices appear in print, challenging Standard English and received ideas of what constitutes 'English literature'. Elizabeth Bishop's female voice similarly challenges the male-dominated canon, further opening up ideas of literatures in English. In the poems taken from her volume *Questions of Travel*, Richard Danson Brown suggests that her use of poetic techniques and devices is intimately bound up with the themes of migration and memory, and that her poems dramatise a variety of tensions between people and places. Bishop expands our sense of English literature by writing in such detail and with such attention about Brazil, using Brazilian poetic forms and Portuguese expressions. Absence and presence are rendered visually in Friel's play *Dancing at Lughnasa*. From the formal opening tableau to the soft-focus golden haze of the final still life, our themes are dramatised with all the ambivalence that moments preserved in snapshot, photographed images entail. This links closely to the use of photographs in Sebald's *The Emigrants*. In that novel (if indeed it can be called a novel) with the use of diary entries and photographs of indeterminate authenticity, but which provide incomplete fragmentary evidence of the past, conspiracies of silence are challenged. Memory and forgetting are explored on a personal as well as collective level. In each of these five texts questions of 'belonging' and identity surface, in each case intimately relating to differing degrees of alienation, dislocation and displacement for the migrant who is unable to forget their place of origin.

References

Phillips, C. (ed.) (1997) *Extravagant Strangers: A Literature of Belonging*, London and Boston, Faber and Faber.

Rushdie, S. (1981) *Imaginary Homelands*, London, Granta Books.

Chapter 5
Sam Selvon, *The Lonely Londoners* and James Berry, *Windrush Songs*

Steve Padley

Aims

This chapter will:

- explore representations of the themes of migration and memory in Sam Selvon's novel *The Lonely Londoners* and poems from James Berry's *Windrush Songs*
- relate these texts to the context of Caribbean migrant experience
- give you further practice in critical analysis of prose fiction and poetry
- discuss the novel in relation to the concept of literatures.

Introduction

In June 1948 the SS *Empire Windrush* arrived at Tilbury Docks in England at the end of a journey from Jamaica that brought around 500 West Indians to Britain. The British Nationality Act earlier that year had granted free entry to Britain for all Commonwealth citizens, as the government tried to recruit extra labour to help national reconstruction after the Second World War. This led to a large increase in the immigrant population of Britain, mostly from the Caribbean, India and Pakistan. Although the *Windrush* brought the first substantial migrant influx from the Caribbean, it was not until the mid-1950s that others followed in large numbers, with over 100,000 migrants arriving between 1954 and 1958.

During the war, some 10,000 West Indian servicemen were based in Britain. As Robert Winder has shown, the reception offered to these servicemen was generally hospitable; those West Indian soldiers posted to RAF bases, for example, 'were embraced as friends by their neighbours; some even resolved to come back once the fighting was over' (2004, p. 330). The story was very different, though, for many who did come back and others who made their first journey to Britain in the early post-war period. They experienced discrimination, and regular employment and decent housing were often hard to find. What, then, was the appeal of England for those Caribbean migrants who uprooted themselves from their homelands to travel thousands of miles to a country so different in terms of its social structure, cultural norms and values, and climate? The discussions of the texts in this chapter will offer some possible answers to this and other questions, through an emphasis on the themes of migration and memory.

This chapter focuses on Sam Selvon (1923–1994) and his novel *The Lonely Londoners*, published in 1956, and on James Berry (b. 1924) and some of the poems from his collection *Windrush Songs*, published in 2007. The edition of *The Lonely Londoners* that is referred to in this chapter is the Penguin Modern Classics (2006) edition, with an introduction by Susheila Nasta. You should read the novel when instructed to do so in the chapter. You can find the relevant poems from *Windrush Songs* located within the chapter, at the points at which you should read them.

Selvon and Berry: leaving home

Activity 1

Read the poem below, 'To Travel this Ship', from James Berry's
Windrush Songs and think about the following questions:

1   What can you discern in this poem about the speaker's motivation for
leaving his Jamaican homeland?

2   What, if anything, does his destination mean to him?

3   How would you characterise the language and form of this poem?

> To travel this ship, man
> I gladly strip mi name
> of a one-cow, two-goat an a boar pig
> an sell the land piece mi father lef
> to be on this ship and to be a debtor.   5
>
> Man, jus fa diffrun days
> I woulda sell, borrow or thief
> jus fa diffrun sunrise an sundown
> in annodda place wid odda ways.
>
> To travel this ship, man   10
> I woulda hurt, I woulda cheat or lie,
> I strip mi yard, mi friend and cousin-them
> To get this yah ship ride.
>
> Man – I woulda sell mi modda
> Jus hopin to buy her back.   15
> Down in dat hole I was
> I see this lickle luck, man,
> I see this lickle light.
>
> Man, Jamaica is a place
> Where generations them start out   20
> Havin notn, earnin notn,
> And – dead – leavin notn.
>
> I did wake up every mornin
> and find notn change.
> Children them shame to go to school barefoot.   25
> Only a penny to buy lunch.
>
> Man, I follow this lickle light for change.
> I a-follow it, man!

(Berry, 2007, p. 33)

Discussion

1   The main motivation is economic. The speaker sees no future in a poverty-stricken Jamaica. He records the futility of trying to make a living from agriculture, and even family ties are not enough to persuade him to stay; he rejects the land his father leaves him and even claims he would sell his own mother to escape!

2   His destination seems to be purely a means to an end; he does not even name it. There is an awareness of cultural difference – 'in annodda place wid odda ways' (l. 9) – but the speaker is clearly driven by financial necessity rather than a desire to see other places and ways of life for their own sake.

3   You will have noticed that this poem uses a dialect voice, rejecting Standard English in order to give a sense of this speaker as an individual Jamaican. You may also have noted the relative simplicity of the **diction** – it lacks the linguistic complexity and rhetorical flourishes you might associate with conventional 'poetic' language. In addition, there is only sporadic use of techniques such as rhyme, and the stanza form is irregular. However, other formal devices, such as compression of expression and the repetition of terms like 'notn', 'likkle' and 'Man', convey a vivid sense of a distinctive speaking voice.

Dialect seems more appropriate to the speaker and subject matter in this poem than would the use of Standard English, but it also brings the text into conflict with more traditional ideas of what constitutes literary language. The issue of finding a 'voice' for the articulation of West Indian migrant experience has preoccupied Caribbean writers in the post-war period, and, as you shall see, Sam Selvon's *The Lonely Londoners* was significant in this respect, though its use of dialect was also one of the factors that led British critics to dismiss its literary credentials when it was first published. As Susheila Nasta points out in her introduction to your edition of the novel, many early reviewers dismissed it as 'an amusing social documentary of West Indian manners' (p. xii). The reaction of contemporary reviewers is instructive in relation to the concept of 'literatures', demonstrating the enduring potency of traditional distinctions between literary and non-literary writing, based on subject matter and linguistic **register**.

In the 'Introduction' to *Windrush Songs*, James Berry describes the situation facing the people of the Caribbean in the late 1940s:

> None of us wanted to grow up poverty stricken. We didn't want to grow up without knowledge of the world. We certainly didn't want to grow up like our fathers who were stuck there, with a few hills of yams, a banana field, and a few animals. That could not feed a family, let alone provide money for anything more. We were a generation without advanced education or training, anxious about our future. Some of us had shown great promise at school, but now we were stuck, most of our parents could not pay for our further education and there were no national projects to employ us. And here we were, hating the place we loved, because it was on the verge of choking us to death.
>
> This was the state of the Caribbean at that time. The culture was suffering from its history. It was in a state of helplessness. In fact we had not emerged from slavery; the bonds were still around us.
>
> (Berry, 2007, p. 9)

Unlike the speaker in 'To Travel this Ship', Berry alludes to a desire among young Caribbean men to widen their horizons, to see the world, and to gain educational opportunities unavailable at home. An ambivalent attitude towards the Caribbean on the part of this generation is also revealed, as the continuing impact of slavery left them 'hating the place we loved'. The prospect of migration evoked conflicting and contradictory emotions in many of those who decided to undertake the journey to what was perceived as a land of opportunity.

Berry goes on to reveal equally ambivalent attitudes towards England:

> Despite the aftermath of slavery there was still a respect for England and a sense of belonging. ... We knew that in England you could continue education while you worked, you could go to evening school. But England was also the home of the slave masters, and we retained a general distrust of white men. However, England was the nearest thing we had to a mother country; we saw in it some aspect of hope.
>
> (Berry, 2007, p. 10)

England was seen as a place of vocation, of education, a place to belong, as well as a place where white men had grown rich through slavery. The image of England Berry presents here had been inculcated into its colonised subjects over a long period, as Winder has explained: 'Years of missionary and educational propaganda, stunning feats of engineering, impressive administrative efficiency, buckets of pageantry, and conspicuous displays of wealth and power had all left their mark. Britain seemed high and mighty, in every sense' (2004, p. 347).

It can be assumed that the troubled emotions towards their real and potential homelands felt by young Jamaicans were shared as well by inhabitants of other Caribbean islands, such as Trinidad, the birthplace of Sam Selvon. As you work through the chapter, keep in mind Berry's recollections of the hopes and fears of his Jamaican contemporaries and try to evaluate how far they are reflected in the experience of Selvon's characters.

Sam Selvon's *The Lonely Londoners*

Like James Berry, Selvon came to Britain during the early days of post-war migration, though not for economic reasons. The son of an Indian father and a Scottish-Indian mother, Selvon had a relatively comfortable middle-class upbringing. After serving in the Trinidadian Navy, Selvon worked on newspapers and literary magazines in Port of Spain, Trinidad. He moved to England in 1950, to avoid 'being lulled into complacency and acceptance of the carefree and apathetic life around me' (Selvon in Nasta and Rutherford, 1995, p. 58).

Although Selvon had published short stories and poems in his native Trinidad, it was not until after he settled in London that his career as a writer began to flourish. His first novel, *A Brighter Sun*, a story of Trinidadian rural life, was published in 1952, followed by another Caribbean-themed novel, *An Island is a World* (1955). *The Lonely Londoners*, perhaps his best-known and commercially most successful novel, followed in 1956, and was his first to address the migrant experience. Trinidad and London continued to serve as the main settings for the majority of Selvon's fiction thereafter.

Selvon's early experiences in London became the foundations for *The Lonely Londoners*. His first home was the Balmoral Hotel in South Kensington, a hostel mostly populated by colonial students, but also housing various other kinds of immigrants. Many of the people Selvon came into contact with provided the raw material for the central

Figure 5.1   Carnival spectators watching from the pavement, Trinidad, *c.*1940s–1950s. Photo: © Bradley Smith/Corbis.

characters in *The Lonely Londoners*. For Selvon, this period was significant for what it taught him about himself and other West Indians, as well as presenting him with some negative first impressions of England:

> It was my first experience of living among other West Indian islanders, happening in the heart of London thousands of miles from our home territory, and I learned as much about them as I learned about the English, whose ignorance of black people shocked me.
>
> (Selvon in Nasta and Rutherford, 1995, pp. 58–9)

It was as a consequence of encountering migrants from other West Indian islands that Selvon for the first time became 'aware of the richness and diversity of Caribbean speech' (Sandhu, 2003, p. 145), an important factor in the writing strategies adopted in *The Lonely Londoners*, enabling him to articulate experiences relatively new to literary fiction at the time.

Selvon was also instrumental in helping to establish a community of West Indian writers in London. It should be noted here that this community was at first overwhelmingly male. In the 1950s most West Indian migrants were men; only when they had settled did some bring their families to Britain. Almost inevitably, there is an emphasis on masculine perceptions in *The Lonely Londoners*. The impact of this on the novel's gender perspectives will be discussed later.

After almost thirty years, growing disillusionment with England led Selvon to emigrate to Canada in 1978. His literary fame brought him a number of awards and academic posts in Britain, the West Indies and Canada. Selvon returned to Trinidad in 1993, dying the following year of pneumonia and lung disease.

Language and form in *The Lonely Londoners*

The Lonely Londoners is regarded by many critics as a pioneering text in Caribbean migrant writing, not only because of its subject matter, but also because of its innovative use of literary form and technique. Before I ask you to read it in its entirety I'd like you to spend some time looking closely at the first few pages of the novel.

Activity 2

First, read from the beginning of the novel to the end of the second paragraph on p. 4 (which ends 'he wish he was back in bed') and then think about the following questions:

1 What type of narrative perspective is used here? Do you find anything immediately striking about the voice of the **narrator**?

   How does the narrative perspective change in this extract?

2 What impression of London is given in this section?

3 How does Selvon develop the character of Moses?

Discussion

1   I hope you recognised this extract as an example of third-person narration. The first thing you probably noticed was that, as in Berry's 'To Travel this Ship', the narrative voice does not adopt a Standard English mode of expression: phrases such as 'when it had a kind of unrealness about London' and 'as if is not London at all' (p. 1) reflect the idioms and rhythms of Caribbean speech.

Although the narration remains in the third person, I think there are some subtle shifts within that perspective in this passage. Frequently, the narrator seems to represent Moses' consciousness. From describing his actions in the second paragraph – 'When Moses sit down and pay his fare he take out a white handkerchief and blow his nose' – the narrative shifts to describe Moses' feelings about the demands placed on him by others: 'That was the hurtful part of it – is not as if this fellar is his brother or cousin or even friend' (p. 1). It is as if we are reading Moses' thoughts, expressed in his own voice. The perspective remains in the third person, but I think our identification with Moses increases here.

2   The London setting seems to me shadowy and ambiguous, effects created by the references to the 'fog' and the 'blur' that makes the setting seem as unfamiliar to the reader as it would have been to new migrants at the time. Note the evasions and qualifications in the description: 'a kind of unrealness'; 'some strange place', and the otherworldliness of the reference to 'another planet' (p. 1). This version of London seems a rather sinister place.

3   As this extract progresses, Selvon's narrative strategies give us a clearer impression of Moses and his status as a well-known figure in the migrant community, an authority on living in London. Moses seems to take on this role grudgingly, blaming himself for soft-heartedness and berating those who send new migrants to him, but the extract also shows him to have a sense of duty towards his compatriots, evidence of a strong community spirit that unites these migrants from all over the West Indies: 'But all the same he went out with them, because he used to remember how desperate he was when he was in London for the first time and didn't know anybody or anything' (p. 3).

The combination here of a non-standard voice and narrative techniques that render what for many readers would be a familiar setting in unfamiliar terms evokes sympathy, or at least empathy with the narrative voice. It seems that the reader is viewing the events and

characters from a perspective within the community that is
being described – the kind of community conventionally denied
a literary voice.

In shifting the narrative focus to represent Moses' consciousness,
Selvon adopts a technique called **focalisation**. Although the **third-
person narrator** can still be described as the 'speaker' in the second
paragraph, Moses becomes the 'focaliser': the character through whose
eyes and perceptions the narrative is mediated:

> He had was to get up from a nice warm bed and dress and come
> out in this nasty weather to go and meet a fellar that he didn't
> even know. That was the hurtful part of it – is not as if this fellar
> is his brother or cousin or even friend; he don't know the man
> from Adam.

> (p. 1)

The level of exasperation in the narrative voice at this point seems to
capture Moses' frustration, rather than reflecting the narrator's view.
This kind of deep focalisation relies on the use of **free indirect style**,
a technique discussed in the first part of this book, in relation to
James Joyce's short story 'Clay' from *Dubliners* (Chapter 2) and Jack
Kerouac's novel *The Town and the City* (Chapter 4). Moses is not
speaking aloud here, but his consciousness is rendered as though he
were speaking, though in the narrator's third-person, rather than in the
first-person. If you are still unsure about techniques such as
focalisation and free indirect style it might be worth looking back at
this point to the discussions of 'Clay' (pp. 43–6) and *The Town and the
City* (pp. 124–5), and then rereading the opening paragraphs of *The
Lonely Londoners* again to see if you can identify similarities in the shifts
of narrative perspective.

The close correlation between the narrative voice and the voices of the
Caribbean migrant characters is for many critics one of the most
innovative elements of Selvon's writing in *The Lonely Londoners*, having
a crucial effect not only on form but also on subject matter.
According to Kathie Birat: 'by placing his characters in an unfamiliar
context, he makes language, and particularly the characters' search for
a language capable of capturing their experience, the subject of the

story' (2009, p. 19). As discussed above, the effect created – making the familiar seem unfamiliar – also impacts on the non-Caribbean reader, rendering the London environment strange even to those who know it.

Selvon was by no means the first writer to explore West Indian migrant experience: as early as 1934 Jean Rhys (1890–1979), in her novel *Voyage in the Dark*, focused on a young woman from the Caribbean struggling to come to terms with life in London. Nor was Selvon the first to adopt innovative uses of free indirect style, but his experimentation with the dialect voice in exploring his subject matter and deploying his narrative techniques was something new at the time: 'I think I can say without a trace of modesty that I was the first Caribbean writer to explore and employ dialect in a full-length novel where it was used in both narrative and dialogue' (Selvon in Nasta and Rutherford, 1995, p. 74). In the opening pages of the novel, the key effect is to narrow the distance between narrator and character.

We will return to Selvon's literary style later, but now I want you to read the novel in its entirety. Don't worry too much about any unfamiliar terms or phrases, but aim for a general understanding of the content and structure of the narrative.

Activity 3

When you have completed your first reading, think about the following questions:

1 How would you describe the structure of the novel? What is Moses' function in the narrative?

2 What is your overriding impression of the characters' experience of London?

Discussion

1 I'd describe the structure of the novel as episodic, consisting of a succession of anecdotes, shifting from character to character, creating a complex web of interrelations between vividly drawn figures from different areas of the Caribbean: Moses, Galahad, Big City and Bart are all natives of Trinidad; Tolroy and his family originate from Jamaica, as does Harris; Five Past Twelve is from Barbados; and Cap is not from the Caribbean at all, but from Nigeria, though 'many times you would mistake him for a West Indian' (p. 35). From the white perspective glimpsed occasionally in the novel, migrants are

reductively categorised as Jamaican, but Selvon is at pains to stress the variety of his characters' origins, often through their reminiscences about the lives they left behind. Formally, this is reflected in the use of a dialect voice that equates to no specific Caribbean location, but amalgamates different dialects. These characters are united by the language, which also forges a link between them and the narrative voice, and by their common struggle to survive in British society. They are also united by their shared connection to the figure of Moses, whose presence links the various narrative threads.

2   These characters' experience of London is largely negative, but the use of exaggeration and comic interludes offers a more life-affirming counterpoint to the recurring **motifs** of disillusionment and alienation in the novel. Despite their disparate backgrounds there is also a sense of kinship connecting these characters.

Critical discussions of the novel's structure have made comparisons that bear in different ways on our concept of 'literatures', relating *The Lonely Londoners* to other narrative forms, both literary and non-literary. For Nasta, in her introduction to your edition of the novel, the fragmentary structure offers evidence of the influence on Selvon's storytelling strategies of Trinidadian calypso, a musical form 'well-known for its wit, melodrama, licentiousness and sharp political satire' (p. xiii), in which, furthermore, as Donnell and Welsh have suggested, 'we can finally locate a working-class uneducated voice representing its own perception of cultural and social issues, as opposed to the conscious downward gaze of the intellectual and writer' (1996, p. 125). This gives the narrative a recognisable oral dimension that, in drawing on a non-Western and non-literary source, reinforces the challenge to conventions of literary language and form posed by the use of a modified Caribbean dialect, and facilitates the articulation of a voice – that of the black working-class immigrant – that had hitherto been largely denied recognition in literary fiction.

Similarly, in his introduction to the 1985 edition of *The Lonely Londoners*, Kenneth Ramchand endorses the idea of a relationship between Selvon's approach and an oral storytelling tradition, prominent in societies that did not privilege the printed word. He also stresses the novel's status as a written text, seeing it as 'feed[ing] on oral literature and on the stuff that oral literature itself also draws upon without losing its identity as writing' (Ramchand, 1985 [1956], p. 10). The connection here with oral literature reflects a challenge to traditional conceptions of the literary that gives primacy to the printed over the spoken word. Despite its 'written' status the language of the text prioritises voices excluded from the literary mainstream at the time it was written.

Sukhdev Sandhu offers yet another slightly different view of the novel's structure, describing it as:

> a series of loosely related sketches of metropolitan life. To read it is to undergo a series of jolts and tumbles as characters flit in and out of view; comic vignette rubs up against mordant reportage. The effect is rather akin to that of a whitewashed wall that, over time, has become a messy riot of colour as fly-posters, graffiti art and community news-sheets vie with each other to adorn it with newer and ever louder information.
>
> (Sandhu, 2003, p. 167)

Sandhu's interpretation invokes a range of textual forms that do not fit into traditional definitions of the literary – 'reportage', 'fly-posters', 'graffiti art', 'community news-sheets', and so on – that further highlights the novel's somewhat problematic status as 'literature' when set against **canonical** expectations. As we shall see later, the novel also engages in subversive interactions with canonical models and references.

The critical perspectives outlined above may differ in emphasis, but the common thread that links them is the close relationship between form and language, subject matter and themes. I want now to explore this relationship further by considering Selvon's techniques of **characterisation**. *The Lonely Londoners* has a relatively large cast of characters, but there is not space here to discuss them all. Instead, I want to focus on how three characters are depicted: Moses, Bart and Galahad, comparing the representation of their migrant experiences: how they respond to the disillusionment that many critics have seen as central to the theme of migration in West Indian writing; the role that memory and reminiscence play in providing a contrast with their experiences in London; and how they are portrayed through Selvon's distinctive use of language and form.

Characterisation, illusion and identity in *The Lonely Londoners*

I have already referred to the disjunction between what Caribbean migrants expected to find in England and their actual experiences. For David Dabydeen and Nana Wilson-Tagoe:

> *The Lonely Londoners* deals with the shattering of the illusion of belonging, the illusion of being English, and indeed the illusion about who the English are. The journey to England is a journey to an illusion, and the sojourn in England is a shattering of that illusion. The illusion is, firstly, a material dream about the wealth of England – the streets are meant to be paved with gold, with work well-paid and readily available. Secondly, it is an illusion about the courtesy, hospitality and human warmth of the English. The illusory hospitality of the English involves an imagined willingness of their white women to readily accept black men. …
>
> Finally, the illusion of England involves a romantic sense of English history. Names like Charing Cross, Waterloo and Trafalgar Square are powerfully seductive. … The seduction of England is the illusion of its romantic or fabulous history, and the illusion that the West Indian could participate in that history. It was a powerful dream especially since West Indians were taught, through colonial education, that there was no history or romance or fable in the islands; that all history resided in England.
>
> In the novel, all the dreams are painfully destroyed by the reality of their encounter with the actual England.
>
> (Dabydeen and Wilson-Tagoe, 1988, pp. 144–5)

These illusions are explored in the novel, linking together the otherwise seemingly fragmented 'ballads', or anecdotes that relate the characters' exploits. However, the novel's treatment of these shattered illusions is not simply a case of recording examples of an idealised vision of England coming up hard against the reality of post-war life in London. Selvon presents this theme in a variety of ways.

Figure 5.2   Piccadilly Circus, London, *c*.1950s–1960s. Photo: Lightworks Media/Alamy.

Activity 4

First, reread the 'Bart' section (from 'During them first days' on p. 45 to 'in the world, too' on p. 52) of the novel.

1   How does Selvon present Bart and develop the reader's sense of his character? How would you describe the different moods and literary techniques used in this section?

2   To what extent is Bart shown to be a victim of the illusions described above by Dabydeen and Wilson-Tagoe?

Discussion

1   Bart is presented initially in comic terms, focusing on his almost pathological meanness with money, which leads him to deny himself food in order to avoid helping a friend in difficulties. Humour is the prevalent element in the first part of this section, with a characteristic anecdote involving Bart and Cap showing the quick, sly wit that Bart shares with a number of other characters – 'Come back by the two

and six ear' (p. 47) – rendering him a more sympathetic character than he first appears.

Bart also appears to be a reluctant member of the West Indian community, trying to pass himself off as 'Latin-American' (p. 46) because of his lighter skin, and avoiding the company of blacker members of the community: 'he always have an embarrass air when he with them in public, he does look around as much as to say: "I here with these boys, but I not one of them, look at the colour of my skin"' (p. 48).

The relatively humorous tone gives way to a darker mood as Bart encounters racial prejudice, ironically described as 'the old diplomacy' (p. 48). His increased exposure to discrimination is accompanied by a physical decline; the comic refusal to eat in case by doing so he will have to share his resources with a fellow sufferer gives way to a more psychologically troubling act of denial as he 'train himself to live only on tea for weeks' (p. 48).

There is another shift of mood once Bart recovers from his illness, and the focus of the narrative moves to his obsession with his white girlfriend, Beatrice. **Pathos** becomes the prevailing mood of the remainder of the extract as Bart loses the object of his affection. His fruitless search for her is rendered movingly, with heightened emotion and diction, while maintaining the Caribbean idiomatic narrative voice:

> He must be comb the whole of London, looking in the millions of white faces walking down Oxford Street, peering into buses, taking tube ride on the Inner Circle just in the hope that he might see she. For weeks the old Bart hunt, until he become haggard and haunted.
>
> (pp. 51–2)

The simple and reflective tone of the narrator's rueful observation – 'It have men like that in the world, too' (p. 52) – concludes this section with what Ramchand calls 'acceptance and a quiet awe' (1985, p. 11).

2 Clearly, Bart falls prey to the shattering of at least the first two of the illusions outlined by Dabydeen and Tagoe-Wilson. The falsity of the belief in plentiful work is implied firstly in Bart's reluctance to help his associates financially. On achieving the coveted security of regular work, Bart even seems to internalise English prejudices and reflect it back in his attitudes: 'Many nights he think about how so many West Indians coming, and it give him more fear than it give the Englishman, for Bart frighten if they make things hard in Brit'n' (pp. 47–8).

He also encounters the lack of 'courtesy, hospitality and human warmth', having doors slammed in his face and being ejected from Beatrice's house by her father. Furthermore, the 'imagined willingness of their white women to readily accept black men' is also brought into

> question by Beatrice's disappearance. Bart's ceaseless quest for
> Beatrice is in one sense heartbreakingly futile, but could also embody
> the resilience that many of these characters demonstrate as a
> response to the prejudice they face on a daily basis.

The character of Beatrice, perhaps, represents an example of the significance of naming in the novel in relation to the canonical literary tradition with which it engages, often subversively. Beatrice shares her name with Dante's (1265–1321) guide through Paradise in the last book of his epic poem *Divine Comedy* (1307–21). The impact on Bart of his Beatrice's disappearance could be seen as a subversion of the role of Dante's Beatrice, in that Bart descends into a personal hell as a consequence of losing her. It is possible here to see Selvon's novel in a complex intertextual negotiation with more canonical forms of literature.

Skin colour is central to these characters' alienation. Bart's denial of the implications of his colour is symptomatic of a destabilising of identity resulting from the experience of racial prejudice, a disassociation by Bart from his own sense of self; his outward alienation is mirrored by an inner one. Bart is forced to recognise that this alienation is what connects him to the other West Indian migrants, forcing him eventually to 'boil down and come like one of the boys' (p. 48).

A disassociation from skin colour is also apparent in Galahad's attempts to come to terms with white attitudes to Caribbean immigrants, as he addresses his colour as though it were something separate from himself:

> And Galahad watch the colour of his hand, and talk to it, saying,
> 'Colour, is you that causing all this, you know. Why the hell you
> can't be blue, or red or green, if you can't be white? You know is
> you that cause a lot of misery in the world. Is not me, you know,
> is you! I ain't do anything to infuriate the people and them, is you!
> Look at you, you so black and innocent, and this time so you
> causing misery all over the world!'
>
> (p. 77)

This is a rare reflective moment for Galahad, a character with a surer sense of self than most in the novel. That even he is affected in such a way as to try to divorce himself from his colour is indicative of the insidious power of racism. Galahad's more usual way of defining himself is very different from Bart's, however, as is his attitude towards women, which is significant in relation to the novel's wider engagement with issues of gender, the subject of the next section of this chapter.

Representations of women in *The Lonely Londoners*

Activity 5

Reread the episode of Galahad's date with a white woman (from 'When that first London summer hit' on p. 71 to 'he tell Sir Galahad' on p. 83) and think about the following questions:

1 Looking back on the three types of illusions faced by Caribbean migrants according to Dabydeen and Wilson-Tagoe above, which are most applicable to Galahad's situation here?

2 Compare and contrast the depiction of Galahad's attitude towards women with that of Bart.

Discussion

1 Galahad seems to be still seduced by 'the romantic sense of English history'. His nickname, Sir Galahad, is taken from a character in Arthurian legend, and constitutes another example of the novel drawing on canonical literary and mythical sources. It is also clear that London place names still carry a thrill for him – a thrill that is validated with reference to yet another kind of literary source:

> Jesus Christ, when he say 'Charing Cross', when he realise that is he, Sir Galahad, who going there, near that place that everybody in the world know about (it even have the name in the dictionary) he feel like a new man.

(p. 72)

Galahad also still seems to take for granted the 'imagined willingness of their white women to readily accept black men', a belief that had been inculcated in Galahad when he was still in Trinidad: 'This was something he uses to dream about in Trinidad. The time when he was leaving, Frank tell him: "Boy, it have bags of white pussy in London, and you will eat till you tired"' (p. 79).

2 While Bart continually scours the metropolis hoping to see his lost Beatrice again, for Galahad, the pursuit of white women is a more casual affair, almost a 'game', to alleviate the hardship and misery of migrant life. Although he is on his way to meet Daisy, his 'first' white woman, he is distracted by what he perceives as the seeming availability of other women: 'He go into the gardens, and begin to

walk down to the Arch, seeing so much cat about the place, laying down on the grass, sitting and talking, all of them in pretty summer colours' (p. 78).

The description of the prelude to Galahad's date is instructive in relation to the rather restricted gender perspectives the novel has to offer. As stated earlier, migration from the Caribbean was initially primarily a male phenomenon. It is male experience with which the novel is concerned; the demeaning and derogatory terms used by Galahad and other characters about women – 'white pussy', 'so much cat about the place', 'a first-class craft' (p. 78) – dehumanise the women with whom the men come into contact. Galahad is not alone in using women for his own ends and gratification. Bart is a rare example in this novel of a man demonstrating genuine emotional attachment to a woman, and his obsession evokes pity in the narrator that the reader is presumably expected to share.

Activity 6

Based on your reading of the novel, how would you describe the depiction of its few female characters?

Discussion

Mostly, representations of women in *The Lonely Londoners* tend towards the stereotypical, characteristically identified with domestic roles. Although Tolroy's mother, named only as 'Ma', does move beyond the family circle, finding work in London, that work is only a kind of domestic labour, washing up in a Lyons Corner House, where she is able to observe, but not participate directly in, London life: 'Ma work in the back, in the kitchen, but she was near enough to the front to see what happening outside of the kitchen' (p. 68).

Tanty, the only female character accorded extended focalisation, is for the most part similarly confined to the domestic sphere, though she is a disruptive force in the immediate environment of the working-class area around the Harrow Road where she lives, subverting cultural norms by forcefully persuading the white shopkeeper to give credit, and using her shopping expeditions to indulge in 'big oldtalk' (p. 67) with the shop assistants. Tanty's refusal to bow to the cultural and social mores of her adopted homeland offer an affirmative alternative to the struggles to conform undertaken by characters like Bart. Her only real encounter with the world beyond the Harrow Road, a journey to Ma's workplace in the centre of London, serves, perhaps, as a **parody** of the migrant theme, and is presented in **mock-epic** terms as she overcomes her fears to take the underground to central London:

> But was plenty different when she find sheself in the station, and the idea of going under the ground in this train nearly make she turn back. But the thought that she would never be able to say she went made her carry on.
>
> (p. 70)

That Tanty is shown to exaggerate the perils attendant on her journey home by bus – 'She was so frighten that she didn't bother to look out of the window and see anything' (p. 71) – indicates that her role in the novel seems to be mainly to provide comic relief. This suggests a marginalisation of black female experience as her fearful progress across London and back contrasts with the confident ease with which characters such as Galahad move around the capital, often in predatory pursuit of white women.

To return to the earlier comparison of Galahad and Bart, Galahad's approach to London life is in direct contrast with Bart's desire to escape his own identity, but Galahad's main function in the novel is to present a life-affirming counterpoint to the world-weariness of the central character, Moses. The two have a symbiotic relationship that reaches a peak of formal complexity in the section of the novel depicting London in the summer.

Style and narrative techniques: London in summer

Activity 7

Now read the 'London in summer' section (from 'Oh what a time it is' on p. 92 to 'what it is all about' on p. 102).

1   How would you describe the differences in the style and narrative techniques used by Selvon in this section from the rest of the novel?

2   How does Selvon represent the characters of Moses and Galahad in this section?

Discussion

1   This section begins with a celebration of the effect of summer on black and white Londoners alike, a rare moment in the novel of communion across ethnic divides. This gives way to a rapid succession of episodes, similar in structure to the novel as a whole, though encapsulated here in a single, unpunctuated sentence running over ten pages. This device gives a more fluid rhythm and faster tempo to the writing here, blurring the individual anecdotes into an impressionistic summary of these characters' experiences. Nasta, drawing on other literary parallels, has described this section as a 'long prose poem to London, a painful and lyrical love song' (p. xv). You may have noticed the prevalence of poetic effects such as repetition – phrases such as 'coasting a lime' that have already become a part of the **lexicon** of the novel recur here frequently – and **alliteration**: 'see all them pretty pieces of skin taking suntan and how the old geezers like the sun they would sit on the benches and smile everywhere' (p. 92).

2   The narrative voice closely echoes the speech patterns of the main characters, particularly Moses and Galahad, taking Selvon's manipulation of narrative techniques to more subtle levels. Phrases associated with each of them are woven into the narrative voice. The references to 'a sort of fog' and 'the streets of London paved with gold' echo the opening pages of the novel, while the description of 'the sun in the sky like a forceripe orange' (p. 93) reminds us of Galahad's first reaction to the English climate (p. 23). The different perspectives of Galahad and Moses are invoked at the end of the section in a passage that, while maintaining the distance of the third-person narrator, also fuses their respective speech patterns:

> all these things happen in the blazing summer under the trees … and in the night the world turn upside down and everybody hustling that is life that is London oh lord Galahad say when the sweetness of summer get in him he say he would never leave the old Brit'n as long as he live and Moses sigh a long sigh like a man who live life and see nothing at all in it and who frighten as the years go by wondering what it is all about.
>
> (pp. 101–2)

Although Moses is the linking factor between the main characters in the novel, the respective narratives of Moses and Galahad are the most closely interrelated, as the London summer section shows. In the later stages of the novel their connection is maintained. Reminiscence is a crucial component in their relationship; their first point of connection is to share recollections of characters and events from their Trinidadian past. Towards the end of the novel, in the midst of 'one bitter season' (p. 116) of scarce employment, they resort again to memories of the Caribbean to raise their spirits.

Memory in *The Lonely Londoners*: Moses and Galahad

In the later stages of the novel the theme of memory comes strongly to the fore, highlighting the stark contrast between these characters' past and present locations and the depths of their alienation. Recalling hardships suffered in his younger days in San Fernando, when his father was reduced to snatching pigeons for food, Galahad's desperation drives him to mimic his father's actions in the more rarefied surroundings of Kensington Gardens. The horrified reactions he provokes illustrate all too clearly the vast cultural differences in time and place between the migrants' homelands and 1950s London. Nevertheless, just as the stolen pigeon provides sustenance for Galahad and Moses, so their reminiscences offer them consolation and affirmation, before Moses lapses into the guilt and despair that increasingly characterise his mood:

> 'Boy,' Moses say, 'look how we sit down here happy, and things brown in general. I mean, sometimes when we oldtalking so I does wonder about the boys, how all of we come up to the old Brit'n to make a living, and how years go by and we still here in this country. Things like that does bother me.'
>
> (p. 124)

Unusually here, it is Moses who lapses into an idealised nostalgic reverie: 'I would get a old house and have some cattle and goat, and all day long sit down in the grass in the sun, and hit a good corn cuckoo and calaloo now and then' (p. 125). Although Moses projects into the future here, it is an idealised future vision of a Caribbean life at odds with the reality of rural poverty that provided the impetus for many to leave the Caribbean behind. Moses here is led by his physical displacement from his native land and his psychological alienation from his adopted city, to create an 'imaginary homeland', a Caribbean of the mind, to appropriate Rushdie's perspective on the migrant experience as quoted in the 'Introduction to Part 2'. By contrast, in a moment of role reversal, Galahad becomes the hard-headed realist: 'It ain't have no prospects back home, boy' (p. 125). The imaginary homelands that live on in the memories of Moses and other devotees of 'oldtalk' like Tanty are, it could be argued, as illusory as the perceptions about the 'mother country' that many migrants held on arrival in Britain. Nevertheless, the significance of memory for these characters is evident throughout the novel and amply demonstrated by Moses: 'This is a lonely miserable city, if it was that we didn't get together now and then to talk about things back home, we would suffer like hell' (p. 126).

Memories play a central role in strengthening the relationships between the central characters as the novel progresses. The overall mood becomes increasingly despairing, and is focalised even more deeply through Moses' jaundiced perspective in the final pages. Alongside this, however, there is also a greater sense of connection between Moses and his fellow migrants. Whereas at the start of the novel Moses seems to be a reluctant good Samaritan, here he shows deep insight into the pain of displacement that these characters feel, shifting between dialect voice and idiomatic expression to more heightened diction and elevated lyricism:

> Under the kiff-kiff laughter, behind the ballad and the episode, the what-happening, the summer-is-hearts, he could see a great aimlessness, a great restless, swaying movement that leaving you standing in the same spot. As if a forlorn shadow of doom fall on all the spades in the country.
>
> (pp. 138–9)

The sense of community endures, however, as the characters assemble around Moses, penetrating so deep into his consciousness that he feels their presence even when they are not there:

> Sometimes during the week, when he come home and he can't sleep, is as if he is hearing the voices in the room, all the moaning and groaning and sighing and crying, and he open his eyes expecting to see the boys sitting around.
>
> (p. 135)

Activity 8

Read the extract below from the introduction to Onyekadu Wambu's *Empire Windrush: 50 Years of Writing About Black Britain* (1998) and then answer the following question:

How far is this a fair assessment of Selvon's *The Lonely Londoners* and its representation of migrant experience?

> Over the years the preoccupation of much of the literature has been with this troubled quest for identity and liberty, as men were wrenched away into a new world, and older notions of self collapsed. This is largely the world of the wretched, having to remake themselves constantly in a hostile world, with wretched tools. It is necessarily bleak, tragic and sad.
>
> (Wambu, 1998, pp. 23–4)

Discussion

As some of the preceding discussions have demonstrated, the instability of identity and the struggle to create a new sense of self in different surroundings is a recurring theme in Selvon's novel, symbolised by Bart's attempts to exploit his lighter skin as a way of distancing himself from his fellow migrants; Galahad's emphasis on dressing sharply and smartly to bolster his sense of self; and Moses' increasingly unfocused yearning for a different way of life. Selvon's characters, ground down by prejudice, could indeed be seen as wretched, and clearly do exist in a 'hostile world'. But the novel also celebrates London, and the characters' determination to struggle on manifests itself through vivid and humorous episodes. 'Bleak, tragic and sad' the novel may be on occasion, but some of the characters, especially Galahad, show at times the positive side of living in London in a dark and often dreary period of English history.

Selvon's novel offers a perspective on the impact of Caribbean migration on its characters and on the 'mother country' in the early post-war era. As the novel draws to a close Moses' meditations add a distinctly self-referential dimension to the text:

> Daniel was telling him how over in France all kinds of fellars writing books what turning out to be best-sellers. Taxi-driver,

porter, road-sweeper – it didn't matter. One day you sweating in the factory and the next day all the newspapers have your name and photo, saying how you are a new literary giant.

He watch a tugboat on the Thames, wondering if he could ever write a book like that, what everybody would buy.

(p. 139)

This ending leads Ramchand to suggest that 'in a sense, *The Lonely Londoners* is the book Moses would have written' (1985 [1956], p. 21), a plausible idea that makes explicit the novel's questioning of traditional notions of what constitutes literature and the literary. Now we will move on to a more recent exploration of the themes of migration and memory, James Berry's *Windrush Songs*, which were published just over half a century after Selvon's novel, demonstrating the enduring impact and importance of these themes.

Memories of migration: James Berry's *Windrush Songs*

James Berry was born in rural Jamaica in 1924, and felt compelled early in life to seek his fortune elsewhere, moving to America in 1942 only to return four years later disillusioned by the treatment of black people he witnessed there. In 1948 Berry emigrated for a second time, on this occasion to Britain, where he settled. Like Selvon, Berry was involved in fostering a sense of community among West Indian migrant writers in Britain. Many of his poems address the migrant experience and, again like Selvon, fluctuate between the Caribbean and Britain for their settings and themes. Berry was awarded the OBE for services to poetry in 1990.

While memory, expressed through the reminiscences of Selvon's migrants, plays a significant role in *The Lonely Londoners*, in Berry's *Windrush Songs* it is a more dominant theme. The emphasis throughout this collection is on the world the migrants left behind them, as the poems explore ways of reconnecting with the traditions and values of Jamaican life, and address the complex historical relationship between the Caribbean and the imperial centre.

Activity 9

Read Berry's 'Empire Day' (reproduced below) and think about the following question: What attitudes towards England and the British Empire are revealed in this poem, and how does Berry use different registers of language to explore the relationship between colonised and coloniser here?

Empire Day is what me rememba, singin
praises to Modder Country, Englan.
At home, me put on mi church shoes
an mi new likkle khaki trousers an shirt
an meet other spruced-up distric   5
children-them. Stiffly, happily on we go.

At school we have prayers. We recite
poems about Englan and Empire. Each
one of us get a likkle Union Jack
and sweets with flags printed   10
all over the tin.

Other schools join we. And, drilled,
marchin around the schoolyard, aroun
our wide and high, high poinciana tree
covered wid red flowers, our likkle   15
Union Jack them a-wave and a-flutta.
We sing we heart out, singing 'Rule
Britannia', glowin with all we loyal
virtue to King, Country and Empire.

In jollification, we play games.   20
We eat jerk pork, fresh bread, candy
an spicy cake. We eat snowball an drink
cool drinks. Mi Union Jack sweets-tin
turn mi treasure, keeping
mi slate pencil an mi marble-them.   25

(Berry, 2007, p. 49)

Discussion

As in 'To Travel this Ship', which we considered at the start of this chapter, and in *The Lonely Londoners*, the use of a non-Standard English register evokes Caribbean speech, and is crucial to the effects achieved. Here, though, Berry also draws on more formal levels of diction in words and phrases such as 'stiffly', 'recite', 'drilled', 'loyal virtue' and 'jollification', which are juxtaposed against vivid indigenous symbols

Figure 5.3   The *Windrush* arrives from Jamaica, 21 June 1948. Photo: Daily Herald Archive/Getty Images.

like 'the high, high poinciana tree / covered wid red flowers' (ll. 14–15). The speaker of the poem makes no overt judgement about the children's enthusiasm for Empire Day, though we might read into the regimented terminology of 'drilling' and 'marching' a mature recognition on the part of the speaker of the implications of these celebrations, where 'poems about Englan and Empire' (l. 9) are recited and Union Jacks are waved unreflectingly by the excited children. Key terms associated with the imperial presence, terms such as 'Modder Country, Englan' (l. 2), are recast into Jamaican dialect, subverting the poem's ostensible endorsement of the children's excitement about Empire Day.

Most of the poems in *Windrush Songs* are concerned with looking back on what these migrants have left behind. After many years of living in England, memories of home seem to carry an increasingly potent charge.

Activity 10

Read Berry's 'Reminiscence Voice' (reproduced below) and try to answer these questions:

1   What aspects of Jamaican life are the subject of the speaker's reminiscences in this poem?

2   How is the intensity of memory and longing for the homeland conveyed here?

> Man, I want to go back to hear
> hilltop cockcrow giving
> answer to bottom yard rooster challenge
> mother cow giving anxious 'moo'
> for a calf keeping cool in the shade   5
>   I want to renew all that.
>
> Man, I want to go back to hear
> cooing of ground-doves in quiet noon-time
> and tree-top nightingales singing
> to the moon long before daylight –   10
>   I want to renew all that.
>
> Man, I want to go back to have
> a curry-goat feed under coconut palms
> rum flowing like a nature stream
> and conchshell blowing for a big sea catch   15
>   I want to renew all that.
>
> Man, I want to go back to hear
> Maama Tunny passing to church
> fanning herself, calling
>   'Good-morning' to our house.   20

(Berry, 2007, p. 43)

Discussion

1   The key images symbolising the speaker's longing are associated with the natural world and rural Jamaican settings; references to birds, animals, trees and natural artefacts indigenous to the West Indies create a vivid sense of place, drawing, perhaps ironically, on the **pastoral** traditions of English literature, and describing a world very different from the British inner cities in which most Caribbean migrants settled. In the last two stanzas a sense of human community comes to the fore. Embodied in Maama Tunny's neighbourly act of 'calling / "Good-morning" to our house' (ll. 19–20) is an evocation of communal values largely lacking in early migrants' experiences of marginalisation and prejudice.

2   Repetition seems to be a key device in this poem, conveying the depth of the speaker's longing to reconnect with his origins. The recurrent phrase 'Man, I want to go back' that begins each stanza emphasises the intensity of the speaker's desire, and the simple but rather formal diction of the refrain 'I want to renew all that' gives the reminiscences an almost ceremonial dimension.

Once again we can see the complex negotiations between writing from a Caribbean migrant perspective and the conventional idea of the canon to which it poses a challenge, with Berry's evocation of pastoral forms associated with the traditions of English literature used to create positive memories of Jamaican village life that endure into the twenty-first century.

Where migration is the key theme of Selvon's novel, and memories of home assume significance at some of the bleakest times for his characters, particularly in the depictions of the gatherings of the 'boys' in Moses' room towards the end of the novel, memory is the central motif of Berry's poems. In both cases, these themes are closely linked to questions of how West Indian identity developed and changed as a result of migration to a 'mother country' undergoing its own crisis of identity in the postcolonial era, with its empire rapidly shrinking and its position as a major world power receding into the past.

Conclusion

The Lonely Londoners details numerous examples of racial prejudice, a disturbing aspect of British society throughout the post-war period. Just two years after *The Lonely Londoners* first appeared, racial tensions erupted into violence in both Notting Hill in London, and Nottingham. While such violent manifestations of racial tensions have been relatively rare, immigrant communities have continued to face persecution in varying degrees; the rise of far-right racist parties such as the National Front in the 1970s and the British National Party in the early twenty-first century have fuelled racial discontent, and criminal cases such as the murder of black teenager Stephen Lawrence in 1993 have revealed the extent of racist attitudes in major British institutions such as the Metropolitan Police Force. Black British writers since Selvon have continued to explore migrant experience against this background, and over the same period black British literature has asserted itself in a more central position in relation to the established canon. James Berry's poems in *Windrush Songs* may look back to an earlier time, but do so informed by half a century of black experience of British society. It is surely indicative of the enduring symbolic power of the SS *Empire Windrush* that it forms the central focus point of a collection of poems written in the early twenty-first century about the birth of contemporary black British experience. Berry's poems celebrate the positive aspects of Caribbean life, however, rather than dwelling on the challenges posed to West Indian identity by over sixty years of struggle to assimilate into British society.

References

Berry, J. (2007) *Windrush Songs*, Newcastle upon Tyne, Bloodaxe.

Birat, K. (2009) 'Hearing voices in George Lamming's *The Pleasures of Exile* and Sam Selvon's *The Lonely Londoners*', *Commonwealth*, vol. 32, no. 1, pp. 9–22.

Dabydeen, D. and Wilson-Tagoe, N. (1988) *A Reader's Guide to Westindian and Black British Literature*, Hatfield, Hansib Publishing.

Donnell, A. and Welsh, S.L. (eds) (1996) *The Routledge Reader in Caribbean Literature*, London, Routledge.

Nasta, S. and Rutherford, A. (eds) (1995) *Tiger's Triumph: Celebrating Sam Selvon*, Armidale, NSW, and Hebden Bridge, UK, Dangaroo Press.

Ramchand, K. (1985 [1956]) 'Introduction' in Selvon, S., *The Lonely Londoners*, New York, Longman.

Sandhu, S. (2003) *London Calling: How Black and Asian Writers Imagined a City*, London, Harper Collins.

Selvon, S. (2006 [1956]) *The Lonely Londoners*, London, Penguin.

Wambu, O. (ed.) (1998) *Empire Windrush: Fifty Years of Writing About Black Britain*, London, Victor Gollancz.

Winder, R. (2004) *Bloody Foreigners: The Story of Immigration to Britain*, London, Little, Brown.

Further reading

Berry, J. (ed.) (1976) *Bluefoot Traveller: An Anthology of West Indian Poets in Britain*, London, Limestone Publications.

Berry, J. (1979) *Fractured Circles*, London, New Beacon Books.

Berry, J. (1982) *Lucy's Letters and Loving*, London, New Beacon Books.

Berry, J. (1985) *Chain of Days*, Oxford, Oxford University Press.

Lamming, G. (1992 [1960]) *The Pleasures of Exile*, Ann Arbor, MI, The University of Michigan Press.

Nasta, S. (ed.) (1988) *Critical Perspectives on Sam Selvon*, Washington, D.C., Three Continents Press.

Phillips, M. and Phillips, T. (1998) *Windrush: The Irresistible Rise of Multi-Racial Britain*, London, Harper Collins.

Selvon, S. (1984 [1975]) *Moses Ascending*, Oxford, Heinemann.

Selvon, S. (1991 [1983]) *Moses Migrating*, Washington, D.C., Three Continents Press.

Selvon, S. (1997 [1952]) *A Brighter Sun*, Harlow, Longman.

Wyke, C. (1991) *Sam Selvon's Dialectical Style and Fictional Strategy*, Vancouver, BC, University of British Columbia Press.

Chapter 6
Elizabeth Bishop, *Questions of Travel*

Richard Danson Brown

Aims

This chapter will:

- extend your awareness of the forms and preoccupations of modern poetry through the work of one of the most influential twentieth-century poets, Elizabeth Bishop

- explore the ways in which Bishop's work negotiates the related themes of memory and migration

- examine her adoption of popular literary forms in relation to the concept of 'literatures'

- examine a group of poems collected at a specific moment in time as a collection with connected themes and preoccupations.

Introduction

The American poet Elizabeth Bishop (1911–1979) always felt herself to be a kind of migrant, an unfixed inhabitant of seashore locations. In an acceptance speech for a small-scale literary prize in 1976, she noted:

> I find it extremely gratifying that, after having spent most of my life timorously pecking for subsistence along the coastlines of the world, I have been given this recognition from so many different countries, but also from Norman, Oklahoma, a place so far inland.
>
> (Bishop, 2008, p. 732)

Many of Bishop's concerns are embedded in this graceful yet pointed acknowledgement. On the one hand, she rather comically identifies herself as a wading bird – as we will see, a sandpiper – desperately 'pecking for subsistence' along varied shorelines. On the other, she emphasises her status as a poet lauded in 'so many different countries', almost to the detriment of the desperately inland Norman, Oklahoma, in the American Midwest. Modesty, distance and perspective are neatly poised in this formulation as the poet gives away something, yet not all, of herself.

This chapter explores Bishop's collection *Questions of Travel* (originally published in 1965) in the light of the themes of migration and memory, as well as our concern with the idea of literatures. Unlike other writers dealt with in this part of the book, Bishop's work does not centre on large-scale human migrations; rather, she explores issues of identity and belonging through her own experience of emigrating as an adult from the United States to Brazil, which, in turn, enabled her to reflect more critically on the Nova Scotia of her early childhood. At the same time, while living and working in Brazil, Bishop's translations opened up Brazilian poetry to audiences in North America and Europe, while some of her original poems show the influence of popular forms on contemporary poetry. Her work is neatly poised between Romantic conceptions of the role of the poet and the broader definitions of 'literature' as something not automatically high culture, which were outlined in the 'Introduction to Part 2' and in the previous chapter on Selvon's *The Lonely Londoners*.

The edition of the collection that is referred to in this chapter is the Chatto & Windus edition (2004).

Bishop and the sandpiper

We begin by reading the poem Bishop alludes to in her speech, 'Sandpiper'. At first glance, this may seem like simply a poem about the natural world, but it has more to tell us about how she saw the role of the poet, and about the interplay between memory and migration in her work.

Activity 1

Read 'Sandpiper' through at least a couple of times, then briefly answer the following questions:

1   What attitude does the poem show to the bird?

2   What evidence does the poem give that it might be concerned with the role of the poet?

3   Based on your answers to these questions, try to come up with a couple of phrases to describe or characterise the poem.

Discussion

It is worth stressing at the outset that my responses are not the only approaches to these questions, so you shouldn't be too concerned if yours are different. My perspectives should help to guide, but not restrict, your own.

1   I would say that the poem is empathetic to the sandpiper, in that it continuously tries to visualise and explain the bird running on an Atlantic beach. Consider the following phrases: 'He runs … in a state of controlled panic' (ll. 3–4); 'He runs … watching his toes. / – Watching, rather, the spaces of sand between them' (ll. 8–9); 'Poor bird, he is obsessed!' (l. 18). In each case, Bishop psychologises the bird's behaviour, deducing quasi-human states of mind from the bird's actions. We might say that the poem is a miniature study in obsession, as the sandpiper repeatedly looks for 'something, something, something' (l. 17). The poem wants to make this ceaseless activity vivid to the reader, so that by the end, we should feel some of the pathos it expresses for the 'Poor bird'.

2   A concern with the role of the poet is evident in two ways. First, Bishop makes an explicit reference to the Romantic poet and artist William Blake (1757–1827) in the first stanza. On a literal level, it's impossible to view a sandpiper as 'a student of Blake' (l. 4), which immediately implies that the bird in the poem is more than just a natural object. Second, the poem's empathy for the bird suggests an analogy between the sandpiper and the poet: as the bird is engaged in a ceaseless struggle for discovery, so Bishop's poem attempts to create a textual, poetic order from 'The millions of grains' (l. 19).

3   My answers to the previous questions suggest some ways of describing it: as a miniature study of a psychological state; as an act of empathy between the poet and the natural world; as a search for order, cleverly expressed in the ordered forms of traditional poetry. I would say that there is a reciprocity between the poem's form and the world it tries to condense into its rhyming quatrains. We might say that it's an act of obsessive attention to detail, trying to get into the shape of the poem those grains of sand, that sheet 'of interrupting water' (l. 6), and the tension between the detail pored over by the sandpiper and the vastness of the roaring Atlantic.

It is worth expanding on the form of 'Sandpiper'. As you probably noticed, the poem is written in rhyming quatrains, or four-line stanzas; the usual rhyme scheme is *abxb*, though the second stanza adopts the more conventional scheme *abab*. This is one of the commonest rhyming structures used in English, as in Thomas Gray's much anthologised 'Elegy in a Country Churchyard' (1751). Bishop's metre is also largely conventional. Though she doesn't write in wholly orthodox **iambic pentameter** in most lines, you should be able to pick out five major stresses, as in:

> x / / x x / x x / x /
> The beach hisses like fat. On his left, a sheet
> x / x / x / x /   x /
> Of interrupting water comes and goes

If the first line has the irregular swing of conversation, with consecutive or **spondaic** stresses on 'beach hiss', the return to a regular iambic pattern in the second line helps to orientate the reader by recurring to a more familiar poetic rhythm. The interplay between technical freedom and constraint is part of Bishop's purpose: she effects a compromise between poetic tradition and formal innovation in the structures of the poem. This is particularly marked in:

```
 /   x   x   /    x    /    x    /    x
looking for something, something, something.
     x   /   x  /  x    /
Poor bird, he is obsessed!
```

The first line lacks one stress, while the second is two stresses short of the full pentameter line (unless one chooses to read 'Poor bird' as a **spondee**, in which case the line is only one stress short). The effect is deliberate: at the moment when the poem clarifies the bird's obsession, the lines lose conventional coherence and structure. We pause over 'Poor bird, he is obsessed!' because the unorthodox shape of the line within the stanza underlines that this is a noteworthy moment. You might say that there is an empathetic join between form and content just as the poem itself is concerned to make the reader empathise with the bird.

Bishop recognised that there was a connection between herself and the sandpiper. In the same speech quoted at the beginning of this chapter, she admitted:

> all my life I have lived and behaved very much like that sandpiper – just running along the edges of different countries and continents, 'looking for something'. I have always felt I couldn't *possibly* live very far inland, away from the ocean; and I *have* always lived near it, frequently in sight of it. Naturally I know, and it has been pointed out to me, that most of my poems are geographical, or about coasts, beaches and rivers running to the sea, and most of the titles of my books are geographical too: *North & South*, *Questions of Travel* and one to be published this year, *Geography III*.
>
> (Bishop, 2008, pp. 731–2)

This implies that Bishop's sandpiper is an elaborate **metaphor** for the poet, and her poetic project. So 'Sandpiper' can be used as a shorthand way of telling the story of Bishop's life, as I will do now. Bishop spent the early years of her life in Nova Scotia. After the early death of her father and her mother's subsequent mental breakdown and death, she was shuttled between her relatives in the Canadian province and her father's family who lived in cosmopolitan Boston in American

New England. From early childhood, then, she had a strong sense of being divided between different cultures and milieus. During her adult life, she travelled widely through Europe and the Americas, spending several years in Key West in Florida. From 1951 to 1967, she lived in Brazil with her lover Lota de Macedo Soares, a wealthy and politically well-connected architect who was to kill herself in 1967. Bishop divided her time between Rio de Janeiro, Lota's mountain property near Petrópolis, a resort to the north-east of Rio, and Ouro Prêto in the interior. It is in this period of Bishop's life that the poems which were collected in *Questions of Travel* were written (for Bishop's life, see Bishop, 2008, pp. 905–19; Millier, 1993).

Figure 6.1   Elizabeth Bishop with her cat, Tobias, 1954. Photographed by J.L. Castel. Photo: Archives and Special Collections, Vassar College Libraries.

Bishop also translated several important Brazilian writers during this period. Her version of *The Diary of 'Helena Morley'* (1957) is an account of provincial life in late nineteenth-century Brazil through the eyes of a teenage girl; she translated the work of several important Brazilian poets, notably Carlos Drummond de Andrade (1902–1987), whom she was to describe as 'the greatest living Brazilian poet' (Bishop, 2008, p. 721). Though she was never a prolific writer, writing was Bishop's central preoccupation throughout her life. Like most modern poets, she

Figure 6.2 Elizabeth Bishop's studio, Samambaia Hillside, Brazil. Photo: Archives and Special Collections, Vassar College Libraries.

was unable to sustain herself through the proceeds of her poems alone ('timorously pecking for subsistence' is jokey but not altogether ironic) and subsidised her writing through various bequests, lectureships, grants and prizes, including the Pulitzer Prize, which she won in 1956. She was highly praised throughout her career by poets such as Marianne Moore (1887–1972) and Robert Lowell (1917–1977), who were among the most significant and widely praised twentieth-century American poets (see Kalstone, 1989). Lowell's blurb for *Questions of Travel* is relevant to all her work, and has obvious connections with 'Sandpiper': 'She has a humorous, commanding genius for picking up the unnoticed, now making something sprightly and right, and now a great monument ... When we read her, we enter the classical serenity of a new country' (Bishop and Lowell, 2008, p. 580).

But why does Bishop compare herself with a sandpiper? Comparisons between birds and poets are familiar in many different kinds of poetry: Percy Bysshe Shelley (1792–1822) in 'To a Skylark' (first published in 1820) counterpoises the 'profuse strains' of the bird's 'unpremeditated art' with the flawed human structures of poetry (1971, p. 602). In contrast, 'Sandpiper' has no interest in song or the notion that the bird might stand for the poet as a kind of spontaneous prophet. Rather, as I noted earlier, the focus is on the bird's obsessive psychology; ornithological detail is 'take[n] for granted' ('Sandpiper', l. 1). Jamie McKendrick observes that the bird is presumably looking for food, 'though the poem pretends not to have thought of this obvious fact' (2002, p. 129), while Tim Dee notes that 'Identifying Elizabeth Bishop's sandpiper is hard … Nearly ninety species of bird might be called sandpiper and behave at the sea's edge as Bishop's birds do' (Armitage and Dee, 2009, p. 301). Sandpipers are waders (or shorebirds in North America) that live by the sea, and which migrate. Figure 6.3 is a photograph of a Purple Sandpiper, a sub-species of sandpiper common in the Arctic and Canada. This may be the closest we can get to the bird that stands behind the textual 'Sandpiper'.

Figure 6.3　Purple sandpiper *Calidris martima* on rocky shore, Portland Bill, Dorset, England. Photo: © Mike Read/RSPB Images.

So at one level, it's easy to see why Bishop might have seen something of herself in these migratory creatures that inhabit the shoreline. But any literal equation between Bishop and the sandpiper is problematic; equally, I would hesitate to endorse the biographical reading Bishop rather grudgingly sketches in her acceptance speech, quoted earlier, because that would reduce the poem to a rather simplistic **allegory** of the poet's own life. How, then, does 'Sandpiper' connect with ideas of memory and migration? In Activity 1, I suggested that the poem is a miniature, an act of empathy between the poet and the natural world, as well as a search for order, showing a particular relationship between poetic form and the world the poem attempts to capture. Building on the sandpiper's obsessive search in the final stanza, I would emphasise the way Bishop positions her subject 'in a state of controlled panic': the sandpiper dangerously poised on the cusp between two opposed milieus is provocative not just because it resembles Elizabeth Bishop, but because in its brittle dance along the hissing beach, it carries with it broader resemblances between the readers of the poem and the worlds we inhabit. 'Sandpiper' isn't a text that describes actual migrations like *The Lonely Londoners*; however, the bird occupies a ceaselessly mobile world of mist, shifting tide and sands.

Questions of Travel: the Brazilian poems

Questions of Travel was Bishop's third collection. In this chapter, we will look at ten of its original nineteen poems, plus two translations from Brazilian texts not included in this volume. It was a short book; as she confessed in a letter, 'I just wish the contents were twice the length – it seems a bit thin' (Bishop, 1996, p. 438). The original edition included the autobiographical short story 'In the Village', but it was later excluded from *Complete Poems* because it was a prose text. The story (which is discussed in the final section) centres on Bishop's childhood in Nova Scotia, specifically the moment when her mother suffered her final mental breakdown.

Although her letters present the inclusion of 'In the Village' as an attempt to fill up the 'thin' volume (Bishop, 1996, p. 431), the story adds to *Questions of Travel*'s complexity by connecting questions of travel with questions of memory in the structure of the volume. The book is divided into two sections: I. Brazil (which included 'Arrival at Santos', 'Brazil, January 1, 1502', 'Questions of Travel', 'Squatter's Children', 'Manuelzinho', 'The Armadillo' and 'The Burglar of Babylon'); and II. Elsewhere (which included 'In the Village', 'First Death in Nova Scotia', 'Sandpiper' and 'Sestina'). Such structures raise the question of how to read volumes of poetry when the constituent parts were written over a number of years. To what extent can individual poems also be read as part of a larger whole? This question underpins the next activity. From 'Sandpiper', you should have a preliminary sense of what Bishop meant by 'Elsewhere': the second part of the volume collects pieces with a broader psychological geography than the first, which includes what Bishop called 'the descriptive Brazilian ones' (1996, p. 431).

Reading poems as a group can be initially disorientating, especially when forms and voices shift from text to text – each poem in *Questions of Travel* tends to construct its own register or particular situation, and understanding the text depends initially on your ability to decode or

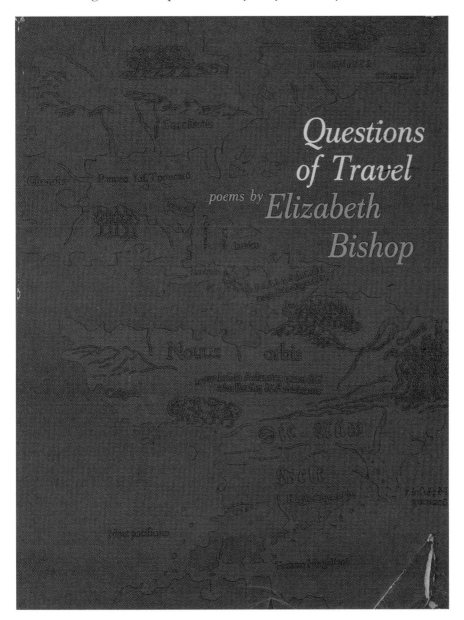

Figure 6.4   Front dust cover of Elizabeth Bishop (1958) *Questions of Travel*, New York, Farrar, Straus and Giroux. Jacket design by Adrianne Onderdonk.

empathise with that perspective. Unlike the Romantics, who frequently frame their poems through a lyrical 'I' with whom the reader can identify, as William Wordsworth (1770–1850) does in 'I wandered lonely as a cloud', Bishop's self is usually more hidden within the poems. It took me several readings to understand that 'The Armadillo' relates to the Brazilian practice of setting fire balloons alight to celebrate saint's days (see Laurens, 1983): I expected the poem to be more squarely and obviously about armadillos than it seems to be on a cursory reading.

So in writing about Brazil, Bishop often explicitly engages her readers with contexts that are far removed from those of North America or Europe. As you read through these poems, you need to bear in mind a number of related factors. Brazil was colonised by Portugal, rather than Spain, in the sixteenth century, so, unlike the rest of South America, its official language is Portuguese. As the world's fifth largest country, it is an enormous land mass, amounting to over 3 million square miles, or 5.7 per cent of the world's total area. It is still characterised by huge contrasts in wealth and opportunity. As you will see from Bishop's poems, though she was living on the peripheries of the small metropolitan political and cultural elite, twentieth-century Brazil was marked by large amounts of poverty, in which poor migrants from the countryside were often forced to live in slums or *favelas*, like the one described in 'The Burglar of Babylon'. Similarly, slavery had been a major part of the Brazilian economy until 1888; it was the last country in the Western world to abolish slavery. Echoes of this brutal past were still present in twentieth-century Brazil and surface in Bishop's poems and translations.

Activity 2

Bearing these contexts in mind, now read through the seven poems in the Brazil section (listed above). Don't be put off if you find any of them difficult: the object of this activity is to get an overview of these poems rather than to have a detailed understanding of each one. Now write some brief notes about the attitude(s) you think the poems display. What is your sense of Bishop's Brazil? Do you agree with her that these poems are predominantly 'descriptive'? Choose three or four illustrative quotations: you might want to come back to these as you go through the chapter.

Discussion

My sense is of a complex place which combines overpowering natural wonders like 'The tiniest green hummingbird in the world' (l. 21) alongside images of poverty such as 'the crudest wooden footwear' (l. 50) (both from 'Questions of Travel'). It's therefore difficult to distil a single attitude towards Brazil from these poems: I would argue that 'descriptive' is too narrow a term to encompass the range of perspectives, characters and poetic modes embraced in these texts. While all the poems include rich descriptions – see, for example, the simmeringly sexual lizards at the end of the second paragraph of 'Brazil, January 1, 1502' – they include much more than just description. As we shall see, this particular text imagines the brutal European colonisation of Brazil in the sixteenth century. In contrast, 'Arrival at Santos' concentrates on the comedy of American travellers arriving in Brazil. 'Questions of Travel' poses larger philosophical questions about the experience and ethics of travel, which we will consider in greater depth shortly. 'Squatter's Children', 'Manuelzinho' and 'The Burglar of Babylon' try to get inside the Brazilian experience of Brazil, either through acts of empathy, or through the more politicised idiom of 'The Burglar of Babylon', with its concentration on urban poverty. Finally, 'The Armadillo' concentrates on the effects of human behaviour on the natural world.

One of the conclusions which I draw from reading these poems together is that, despite their manifest differences, there are connections between them in terms of focus and what might broadly be called political perspective. Though Bishop tended to repudiate the idea that art should serve political or ideological agendas – she remarked in a letter to the poet Anne Stevenson that reading the Chilean Pablo Neruda was her 'only experience of a good communist poet' (Bishop, 2008, p. 857) – recent criticism has identified what Kim Fortuny describes as a 'social aesthetic' in her work (2003, p. 9). Becoming attuned to the presence of such an aesthetic in *Questions of Travel* helps to clarify how these poems engage with issues of migration and memory.

Reading Bishop from this perspective demands subtlety, since her writing avoids polemic. Consider 'Brazil, January 1, 1502', which, as I mentioned above, partly addresses the European colonisation of Brazil. At the end of the poem, Bishop elliptically describes the arrival of a Portuguese fleet under the leadership of Pedro Álvares Cabral at Guanabara Bay on New Year's Day 1502, at which point the area was baptised, or rather appropriated, as 'Rio de Janeiro' ('river of January').

The end of the poem evokes conflict between European Christians and the indigenous population:

> Directly after Mass, humming perhaps
> *L'Homme armé* or some such tune,
> they ripped away into the hanging fabric,
> each out to catch an Indian for himself –
> those maddening little women who kept calling,
> calling to each other (or had the birds waked up?)
> and retreating, always retreating, behind it.

(ll. 47–53)

The challenge here is partly to do with **allusion** – '*L'Homme armé*' was a popular song in the Renaissance, which was used as the basis for masses by composers such as Guillaume Dufay (*c*.1397–1474) and Josquin des Prez (*c*.1450–1521). So Bishop's conquistadors are humming a contemporary hit on a chivalric theme as they pursue the 'brand-new pleasure' of raping Indian women. This formulation gets to the other difficulty of the passage, which is one of tone. While it's clear that Bishop presents the Portuguese Christians as archetypal tough guys – 'hard as nails [...] glinting, / in creaking armor' (ll. 37–9) – and hypocrites, who can move 'Directly after Mass' to the pursuit of the women, the poem's tone eschews any categorical statement of position. While we may infer moral disgust as Bishop ventriloquises the conquistadors' frustration at the 'maddening little women', the end of the poem focuses on the calls of the women hiding behind 'the hanging fabric', which in turn threaten to metamorphosise into the calls of the waking birds in the penultimate line. While this is clearly a text that engages with colonial history from its title onwards, it's also the case that – as in the epigraph from the work of the art historian Kenneth Clark – Bishop is still concerned with the sensual evocation of an alien environment. In this respect, although the poem repudiates the Christians, there is also a residual sense that it and the reader follow them in trying to capture the pleasurable essence of a strange yet 'always retreating' world.

At one level, 'Brazil, January 1, 1502' re-imagines a distant past. Yet, as Fortuny's work suggests, the tensions in the poem remain relevant to an understanding of how Bishop represents questions of migration and identity in the twentieth century. Fortuny discusses Bishop's work in relation to recent anxieties about the ethics and politics of travel, especially when writers from the rich, 'developed' world travel to poorer countries in search of 'exotic' copy. Fortuny summarises these debates while arguing that Bishop's response to these problems is rather different from that of her contemporaries. Drawing on the work of cultural theorists like Michel Foucault and Edward Said, Fortuny suggests that conventional travel writing reinforces traditional power relations, as typically white male writers reproduce 'the foreign or exotic landscape as a museum piece' (2003, p. 26). From this perspective, travel writing is inherently political because of the 'imbalances of worldly power' that such writing necessarily reflects, whether consciously or not. However, Bishop's work does not altogether fit in with this account of Western travel writing:

> Bishop differs from many of her contemporaries and predecessors in the field of travel literature because she approached the subject fully conscious of her position as a colonial writer. To be a 'First World' North American after World War II and to write from within about circumstances without was to write against the discourse of political victory and expansion.
>
> (Fortuny, 2003, p. 27)

Bishop therefore did not write with any unanalysed assumption of the superiority of North America to Latin America. Fortuny goes on to make the more complicated claim that through labouring 'to expose the philosophical biases of the Western traveler', Bishop constructs 'a highly conscious consideration of the processes of observation' which, in turn 'decenter[s] the self' (Fortuny, 2003, p. 27). That is, because Bishop's focus is on the ambiguities of perspective – how she makes sense of what she sees – she is more aware of the problems of that perspective than many other writers, in the process problematising the idea of the writer's self as a neutral observer of other places. I want to test these claims now by rereading 'Questions of Travel'.

'Questions of Travel'

'Questions of Travel' is one of Bishop's most elusive, quicksilver poems. It has four distinct sections, of varying shapes, sizes and forms. The first verse paragraph concentrates on a sense of the excess of the Brazilian landscape – 'There are *too many* waterfalls'; 'the pressure of *so many* clouds' [my emphases] (ll. 1, 3). The speaker attempts to frame these natural wonders through the devices of poetic comparison into terms that render them slightly more comprehensible: 'the mountains look like the hulls of capsized ships, / slime-hung and barnacled' (ll. 11–12). Capsized ships are not everyday objects, but through the process of comparison, Bishop tries to contain and explain the excesses noted in the opening lines. Note, too, that the verse restlessly moves between long and short lines that seem to mimic the shape of the waterfalls as well as the unsettled quality of the speaker's meditation.

The second verse paragraph raises the questions of travel of the title more directly: 'Should we have stayed at home and thought of here?' (l. 14). This is the key question both of the poem itself and of the collection as a whole, and relates to Fortuny's point about Bishop's 'consideration of the processes of observation'. This part of the poem seems dismissive of the usual reasons given for travel: 'Is it right to be watching strangers in a play / in this strangest of theatres?' (ll. 16–17). In the next line, the impulse to travel is seen as a kind of 'childishness', while the touristic ambition 'To stare at some inexplicable old stonework' (l. 22) is symptomatic of the same disease. If the poem had ended here, you might reasonably have concluded that yes, 'we' should have 'stayed at home' and only '*thought* of here' [my emphasis], rather than actually travelling.

But the much longer third paragraph starts to give a more substantiated response to these criticisms: 'surely it would have been a pity' (l. 30) to have missed the various wonders of Brazil itemised in succeeding lines: the 'noble pantomimists', the 'sad, two-noted, wooden tune / of disparate wooden clogs', and so on (ll. 34, 36–7). As answers to the central questions of travel, you might legitimately say that the third paragraph is relentlessly descriptive – Bishop defends travel in terms of things seen, sounds heard, and objects admired. It's important to note, however, that this list of things – cued by long hyphenated clauses that rhetorically punctuate the text, signalling a departure in thought as well as place – is itself a consideration of thought processes prompted by travel:

> – Yes, a pity not to have pondered,
> blurr'dly and inconclusively,
> on what connection can exist for centuries
> between the crudest wooden footwear
> and, careful and finicky,
> the whittled fantasies of wooden cages.

> (ll. 47–52)

What makes this part of the poem difficult is that it stresses the fact that the traveller questions 'blurr'dly and inconclusively'; there is no conclusive answer to 'Should we have stayed at home and thought of here?' Rather, Bishop assembles a series of potentially connected images which, in turn, are connected with the traveller's inconclusive thought processes. There is another connection worth making here – between the 'finicky' wooden cages and the 'finical, awkward' sandpiper. If you look up these words in the *Oxford English Dictionary* (*OED*), you will see that they mean fastidious or over-particular, and that 'finicky' is associated with American English (see online *OED*, 'finicky' a.). Bishop, it seems, is a poet who is drawn to 'finicky' subjects, but the larger point is that the almost culpable fussiness of the objects the poem describes mirrors the way in which the poem as a whole refuses to come up with clear-cut answers. As Bishop saw something of herself in the sandpiper, so I would argue, 'Questions of Travel' recognises and draws attention to its own poetic 'finickiness'.

The last two italicised stanzas are presented as being a record of the traveller's thoughts in her notebook. They are distinct from the rest of the poem by virtue of those italics, their reference to the work of the French philosopher Blaise Pascal (1623–1662), and because they seem to return to the traditional structures of rhyming verse. As Fortuny explains, Bishop adapts a famous remark from Pascal's *Pensées* (a collection of short texts meaning 'Thoughts' or 'Observations', that was published in 1670), that human misery stems from 'the inability to remain at peace in a room' (Fortuny, 2003, p. 79; see also Pascal, 1958 [1670], no. 139).

Activity 3

With this in mind, now reread the final two stanzas of 'Questions of Travel'. What conclusion do you think the poem reaches about its 'questions of travel'?

Discussion

Your response to this question may well be to have noticed that the final eight lines include no fewer than three questions:

1 Do we travel through lack of imagination?

2 Should we stay in our rooms like Pascal?

3 Should we have stayed at home? (A repetition of a question asked in the second paragraph with the supplementary query *'wherever that may be?'* (l. 67))

Since the poem offers no response to these questions, it's probably misguided to expect it to reach 'conclusions'. What is different about these lines is, as we've noted, the use of rhyme and conventional stanza form, alongside the italics that mimic the words in the traveller's notebook: notebook entries are almost invariably inconclusive – fragments of thought and observation rather than fully worked-through arguments. This suggests that the poem is deliberately inconclusive; even the more traditional poetic forms employed do not disguise the fact that the poem doesn't offer a determined conclusion.

While this is a reasonable position, there are differences between the two questions: 'Should we have stayed at home …?' (l. 14) in the second paragraph and '*Should we have stayed at home …?*' (l. 66) at the end of the poem. In the former, 'home' is made tangible by virtue of 'the long trip' back: this is a known home with distinct conventions and assumptions. In the latter, Bishop destabilises any notion of home by the final half-line, '*wherever that may be?*' This implies that 'Questions of Travel' is in the process of metamorphosising from a piece of travel writing to a text about migration. Notice the couplet immediately preceding the final lines: '*Continent, city, country, society: / the choice is never wide and never free*' (ll. 64–5). Bishop reverses the usual conceit of travel writing that the metropolitan norms of the 'civilised' writer define how the exotic foreign country should be seen. In doing so, she queries the notion of 'choice': where we live is never as wide or as free as 'we' (whoever 'we' may be) might think. In this formulation, migration – even a chosen emigration such as Bishop's own – is more an action of necessity than volition.

'Manuelzinho' and 'The Burglar of Babylon'

It's relevant in this context that Bishop's emigration was more impulsive and opportunistic than a settled decision (Millier, 1993, p. 235). As I noted earlier, traditional poetry is often more at home with the notion of a first-person speaker who is ultimately 'free' to create in verse their own account of the world they inhabit. 'Questions of Travel' works hard to resist this Romantic notion through its melange of competing styles, images and voices. Thus we can suggest that the *Questions of Travel* volume includes poems that move from the normative expectations of travel writing to poems that reflect on Bishop's migration to Brazil and her attitudes to Brazilians as much as to its intoxicating geographies. To illustrate this shift in perspective, I want you now to compare 'Manuelzinho' with 'The Burglar of Babylon'. As you will have noticed in Activity 2, these poems are less descriptive than 'Questions of Travel'. In each case, Bishop focuses on individual Brazilians: 'The Burglar of Babylon' is a narrative poem, while 'Manuelzinho' is a character sketch with elements of storytelling.

Activity 4

Reread the two poems, then answer the following questions:

1   How would you differentiate these poems from the others in the 'Brazil' section?

2   Where do you think Bishop's sympathies lie – with the main characters, Micuçú and Manuelzinho, or elsewhere?

Discussion

1   I would say that these poems are much more direct in idiom and intention than others from the 'Brazil' section. This is evident in focus – 'Manuelzinho' is a **monologue** in the voice of 'a friend of the writer' (in fact Bishop's lover, Lota), while 'The Burglar of Babylon' tells the story of the deaths of Micuçú and one of the soldiers sent to hunt him. This directness is also evident in poetic form. 'The Burglar of Babylon' uses one of the simplest forms, the **ballad stanza**, rhyming *abxb*, with three beat lines that are usually end-stopped. This makes the writing unusually easy to follow, as in 'He could hear the goats *baa-baa*-ing, / He could hear the babies cry' (ll. 61–2); ballad stanza is closely related to popular forms like nursery rhyme and folk song. Though 'Manuelzinho' is written in freer verse without any strong or fixed metrical pattern, it's no less direct, using occasional rhymes to punctuate its comic address: 'You helpless, foolish man, / I love you all I can' (ll. 140–1). So these are poems written in deliberately simple idioms. Moreover, there is a connection between this simplicity and the central characters: the eccentric gardener Manuelzinho, and unsuccessful burglar Micuçú.

2   In each case, I would say that Bishop's sympathies are squarely with these characters. 'Manuelzinho' is a comedy of manners, in which Lota's exasperation at Manuelzinho's eccentricities is continuously offset by the pathos of the human relationship between the rich speaker and the poor **protagonist**. In this context, it's relevant that the name 'Manuelzinho' is a diminutive of the name 'Manuel', which, perhaps, underlines the speaker's condescending attitude towards her gardener. While the poem gets much comic capital from

Manuelzinho's unlikely reactions (consider his take on his dead father: 'no, you "don't think he's dead!" / I look at him. He's cold.' (ll. 59–60), it's also the case that moral sympathy in the poem works away from the educated wit of the speaker towards the recognition of Manuelzinho's weather-beaten dignity: 'Unkindly, / I called you Klorophyll Kid. / My visitors thought it was funny. / I apologize here and now' (ll. 136–9). Similarly, although 'Micuçú was a burglar and killer' (l. 21), 'The Burglar of Babylon' frames his actions in ways that mobilise the reader's sympathy on his behalf. To begin with, the poem identifies 'the hill of Babylon' as a 'fearful stain' on 'the fair green hills of Rio' because of the poverty in which migrant workers like Micuçú must live; the force of this framing device is intensified by the word-for-word repetition of stanzas 1 and 4 at the end of the poem. This underlines the sense that Micuçú's story is an illustration of the plight of 'The poor who come to Rio / And can't go home again' (ll. 3–4). Other qualifying devices include the denial that Micuçú was a rapist; the death of the officer as the result of the nervousness of one of the soldiers rather than any action by Micuçú; and the rather pathetic detail in the voice of one of the inhabitants of Babylon that '"He wasn't much of a burglar, / He got caught six times – or more"' (ll. 171–2). In sum, 'The Burglar of Babylon' is an outlaw ballad, in which Micuçú emerges as much a victim as a villain.

Bishop's 'social aesthetic' is therefore clearer in these poems. Yet it would be misleading to think that they are uncomplicated gestures of class solidarity: Bishop remained a wealthy emigrant in comparison with the people described in 'The Burglar of Babylon':

> On the hills a million people,
>   A million sparrows, nest,
> Like a confused migration
>   That's had to light and rest,
> Building its nests, or houses,
>   Out of nothing at all, or air.

(ll. 5–10)

In terms of *Questions of Travel* as a whole, the differences between Bishop and 'The poor who come to Rio' are partly registered by different birds: where Bishop saw aspects of herself in the solitary sandpiper, the poor migrants are 'a confused migration' of that most demotic of birds, the sparrow. This is not to say that the outrage of 'The Burglar of Babylon' is not genuine; it's more to make the point that Bishop's view of Brazilian society depends on her own privileged position, a little like 'The rich with their binoculars' (l. 133) who watch the manhunt 'standing on the rooftops, / Among TV antennae' (ll. 135–6). This is implicit in the subtle discriminations in 'Manuelzinho' between Lota's urbane voice of civilised dismay and the reality of Manuelzinho's hand-to-mouth existence. What we're left with at the end of the poem is one of Bishop's characteristic gestures of politeness, in which Lota's figurative removal of her hat symbolises a poetic connection between employer and employee that may not work in real life:

> I take off my hat, unpainted
> and figurative, to you.
> Again I promise to try.

(ll. 143–5)

In the desperate situation of 'The Burglar of Babylon', 'promising to try' would not look like very much, and there is little sense even in this poem that Lota or Bishop think of it as any more than a gesture. Yet it is a commitment to a more generous ideal, and that is what I would argue Bishop is trying to articulate in these poems. Bishop could not become Brazilian or indeed poor and uneducated, but in both of these poems she tries to empathise and ventriloquise on behalf of the excluded.

Translation and literatures

Translation is a different form of ventriloquisation, mediating between different languages and cultures to enable texts written in one language to find new audiences. Bishop translated a number of Brazilian poems, and in this chapter we will look at her versions of Carlos Drummond de Andrade's 'Infancy' and the anonymous 'Four Sambas'. The Andrade poem first appeared in *An Anthology of Twentieth-Century Brazilian Poetry* (1972), which Bishop co-edited with the Brazilian writer Emanuel Brasil, and for which she wrote the introduction, while 'Four Sambas' first appeared in the *New York Times* in 1965 (Bishop, 2008, p. 927). In the introduction Bishop explores the differences between Brazilian and American literary cultures:

> It may seem to the American visitor that the educated people whom he meets in Brazil read more poetry and *know* more poetry (often by heart) than people in the same walks of life at home. But it should be remembered that the educated elite is still a very small class, living almost entirely in five or six coastal cities, and that in a country of widespread illiteracy (forty per cent the figure usually given), the potential book-reading, book-buying public is limited.
>
> (Bishop, 2008, p. 720)

Bishop's emphasis is on the value Brazilians place on poetry and on the small size of the poetry-reading public. As in 'Manuelzinho', there is an element of condescension as Bishop tries to explain 'a country of widespread illiteracy' to a more sophisticated American audience. Brazilian literary culture is, however, far from monolithic: 'Brazil has produced in recent years some of the best popular songs ever written' (Bishop, 2008, p. 728). Nevertheless, the implication throughout the introduction is that in some ways Brazil is an environment more conducive to poetry than America; as she remarked in a letter to Marianne Moore written shortly after her arrival in Brazil: 'Poets – even when they're bad, as they mostly are – are much more highly thought of here than in the U. S., a nice old-fashioned romantic idea of the *Poet*' (Bishop, 1996, p. 281). At the same time, such old-fashioned notions coexist with a more plural literary culture, in which the dividing line between high and popular culture is not as clear-cut as elsewhere.

Activity 5

To explore these ideas, you should now read 'Four Sambas' and 'Infancy'. What do they remind you of and why? Don't restrict yourself only to Bishop's work.

Discussion

You may have connected the 'Four Sambas' with the Brazilian dance, which is often accompanied with song; these texts are song lyrics. Bishop's headnote states that the Sambas were composed for Rio's annual carnival, and that these texts from 1965 are linked by their satirical intention against a right-wing military coup that took place in April 1964. They are, however, reminiscent of the style and register of both 'The Burglar of Babylon' and 'Manuelzinho': in the first samba, 'Rio de Janiero, / My joy and my delight! / By day I have no water, / By night I have no light' (ll. 1–4) echoes the former, while in the third samba the witty empathy of 'I'm sorry for poor Juvenál / Hanging in the old Central / All year long …' (ll. 16–18) recalls the urbane wit of the latter. The final samba shows a different kind of wit, in this case recalling the extravagant conceits of jazz songs like 'Anything Goes' or 'You're the Top' by Cole Porter (1891–1964), as when the speaker describes his mulatta (mixed-race girlfriend) as 'The prune in my pudding, / Pepper in my pie' (ll. 28–9). The second samba is different again, reading as a zestful satire on political corruption: 'Kick him out of office! / He's a greedy boy!' and '"Pull" won't work again' (ll. 5–6, 10). In each case, these are urgent, demotic voices rather than those of high literary culture. You might reasonably suggest, therefore, that both in her translations and in original poems like 'The Burglar of Babylon' and 'Manuelzinho', Bishop expands received notions of the literary by making room for demotic and popular registers.

'Infancy' is much more clearly a literary poem. Its **free verse** recalls the shifting, unsettled and unpredictable verse paragraph shapes of 'Questions of Travel', while the speaker's allusions to Daniel Defoe's *Robinson Crusoe* (1719) mark it as a text that expects readers both to understand the allusion and to compare the situation described in the poem with Defoe's famous narrative of shipwreck and rescue. Indeed, *Robinson Crusoe* is crucial to the poem, as the speaker juxtaposes his boyish absorption in 'the long story that never comes to an end' (l. 6) with the unseen reality of his own story, which 'was prettier than that of Robinson Crusoe' (l. 21). You may also have heard echoes of Bishop's 'social aesthetic' in the second paragraph, as the speaker remembers 'a voice that had learned / lullabies long ago in the slave-quarters' (ll. 7–8) calling him to coffee. In this way, and in the image of 'Coffee blacker than the black old woman / delicious coffee' (ll. 10–11), the poem gestures towards the colonial history of slavery that it never fully discusses. Rather, like the poems we will discuss in the next section, 'Infancy' is a lyrical exploration of the workings of memory in relation to high culture and contested histories.

As I argued in relation to 'The Burglar of Babylon' and 'Manuelzinho', Bishop inevitably views Brazil from the position of an outsider. Nevertheless, since poetry is an art of ventriloquisation – in which the poet throws his or her voice into different characters, places and situations – there is a sense in which the Brazilian poems of *Questions of Travel* and these translations show a commitment to Brazilian culture alongside an awareness of the complex social realities of twentieth-century Brazil. Bishop's skill as a poet lies partly in the ways these disparate texts refuse to sentimentalise social relationships. Manuelzinho is patronised in the poem that bears his name, while Lota 'promise[s] to try' (l. 145) to do better by him; Micuçú remains a thug, even as the poem partially exculpates him from his killings. Similarly, the translations attempt to make English-speaking readers more conscious of Brazilian culture and history, and thus to share something of Bishop's own experience as an emigrant writer.

Memories of Nova Scotia

Bishop's childhood in Nova Scotia provides the setting for many of her most striking texts, and as Jonathan Ellis notes, much of this work was written while she was living in Brazil:

> Bishop's sense of being an outsider in Brazil reawakened her childhood sense of always being a 'guest' in other people's homes. While she spent some time probing her appropriation of Brazilian subjects ... in poems like 'Arrival at Santos' and 'Questions of Travel', she devoted most of her energies to work set in Nova Scotia and New England, re-examining her identity. ... This period in her life produced some of her most autobiographical writing, from stories like ... 'In the Village' to poems such as 'First Death in Nova Scotia' ... and 'Sestina'. ... Her experience of living in Brazil somehow made writing about childhood exclusion easier.
>
> (Ellis, 2006, p. 92)

As I noted earlier, *Questions of Travel*'s two sections are intimately connected. The Nova Scotia of 'In the Village' and 'First Death in Nova Scotia' is structurally presented in the format of the volume as the flipside of the Brazil explored in the first section. 'In the Village' is interesting both as a piece of life writing – it focuses on a key moment during her mother's mental breakdown – and for the overlaps it displays between Bishop's poetry and fiction. In this extract, Bishop fuses the 'beautiful sounds from the blacksmith's shop at the end of the garden' with her mother's terrible scream:

> … a smell of red-hot metal and horses' hoofs.
> *Clang.*
> The pure note: pure and angelic.
> The dress was all wrong. She screamed.
> The child vanishes.
> Later they sit, the mother and the three sisters, in the shade on the back porch, sipping sour, diluted ruby: raspberry vinegar. The dressmaker refuses to join them and leaves, holding the dress to her heart. The child is visiting the blacksmith.

(Bishop, 2008, p. 100)

Bishop's prose is similar to her poetry in its sensitivity to detail, which is related to what Lowell, as we saw in the section on 'Bishop and the sandpiper', calls her 'genius for picking up the unnoticed' (Bishop and Lowell, 2008, p. 580). Here it is the vanishing child who is unnoticed in the drama of the mother's mental deterioration (the mother is the 'she' who screams); by focusing on competing sounds in a simple, childlike register, Bishop manages economically to convey the emotional complexity of the childhood experience.

The story as a whole meditates on the work the memory does to try to capture and re-interpret the past. At the end, the adult voice of the narrator poses a critical question about this work of memory: 'All those other things – clothes, crumbling postcards, broken china; things damaged and lost, sickened or destroyed; even the frail almost-lost scream – are they too frail for us to hear their voices long, too mortal?' (Bishop, 2008, p. 118). As the physical texture of lost treasures is irretrievably decayed, so the sounds of the past – and the emotions that they symbolise within the memory – are too frail and mortal for us to hold on to. This concern with how we remember is crucial both to 'In the Village' and the poems that follow it, which are also almost obsessively concerned with 'things damaged and lost'.

These poems are among Bishop's most popular. Robert Lowell first saw a manuscript of 'First Death in Nova Scotia' in September 1961, when Bishop noted that it 'undoubtedly shows your influence'; she also explains to the non-Canadian reader that the line 'the Maple Leaf (Forever)' alludes to 'the un-official Canadian anthem' of the same name 'sung in school constantly' (Bishop and Lowell, 2008, p. 379). Bishop was partly indebted to Lowell's 'My Last Afternoon with Uncle Devereux Winslow' from the *Life Studies* (1959) volume, which was seen as heralding the 'confessional' movement in modern poetry, affecting poets such as Sylvia Plath (1932–1963) (see Lowell, 2003, pp. 163–7; see also Kalstone, 1989, p. 219). Confessional poetry is explicitly poetry that engages questions of memory. Thus, like 'First Death in Nova Scotia', Lowell's poem is an account of a child's first encounter with mortality. On receiving a copy of *Questions of Travel* in October 1965, Lowell emphasises the impact the poem made on him in the printed book:

> 'Death in Nova Scotia' haunts me (It was weird this summer when I drove through New Brunswick and Nova Scotia on a short salmon fishing trip, to see everywhere the pale Maple Leaf Flag, more like (and pleasantly at last) a boy scout flag than a nation's – embittered anglophiles still fly the old Union Jack) – the poem is doubly provincial and remote, in time, the Prince of Wales and all, and in place, very sad and lovely
>
> (Bishop and Lowell, 2008, p. 591)

Despite the incoherence of his letter-writing syntax and punctuation, Lowell does a useful job in locating the poem geographically and culturally and in terms of the structure of *Questions of Travel*. He writes partly as a member of the New England aristocracy, for whom Nova Scotia was necessarily 'provincial' (see Hamilton, 1982, p. 4). But in this context, 'provincial' is not meant pejoratively; it's more that Lowell is conflating Nova Scotia's geographical isolation from the land mass of North America with the isolation depicted in the poem. Note, too, Lowell's emphasis on the poem's haunting remoteness: another way of putting this would be that 'First Death in Nova Scotia' is explicitly concerned with childhood memory.

Activity 6

Now read 'First Death in Nova Scotia'. To what extent does it modify your impression of Bishop's work from the Brazil poems?

Discussion

This activity is particularly subjective; there is no single right answer. You may feel that the different setting of 'First Death in Nova Scotia' demands a different poetic voice and form. The poem is marked by the traditional structures of metre, stanza form and rhyme, albeit with many slant- or **half-rhymes**, where the paired words fail fully to match with one another, as in the opening clinch of 'parlor' with 'Arthur'. You might stress the bitter cold evoked in this poem as against the tropical heat of the Brazilian poems: 'the *cold, cold* parlor'; 'his white, *frozen* lake'; 'the roads deep in *snow*' [my emphases] (ll. 1, 15, 50). There's a glacial feel to the poem that runs from its setting, its descriptions, and its focus on Arthur's small, frozen body: 'Jack Frost had dropped the brush / and left him white, forever' (ll. 39–40). This is connected with the simple, almost childlike syntax Bishop adopts, as though mimicking the child's thought processes: 'how could Arthur go, / clutching his tiny lily, / with his eyes shut up so tight / and the roads deep in snow?' (ll. 47–50). From this perspective, the poem recalls 'In the Village' in the way it inhabits the child's **point of view** and circles around questions of memory. This suggests a contrast with the Brazilian poems that tend to be cast in an imagined present tense, as in 'The Burglar of Babylon'. If you emphasised these elements, you will probably want to argue that 'First Death in Nova Scotia' suggests a different way of reading Bishop – as a poet of sharp contrasts in method and location, a contrast that is also signalled by the structure of the *Questions of Travel* volume.

You may, however, have seen more continuity between 'First Death in Nova Scotia' and the Brazilian poems. Certainly, the poem's elaborate formal construction has parallels in 'The Armadillo' and 'Questions of Travel'. The poem also encourages readers to visualise an alien world. It has clear connections with the Brazilian poems in terms of its focus on the position of the observer, and its concern to bring into the reader's mind potentially unfamiliar perspectives and objects. This is apparent in the terrific description of the stuffed loon (loons are North American aquatic birds known as divers in the UK and Ireland), where Bishop configures the dead bird as both a seductive object ('his eyes were red glass, / much to be desired' (ll. 19–20)) and as a silent chorus that impassively observes what happens in the parlor: 'He kept his own counsel / on his white, frozen lake, / the marble-topped table' (ll. 14–16). The point which the poem doesn't need to labour is that the loon and Arthur are linked in stasis and deadness, their inability to do anything other than keep their own counsel. The poem dramatises the psychological realisation of the absolute distinction between life and death. If you follow this approach, you are likely to see 'Brazil' and 'Elsewhere' as different sides of the same question or questions: Bishop is a poet preoccupied with the process and perspective of observation, whether she is evoking a different country or the distant past of her own life. The major difference of Nova Scotian texts like 'In the Village' and

'First Death in Nova Scotia' is, perhaps, their explicit engagement with issues of memory, and specifically Bishop's attempt to transform incidents from her own childhood into literature.

Following this train of thought, you might argue that 'First Death in Nova Scotia' responds to the end of 'Questions of Travel'. Where the latter queries where home may be, the former goes back to the start of Bishop's life to suggest the child's alienation from home both in its 'frosted' description of Arthur in the parlor, and in its fearful implication that leaving Nova Scotia will be impossible with 'the roads deep in snow' (l. 50). The fantasy of Arthur as a page at the British court intimates the speaker's desperation to go to the 'warm' court of 'The gracious royal couples' (l. 41), so that a fantasy home of elaborate formality displaces a real home overshadowed by death.

We end with another Nova Scotian poem, 'Sestina', which is printed immediately before 'First Death in Nova Scotia' in *Questions of Travel*. The poem's title describes its poetic form: a **sestina** is an elaborate poem constructed of six-line stanzas (or sixains) followed by a final three-line **tercet**. Within this structure, a series of six non-rhyming words is repeated at different positions within the seven stanzas to produce an effect of repetition with a difference. The form was first developed by the Provençal troubadour Arnaut Daniel in the twelfth century, and has remained one of the most challenging poetic forms properly to master. In the case of Bishop's 'Sestina', the six words are '*house*', '*grandmother*', '*child*', '*Stove*', '*almanac*', '*tears*' [my emphases], and you can gauge some of the effects of variety and recurrence by comparing the first and fifth stanzas:

> September rain falls on the house.
> In the failing light, the old grandmother
> sits in the kitchen with the child
> beside the Little Marvel Stove,
> reading the jokes from the almanac,
> laughing and talking to hide her tears.
>
> ...
>
> *It was to be*, says the Marvel Stove.
> *I know what I know*, says the almanac.
> With crayons the child draws a rigid house
> and a winding pathway. Then the child

puts in a man with buttons like tears
and shows it proudly to the grandmother

(ll. 1–6, 25–30)

The technical difficulty of the sestina often results in poems that amplify stasis, as the poet must relentlessly return to the same words. I would suggest that Bishop chose the form because she wanted to emphasise the stasis of the Nova Scotia of her childhood: the child's drawing of 'a rigid house' is emblematic of this stifling terrain. Similarly, the child's repressed 'tears' echo differently through each changing stanza. The overall effect, therefore, is one of a closed circuit as the poem reworks and repositions the same words, but ultimately with very little change or development. If 'First Death in Nova Scotia' emphasises the fixity of death, 'Sestina' implies that the memory of childhood is locked into an almost unbearable cycle of repeated human transactions that frame the child's experience. The chilling phrase *'Time to plant tears'* (l. 37) sums up both the Nova Scotia represented in these poems, and the curious amalgam between high cultural forms and more immediate voices. Although 'Sestina' seems remote from the idioms of 'The Burglar of Babylon' and the 'Four Sambas', what keeps it anchored in a comprehensible world is the juxtaposition of everyday objects like the 'marvellous stove' and the 'house' with the familiar practical voices of the almanac and the well-intentioned, yet inadequate, grandmother.

These Nova Scotian poems are, perhaps, closer to what Lowell (quoted in the section on 'Bishop and the sandpiper' above) meant by 'the classical serenity of a new country' (Bishop and Lowell, 2008, p. 580). As I suggested in the previous section, Bishop's Brazil doesn't altogether mesh with the idea of 'classical serenity', a phrase that suggests a beautiful and even an unproblematic terrain. I wouldn't argue that the Nova Scotia of 'First Death in Nova Scotia' or 'Sestina' is any more unproblematic – this is a world of deadly stasis and repressed griefs. However, 'classical serenity' is in part a way of trying to capture the formal quality of Bishop's writing, and the way she uses poetic devices to structure and represent painful emotions.

Conclusion

As this chapter has tried to show, Bishop's employment of a wide range of poetic devices – from high cultural forms like the sestina through to popular forms like the ballad and the samba – is closely related to her engagement with the themes of migration and memory, as she seeks to verbalise tensions within different peoples and places. This does not always make for easy reading. But the richness of Bishop's work lies in the challenges it holds out to its readers – to move from what 'The Armadillo' calls *'pretty, dreamlike mimicry'* (l. 37) to a deeper understanding of the difficult liaisons between art and life.

References

Armitage, S. and Dee, T. (eds) (2009) *The Poetry of Birds*, London, Viking.

Bishop, E. (1996) *One Art: The Selected Letters* (ed. R. Giroux), London, Pimlico.

Bishop, E. (2004 [1983]) *Complete Poems*, London, Chatto & Windus.

Bishop, E. (2008) *Poems, Prose, and Letters* (ed. R. Giroux and L. Schwarz), New York, Library of America.

Bishop, E. and Lowell, R. (2008) *Words in Air: The Complete Correspondence between Elizabeth Bishop and Robert Lowell* (ed. T. Travis and S. Hamilton), London, Faber and Faber.

Ellis, J. (2006) *Art and Memory in the Work of Elizabeth Bishop*, Aldershot, Ashgate.

Fortuny, K. (2003) *Elizabeth Bishop: The Art of Travel*, Boulder, CO, University Press of Colorado.

Hamilton, I. (1982) *Robert Lowell: A Biography*, New York, Random House.

Kalstone, D. (1989) *Becoming a Poet: Elizabeth Bishop with Marianne Moore and Robert Lowell* (ed. R. Hemenway), London, Hogarth.

Laurens, P. (1983) 'On "The Armadillo"' [online], http://www.english. illinois.edu/maps/poets/a_f/bishop/armadillo.htm (Accessed 7 July 2011); originally from Laurens, P. (1983) '"Old correspondences": prosodic transformations in Elizabeth Bishop' in Schwartz, L. and Estees, S.P. (eds) *Elizabeth Bishop and Her Art*, Ann Arbor, MI, University of Michigan Press.

Lowell, R. (2003) *Collected Poems* (ed. F. Bidart and D. Gewanter), London, Faber and Faber.

McKendrick, J. (2002) 'Bishop's birds' in Anderson, L. and Shapcott, J. (eds) *Elizabeth Bishop: Poet of the Periphery*, Newcastle upon Tyne, Bloodaxe.

Millier, B.C. (1993) *Elizabeth Bishop: Life and the Memory of It*, Berkeley, CA, University of California Press.

Pascal, B. (1958 [1670]) *Pensées* (intro T.S. Eliot), New York, E.P. Dutton; ebook version (2006) Project Gutenberg [online], http://www.gutenberg.org (Accessed 7 July 2011).

Shelley, P.B. (1971 [1820]) *Poetical Works* (ed. T. Hutchinson and G.M. Matthews), Oxford, Oxford University Press.

Further reading

The cheapest and most widely available edition of Bishop's poetry is *Complete Poems*; *Poems, Prose, and Letters* is a more expensive and comprehensive selection of her work. 'In the Village' is in *Poems, Prose, and Letters*, but can also be found in Bishop, E. (1984) *Collected Prose* (ed. and intro. R. Giroux), New York, Farrar, Straus and Giroux. For unpublished writings, see Bishop, E. (2006) *Edgar Allan Poe and the Juke-Box: Uncollected Poems, Drafts, and Fragments* (ed. A. Quinn), New York, Farrar, Straus and Giroux.

Chapter 7
Brian Friel,
Dancing at Lughnasa

Suman Gupta

Aims

This chapter will:

- place *Dancing at Lughnasa* not only with regard to its 1936 setting and its appearance in 1990 in Ireland, but also in terms of its inspirations from and resonances beyond the Irish context
- explore notions of memory and migration at the formal and thematic levels in the play
- discuss the textual qualities of the play
- briefly consider language and performance in the play.

Introduction

This chapter looks at the play *Dancing at Lughnasa* (1990) by Brian Friel (b. 1929). Its main focus is on the play as a text, and in this regard it reads the play text closely, with the main themes of this part of the book, migration and memory, in view. The concluding section by Anita Pacheco discusses language and performance in the play.

An underlying concern of this part of the book is also the various ways in which literature is produced, approached and studied, so that it is often more appropriate to think of the academic field in terms of the plural 'literatures' rather than the singular 'literature'. In the following chapter you will find such a pluralistic understanding of literatures exemplified in a number of ways. Though *Dancing at Lughnasa* is justifiably regarded as squarely placed within an Irish literary tradition, the play deliberately draws upon a cosmopolitan sense of theatre and its developments in Russia and the United States. Moreover, a question that is implicit below is whether the Irish literary tradition itself can be regarded as a singular one or as consisting in a number of strands. Like any literary text, this one is subject to a range of readings, including contrary ones: for example, take note of the discussion below on whether the play should be regarded as a departure from or continuation of Friel's Field Day plays, or on how 'home' should be understood in the play.

The edition of the text that is referred to in this chapter is the one published by Faber and Faber in 1990. You should read the entire play text before proceeding with this chapter. The chapter begins with a background section that places the play within its contexts. Activities appear and points of critical discussion regarding the play are outlined in the subsequent three sections, on the themes of memory, migration, and language and performance in the play, respectively.

Background

Brian Friel's play *Dancing at Lughnasa* was first performed at the Abbey Theatre, Dublin, on 23 April 1990. This choice of venue was immediately recognised as significant. The Abbey Theatre, founded in 1903 by William Butler Yeats and Augusta Gregory, is closely associated with Irish national cultural history and is rightly regarded as the dominant theatrical establishment of the Republic of Ireland. Friel's work was no stranger to the Abbey Theatre; four of his earlier plays had been produced there in the 1960s and 1970s. However, his plays in the 1980s – from *Translations* (1980) to *Making History* (1988) – were first performed under the Field Day Theatre Company's banner. This company, based in Derry in Northern Ireland, had been founded by Friel with the actor Stephen Rea in 1980 and grew into a forum for both theatre productions and intellectual debate. The impact of the Field Day collective amidst the Troubles in Northern Ireland was profound, and Friel's 1980s plays were largely received as setting its agenda and articulating its purposes. So, Friel's decision to have *Dancing at Lughnasa* produced at the Abbey first was seen as a break from the Field Day: it seemed to announce a new turn in Friel's art and a loss of verve in the Field Day's role. The play's place in Friel's **oeuvre** is usually understood accordingly, and it is therefore expedient to begin this exploration of *Dancing at Lughnasa* with a few notes on the Field Day's significance.

The Troubles refer to the prolonged period of violent confrontations between Catholic Republican and Protestant Unionist alignments, complicated by police and British army support for the latter, in Northern Ireland. These escalated from the late 1960s, peaked in the early 1970s (especially after Bloody Sunday on 30 January 1972, when fourteen unarmed Republican civil rights protesters were shot dead by British soldiers in Derry), and continued until the Good Friday Agreement of 1998 (and sporadically thereafter). Friel's first explicitly political play, *The Freedom of the City*, was produced in 1973 at the Abbey Theatre, and was obviously addressed to the Bloody Sunday killings. Friel and Rea set up the Field Day Theatre Company in 1980, against the backdrop of the Troubles, to make a specific sort of intervention in that context. According to Marilyn Richtarik, in her history of the early phase of the Field Day company, it was founded with 'the intention of finding or creating a space between unionism and nationalism and proving by example the possibility of a shared culture in the North of Ireland' (2001 [1995], p. 7). Within this broad intention she notes a twofold impulse: that the founders, first, 'wished to bring professional theatre to people who might otherwise never see it', and second, thereby to cultivate a sort of '"parochialism", which is content in itself and feels no need to compare itself with more powerful or cosmopolitan areas' (Richtarik, 2001 [1995], p. 11). In the course of the 1980s, these intentions materialised as an engagement with Irish history and reconsideration of Irish identity in terms of its colonial past and colonial/postcolonial present (more precisely, colonial present in

Northern Ireland and postcolonial present in the Republic). Such understanding could, in itself, be expected to bridge sectarian schisms and enable the Irish to think of themselves and their allegiances differently. Friel's play *Translations*, as a vehicle for which the company was initially established, gave flesh to the intellectual ambition of the Field Day company, as did other 1980s plays by Friel and others (Tom Paulin, Derek Mahon, Thomas Kilroy, Stewart Parker, for instance). These were first produced in Derry and then performed on successful theatre tours. Throughout, in Robert Welch's words, 'Field Day studiously avoided the Abbey', and sought 'to dislodge the concentrations of gravity, in the field of culture, from Dublin and Belfast' (1999, p. 197).

Friel had probably regarded the Field Day Theatre Company as primarily devoted to fulfilling its intellectually and culturally transformative ambition *through theatre*; hoping thereby to contribute, as he once observed in an interview on 6 September 1981, to: 'The decolonization process of the imagination [which] is very important if a new Irish personality is to emerge' (quoted in O'Connor, 2000 [1981], p. 159). However, that ambition became a matter for direct analytical debate with the appearance of a series of influential Field Day pamphlets, in the first instance in September 1983, penned by three of the company's directors (Tom Paulin, Seamus Heaney and Seamus Deane). The pamphlets, and debates surrounding them, continued in subsequent years, and eventually attracted contributions from highly regarded scholars beyond Ireland and Britain (such as Fredric Jameson and Edward Said). As the 1980s waned, much of the Field Day's energies were absorbed by the gigantic project, driven by Seamus Deane, to create a broader canon of Irish literature, which resulted in the three volumes of *The Field Day Anthology of Irish Writing* (1991). In brief, intellectual analysis – and ideological definition – seemed to become as, if not more, important in the Field Day's activities as theatre. Further, as the Field Day's principal members acquired international fame and influence, it appeared in the early 1990s that:

> What had started out as a regionally based touring company, had become part of a new transnational diaspora, still rooted in Irish concerns and images, but as likely to be found in London or Los Angeles as in Dublin or Derry.
>
> (Morash, 2002, p. 265)

These changes in Field Day around the turn of the decade were brought sharply into focus, and came to be marked by, Friel's decision to have *Dancing at Lughnasa* performed at the Abbey Theatre: in a way, it seemed that both the company and its founding playwright had outgrown each other and had to part ways. *Dancing at Lughnasa* was received not simply as a new turn in Friel's writing, but as a new turn defined in terms of Friel's contribution to the Field Day enterprise.

Placing *Dancing at Lughnasa* vis-à-vis the Field Day is a somewhat complex matter, and several different ways of doing this have been suggested. First, the play has been seen as a sort of liberation from the constraints of the company, as seeking expression *against* or *beyond* its ideological thrust. That's the view taken by Richtarik:

> I suspect he felt constrained by the ideological framework Field Day had developed by 1989. *Dancing at Lughnasa* is simply not a 'Field Day play' as described by Rea in 1989 ('a play of ideas, involved with language, involved with looking at imperialism, and looking at men who have one foot in Ireland and one in England') or by Deane in 1990 ('a political crisis produces a clash of loyalties that is analyzable but irresolvable … the dramatic analysis centres on anxieties of naming, speaking, and voice and the relation of these to place, identity, and self-realization.').
>
> (Richtarik, 2001 [1995], p. 268)

Friel himself spoke of his reluctance to be identified with institutions, observing in an October 1991 interview that:

> Institutions are inclined to enforce characteristics, impose an attitude or a voice or a response. I think you're better to keep away from all of them. It's for that reason that I didn't give *Dancing at Lughnasa* to Field Day to produce.
>
> (Friel quoted in Lahr, 2000 [1991], p. 216)

Second, others saw in Friel's move away from the Field Day a desire to *return* to themes that had occupied him prior to establishing the company. The theatre critic Fintan O'Toole's review of the play on 28 April 1990, for instance, noted that its first performances were appropriately undertaken at the Abbey because it is:

a Southern play rather than a Northern one. The essential tensions are the ones with which Friel's work as a playwright began over 30 years ago: the tensions of Southern society modernizing itself, the clash between a traditional culture and a modern, industrial one.

(O'Toole quoted in Furay and O'Hanlon, 2003 [1990], p. 94)

Third, a somewhat conciliatory direction has been taken by numerous commentators (Seamus Deane, Seamus Heaney, Declan Kiberd, Richard Pine and others) who discerned in the play both *continuities* with Friel's earlier work (including the Field Day plays) and *departures* (especially from the Field Day plays). For such commentators the continuities are clarified by identifying the departures, and both appear as much in the themes as in the language and form. In particular, *Dancing at Lughnasa* seems to express/perform the nuances of memory and migration in ways that both resonate with and stand out as distinctive within the body of Friel's plays.

The next two sections of this chapter analyse *Dancing at Lughnasa* in terms of its treatment of memory and migration, respectively, noting where useful how the treatment of these may be understood as a departure from the Field Day plays. This does not mean that you need to read the latter; the significance of references to Friel's other plays, and indeed plays by other authors, in the following can be grasped to a necessary extent by focusing on *Dancing at Lughnasa* itself and the explanations given below.

The play was enormously successful and popular internationally. It is consequently one of the few Friel plays (the early *Philadelphia, Here I Come!* (1964) is another) that has been adapted as a film (in 1998, directed by Pat O'Connor, with the screenplay by Frank McGuinness). I have to warn you here against watching the film in the context of this chapter. Though it uses dialogue from Friel's play, the visual impression and dramatic effect of the film is significantly different from the play's. A detailed consideration of it alongside the play leads Joan Fitzpatrick Dean to observe accurately that the 'uniquely theatrical elements of Friel's play succumbed to the Classical Hollywood Style' in the film (2003, p. 2). The film cannot serve as a replacement for watching the play on stage; if you don't have an opportunity to see it in the theatre, it is still best not to let the film interfere with your imagining of the play.

Figure 7.1   *Dancing at Lughnasa*, dir. Patrick Mason (Abbey Theatre, Dublin, 1991). Photo: JSTOR.

Figure 7.2   *Dancing at Lughnasa*, dir. Patrick Mason (Abbey Theatre, Dublin, 1991). Photo: JSTOR.

Memory

The role of memory in *Dancing at Lughnasa* has received considerable critical attention, especially in relation to the sense of history that is evident in it. For the purposes of this chapter you may think of history as a mode of understanding the past in a structured and consensual way, whereas memory is a somewhat fluid and individual way of recalling the past. The following two activities, focused on memory and history respectively, are designed to help you organise your thoughts in this regard.

Activity 1

With close reference to the play, make a list of the various ways in which memory (i.e. remembering incidents or persons from the past) works as a theme or through characters.

Discussion

1   The obvious theatrical device in the play which foregrounds the theme of memory is that of *not* having the boy Michael present onstage. His presence is registered by the others pretending that he's there and talking to and about him, and by the narrator Michael speaking his lines. Michael's memories *are* obviously the substance of the play – recalling the time when he was a boy in the Mundy sisters' household. Since it is the narrator Michael who recalls what happened around his childhood self, he cannot visualise the boy clearly. One doesn't, naturally, *see* oneself as a child in one's memories, one simply *is* a child in them. The fact that the play constitutes Michael's memories is evident throughout to the audience by the constant absence of the boy, by the oddness of everyone pretending he's there and an adult voice speaking for him – by, so to speak, the boy's absent-presence onstage.

2   To underpin that device, in his narrative monologues Michael makes an explicit theme of memory. He speaks of his memories *as* memories, seeming to reflect on memory itself at times. He starts by mentioning the 'different kinds of memories' (p. 1) of 1936, and then singles out 'these two memories' (p. 2); he talks of what happened before (apropos Jack, pp. 8–9) and after (pp. 41–2; pp. 59–61) the events in view; and he ends the play by returning to 'different kinds of memories' and dwelling at length on a memory that 'owes nothing to fact', a memory simply of 'dancing' (p. 71).

3   Characters in the play make sense of their 1936 present in Ballybeg, and their relations to each other, by recalling their pasts. Thus, the

sisters contemplate going to the harvest dance because of their memories – 'Just like we used to. All dressed up' (p. 12); mention of her old friend Bernie O'Donnell brings back to Maggie memories of the time when she was sixteen (p. 20); Jack reminisces about their mother and Chris as a baby (p. 38); and so on.

4   Jack's memories of his life in Kyanga village in Uganda are a separate matter from those memories in the point above. These do not quite fit into the world of Ballybeg in 1936, and are not shared by others – they evoke effectively a distant and exotic world, entirely enclosed in Jack's mind. This sense of a discrete world of Jack's Kyanga memories is accentuated by his alienation from the surroundings and everyday life of Ballybeg, particularly by his uncertainties with the English language.

5   When Jack recalls their mother and Chris as a baby, the memory comes to him, 'like a – a picture? – a camera-picture? – a photograph! – it's like a photograph in my mind' (p. 38). This is a familiar way of thinking about memories, in terms of still images that recall photographs just as photographs recall the past (family photographs are powerfully associated with memories). And, in fact, this association gestures towards another 'memory device' in the play: it begins and ends with the narrator Michael speaking before a 'formal tableau' of the dramatis personae standing or seated, almost motionless, lit by a soft unnatural light, as in a photograph. It is as if the memories that are the play are set off by and return to an image very like a family photograph.

Having considered the role of memory and the devices through which Friel gives it dramatic form onstage, now turn to Activity 2 to contemplate the ways in which a sense of history works in the play. For the purposes of this activity, history consists in, for instance, being clear about periods and places (contexts), referring to well-documented personages and events, being authentic to or consistent with more or less agreed knowledge of the past (deriving from available evidence and the interpretation thereof).

Activity 2

In what ways is the past accounted for in historical terms in the play, that is, through references to historical periods, places, events and persons?

Discussion

1   There is, of course, a specific period and place that the narrator
    Michael recalls: August 1936 in the imaginary village of Ballybeg in
    the real County Donegal. However, the historical perspective
    assumed for this specific context is only loosely presented. There is,
    significantly, no indication of what chronological vantage point the
    recalled past is seen from: the audience isn't informed what year or
    place the narrator Michael is speaking from; they know only that it
    must be after the mid-1950s because Michael recalls receiving a letter
    from his half-brother '[s]ometime in the mid-fifties' (p. 61). We may be
    tempted to think of narrator Michael's present as the date of the play's
    production in 1990, but he is described as a 'young man' in the
    Character listing, and a sixty-one-year-old (as Michael would have
    been in 1990) could scarcely be regarded as young. There simply
    aren't enough clues about narrator Michael's present. Further, little
    mention is made of political events or socio-historical observations
    related to the village, county or Ireland generally in the play. Apart
    from the vague comment that 'Aunt Kate had been involved locally in
    the War of Independence' (p. 8), there isn't any direct reference to
    recognisable events of Irish history. On the contrary, the historical
    events mentioned are deliberately outside the local sphere and even
    outside the nation: Jack's involvement in the First World War 'when
    he was chaplain to the British army in East Africa' (p. 1), and Gerry's
    joining up with the International Brigade for the Spanish Civil War
    (1936–39) (p. 31). And in Act 2, Gerry recounts the signing-up
    interview in a way that entirely disinvests the Spanish Civil War of its
    political momentousness:

    > 'I take it you are a Syndicalist?' 'No.' 'An Anarchist?' 'No.' 'A
    > Marxist?' 'No' 'A Republican, a Socialist, a Communist?' 'No.'
    > 'Do you speak Spanish?' 'No.' 'Can you make explosives?' 'No.'
    > 'Can you ride a motor-bike?' 'Yes.' 'You're in. Sign here.'
    >
    > (p. 50)

2   It is in relatively small, everyday details that the play's sense of period
    and location is created, details that hold in a general way with any
    awareness of Ireland's social history that an audience may have. The
    importance of the radio; Gerry's reflections on selling gramophones
    (p. 29); the persistence of pagan rituals like the Festival of Lughnasa;
    Agnes's fondness for 'Annie M. P. Smithson novels' (a prolific
    Republican Irish novelist, 1873–1948) (p. 11); Maggie's Wild
    Woodbine cigarettes; Kate's allegiance to her Catholic heritage and
    neighbourhood; the prospect of the local glove-maker going out of
    business because a factory opens (pp. 52–3) – these small, everyday
    details accrue to convey a strong socio-historical sense of the
    context. It is evidently a context caught in transition; a rural society in

which a passing way of life contends with the appearance of mechanisation and modernity. In fact, these everyday details are exactly of the sort where memories merge with history. These details may be recalled by those who lived then and such details have a place in historical narratives.

A close consideration of the role of memory and history in the play suggests that the former dominates over the latter (do you agree?). *Dancing at Lughnasa* is structured around memory and attends to the workings of memory considerably more emphatically than it dwells on historical events and narratives. The manner in which I have distinguished between 'memory' (fluid and more individual) and 'history' (organised, evidenced and relatively consensual) here may appear artificial. Indeed, it has been argued persuasively that historical narrative can be fluid too, and is often divisive, that history may be regarded as an aspect of memory (a sort of 'collective memory'), and that a reasonable understanding of the past or present should be aware of both the individual and the collective dimensions of memory. Ultimately, perhaps, it is mainly what is emphasised in looking back that distinguishes memory from history. Such different emphases have, however, a particular significance for engaging with *Dancing at Lughnasa*.

In Friel's Field Day plays the emphasis was, as noted above, on history. The Field Day project of undertaking a 'decolonization process' whereby a 'new Irish personality' may emerge (that Friel spoke of – see the section 'Background' above) meant re-examining the historical tensions in colonial and postcolonial Ireland from a larger- or deeper-than-sectarian perspective. There was a calculated nationalist investment in this project, apparent in the 1980s plays: a focus on the history *of* Ireland to serve an agenda to do primarily *with* Ireland. Each of Friel's three original plays of the period – *Translations* (1980), *The Communication Cord* (1982) and *Making History* (1988) – were about Irish history, with close attention to how historical understanding and misunderstanding have been generated. And in each, the idea was thereby to crystallise the present and future of Ireland as a nation and the Irish as its people. *Making History* particularly, as its title suggests, was effectively a contemplation both of a key period in Irish history and of the nuances of recording history. Coming after it, *Dancing at Lughnasa* seemed to provide a pointed counterpoint in emphasising memory over history. The questions that immediately arose were what this move did to Friel's investment in a 'decolonization process' (see above) for Ireland and how this new emphasis fitted into Friel's *oeuvre* thus far. Critics responded to these questions variously. Richard Pine, whose first extended study of Friel was published soon after the play appeared, pondered its implications in an Afterword. Pine saw in it a strong investment in the autobiographically personal as opposed to the historical, and read it as using memory to articulate the everydayness of 'home' in Ireland: 'a "home" because everything is both rehearsed and enacted there: a place where memory is shaped hourly, weekly, monthly. … It concentrates, as did *Making History*, on forms of truth, on different kinds of memory' (1990, p. 228 – this passage appears verbatim in *The Diviner: The Art of Brian Friel* (1999, p. 272), Pine's later book on Friel). Evidently, however, Pine regarded *Dancing at Lughnasa* as nevertheless similar to *Making History* in focusing on 'forms of truth, on different kinds of memory'. Taking a similarly inclusive view of history *within* memory as an overarching theme of Friel's work, the poet Seamus Heaney (b. 1939) observed in an essay:

> A great deal of his dramatic writing demonstrates the way his characters either retrieve or reconstruct a past, sometimes in order to indulge and absolve the characters, sometimes to expose and judge them, but mostly in order to exercise judgment and absolution at the same time. Friel is intent upon showing how easy it is for them to evade reality by taking the wrong memory-turn; and he is also intent upon confronting audiences and readers with the possibility that they too have been prone to the same evasions and trials.
>
> (Heaney, 1993, p. 231)

In general, though, critics have been inclined to discern a definite retreat from the earlier national and historically focused agenda in the play's emphasis on memory. For instance, Scott Boltwood, in a book-length study of Friel's complex relation to the Irish nation, suggested that he was 'alienated from both [north and south] Irish states and unable to identify with either' (2007, p. 2), and felt that *Dancing at Lughnasa* showed 'a sanitized past from which the narrative of academic history has been erased' (p. 170) and exemplified Friel's retreat from 'seeking to envision Irishness supplemented by Northern identity' (p. 182).

The autobiographically personal dimension of *Dancing at Lughnasa* mentioned above may suggest that some knowledge of Friel's life could help illuminate the play. In fact, though there is a broad resemblance between Friel's childhood experiences and events in the play, there are also factual slippages between these. After examining the autobiographical in relation to the play, Helen Lojek thus concludes that: 'The play, however, is neither autobiography nor documentary, but a drama that explores complex issues in the lives of invented characters' (2006, p. 79).

The influences that fed into *Dancing at Lughnasa*, and in different ways coalesced into its emphasis on memory over history, derived from both the Irish context and from a cosmopolitan sense of theatre. In 1986 Friel edited and published the memoirs (covering 1861–1954) of a tailor and weaver in Cluainte village, Charles McGlinchey, as recorded by schoolmaster Patrick Kavanagh. What struck Friel, as he observed in his introduction, was McGlinchey's indifference to the important events of Irish history in his memories:

> They [historical events] are overlooked in a manner that is almost Olympian. They do not merit his notice. But by his concentration on the everyday, the domestic, the familiar, the nuance of a phrase, the tiny adjustment to a local ritual, the momentous daily trivia of the world of his parish, he does give us an exact and lucid picture of profound transition: a rural community in the process of shedding the last vestiges of a Gaelic past and of an old Christianity that still cohabited with an older paganism, and of that community coming to uneasy accommodation with the world of today, 'the buses, the cars, the silk stockings'.
>
> (Friel, 1986, pp. 1–2)

This could well be a description of *Dancing at Lughnasa*. Incidentally, it is oft-noted that as opposed to the collective memory of history, Friel evokes here the collective memory that persists in rural Ireland through pagan rituals, such as the Festival of Lughnasa. An extended ethnographic study, *The Festival of Lughnasa* by Máire MacNeill, which drew upon an Irish Folklore Commission Survey of 1942 and noted the 'survival of Lughnasa at a hundred and ninety-five sites in Ireland' (1962, p. 427), was evidently in Friel's view when writing the play.

As interestingly, the emphasis on memory to draw away from a narrow historical focus on Ireland – or, perhaps, to imbue the Irish focus with wider resonances – appears through two influences from theatre outside Ireland. *Three Sisters* (1981 [1901]) by Anton Chekhov (1860–1904) comes to mind as resonating with *Dancing at Lughnasa* in various ways: in its focus on a predominantly female household of sisters; as a 'lucid picture of profound transition' (Friel, quoted above) without explicit allusions to historical events; and in the manner in which characters articulate their desires and relationships and losses through a web of memories. It seems impossible that the parallel wouldn't have been in Friel's mind, since he had adapted Chekhov's play for the Field Day stage in 1981– rendering it, as he observed at the time, 'in an Irish idiom because with English translations Irish actors become more and more remote. They have to pretend, first of all, that they're English and then that they're Russians' (Friel quoted in O'Connor, 2000 [1981], p. 159). Numerous critics have discussed the resonances between provincial Russia and Ireland that Friel exploited through adaptations and allusions to Chekhov and other Russian authors (see, for example, Csikai, 2005; Pine, 1999, pp. 333–43; Richtarik, 2001 [1995], pp. 113–27). Parallels were also drawn by reviewers, immediately after the first production of the play, with *The Glass Menagerie* (1988 [1945]), the 'memory play' by Tennessee Williams (1911–1983) – the parallels were discussed at some length by Fintan O'Toole (2000 [1993], pp. 207–11). The obvious parallel is in using the device of a narrator looking back from an indefinite present, a narrator who is also a character in the events recalled onstage. In fact, the narrator Tom in *The Glass Menagerie* introduces the form of the 'memory play' for audiences in his opening words:

> The play is a memory.
>
> Being a memory play, it is dimly lighted, it is sentimental, it is not realistic.
>
> In memory everything seems to happen to music. …
>
> I am the narrator of the play, and also a character in it.
>
> (Williams, 1988 [1945], p. 14)

Williams's production notes for the play dwelled at greater length on what he regarded as the new form of the 'memory play', and noted, in particular, that though not realistic, and departing from the conventions of **realism**, such a play

> is not, or certainly shouldn't be, trying to escape its responsibility of dealing with reality, or interpreting experience, but is actually or should be attempting to find a closer approach, a more penetrating and vivid expression of things as they are.
>
> (Williams, 1988 [1945], p. 8)

The manner of dealing with reality in a 'memory play', in other words, is not simply a coherent rendering of the recalled past but also, at the selfsame time, a reckoning with the operations of memory itself. The quotation from Heaney above observes that this is precisely what Friel does. As it happens, *The Glass Menagerie* is also set in the period of the Spanish Civil War, which Tom refers to several times as a field of action and significance that contrasts with his limited, poverty-stricken existence.

In *Dancing at Lughnasa* Friel uses the form of the 'memory play' in a similar though distinctive fashion. It, too, presents a coherent and realistic picture of the domestic setting of the Mundy household while simultaneously foregrounding the slippages and distortions of memory – smoothed over by narrator Michael's linking speeches. To consider some of the ways in which Friel does this in the play, work through the following activity.

Activity 3

Can you identify any examples where the realistic features of the play seem to be in tension with the role of memory? You may like to consider particular characters, conversations or the features of the setting of the Mundy household to find such examples.

Discussion

1   If the memories of conversations recorded in the play are those witnessed by the boy Michael and recalled by the narrator Michael, then it is odd that at times they both appear to be missing from the space where the conversations took place. During the dialogues in the kitchen in Act 1 (pp. 3–6), for instance, the narrator Michael is offstage, and the boy Michael is outside making his kites (Agnes taps on the window '*and blows a kiss to the imaginary child*', (stage direction, p. 5)). Only later

(p. 7) does Maggie, who goes out of the kitchen to feed the chickens in the yard, have a conversation with the boy, and shortly before that the narrator Michael re-enters to speak the boy's lines. None of the exchanges on pp. 3–6 can possibly have been witnessed by the boy or recalled by his adult version.

2   In any case, it is implausible that the boy Michael would have the kind of photographic memory that his adult self would be able to recall accurately. This is particularly so since the boy lives in his own child-world, making kites and given to childlike imagining. The power of the child's imagination is vividly conveyed when he feels, despite a bit of uncertainty, that he has actually seen the imaginary bird Maggie had pretended to let fly (p. 14). Maggie is playfully retaliating here to the boy's attempt to scare her earlier by pretending there was a rat nearby (p. 8). She is momentarily taken in by her fear, while the boy remains convinced for a while that there was a bird because of his desire to see something wonderful.

3   I have noted above that the flow of memories that the play seems to be set off by and returns to still photographic moments at the beginning and end of the play. It is not insignificant that in the still tableau at the end '*The characters are now in positions similar to their positions at the beginning of the play – with some changes*' (stage direction, p. 70): as if the photographic images of the memory are less stable and consistent than real photographs.

4   The memories that characters speak of within the play are nostalgic, imbued more with the pleasure they evoke than the abrasions and equivocations of reality: Maggie's memory of her escapade with Bernie when she was sixteen (p. 20) is a memory of a youthful and exciting past; in Jack's memory everything to do with Ryanga is painted in idyllic colours, untainted by cultural and colonial conflicts; nothing about Chris's memories of Gerry sullies her love for him. And at the end of the play, the narrator admits that the memories it consisted in are superseded by one which 'owes nothing to fact', in which 'the air is nostalgic with the music of the thirties' – 'When I remember it, I think of it as dancing' (p. 71).

Evidently, what is given as the memories of this 'memory play' is not a verbatim report of what happened in 1936; it is a retrospective interpretation based on memories whereby the narrator (re)constructs a coherent and realistic picture of the Mundy household then. In the unfolding of the play, memory provides an interpretive structure and is itself a theme.

Migration

The play's structuring through and thematic preoccupation with memory is inextricably bound to the theme of migration. In an introduction to a collection of Friel's plays, Seamus Deane has noted the importance of the 'theme of exile' in the playwright's early work, inherited from 'Irish theatrical tradition': as a reckoning with the 'conflict between emotional loyalties to the backward and provincial area and obligations to the sense of self which seeks freedom in a more metropolitan, if shallower, world' (1984, p. 13). The experience of migration is deeply rooted in Irish colonial/postcolonial history and collective/individual memory, and naturally impinges on all of Friel's plays in more or less direct ways. In *Dancing at Lughnasa* migration is thematised in a number of unmistakable ways: 'The world of the Mundy sisters is filled with absences brought on by emigration', Declan Kiberd has observed in an extended essay on the social background of the play (2001, p. 22).

Activity 4

Make a list of the characters who are or become migrants in the play, with brief notes on what the reasons for migration are and/or what effects it has on them.

Discussion

My attempt to come up with a character-by-character list follows.

1   The narrator Michael: It is clear from the beginning that he is recalling 1936 from a significant distance in time and place; his vivid memories are not merely of a distant childhood but of a distant home that he has left behind. No clear explanation of his reasons for leaving or his career away from the childhood home emerges, except the briefest note on the simple desire to leave: 'when my time came to go away, in the selfish way of young men I was happy to escape' (p. 71). There is an air of inevitability about this note, as if his life in Ballybeg was no more than biding time before he left. And this desire and sense of inevitability actually needs no further explanation than the one given by Deane above. That feeling of being torn between loyalty to a backward area and obligation to the self seeking freedom saturates the play as a whole – both in the narrator's nostalgic reminiscing and in what's revealed of each character.

2   Jack: The returned émigré Jack's alienation in Ballybeg demonstrates that migration is not merely about physical movement but, more importantly, about cultural displacements and replacements. Every

aspect of Jack's sensibility had migrated: his linguistic ability, religious convictions, cherished memories, relationships, adaptation to everyday life. The return is a process of incomplete re-adaptation wherein he is unable to accept Ballybeg as home again or regain his sense of belonging to the family. In fact, for Jack the missionary purpose of migration – cultivating Christian religious beliefs and practices in Kyanga – has been subverted by the comprehensiveness of his migration. The depth of this subversion is conveyed both in his relations with the district commissioner in Kampala, which he recalls (pp. 39–40), and in the social ostracism he encounters in Ballybeg (which his sister Kate fears and suffers from).

3   Gerry: In Michael's 'memory play' Gerry is a perpetual migrant, a drifter always looking for 'a *named* destination – democracy, Ballybeg, heaven' (p. 51). As Chris observes when he asks to marry her: 'But you'd walk out on me again. You wouldn't intend to but that's what would happen because that's your nature and you can't help yourself' (p. 33). And yet, Gerry's constant movement within Ireland, to Spain, back to Wales, the land of his birth, seems to be not so much due to restlessness and alienation as due to an easy and detached ability to adapt quickly wherever he is – the equivalent of the easy charm that he exercises unpretentiously and yet duplicitously over Chris and Agnes (indicatively, he goes through the same flirtatious dialogues with them on pp. 50 and 65, respectively). The itinerant Gerry's home is, evidently, wherever he is: 'Wales isn't my home any more. My home is here – well, Ireland' (p. 31), he tells Chris. 'Ireland' is an afterthought there, the 'here' of the moment. In a way Gerry is both similar to and a counterpoint to Jack, which renders their ritual hat-exchanging meaningful: it makes visible onstage that they are both powerfully and permanently displaced in Ballybeg, though in quite different ways.

4   Rose and Agnes: Their emigration and sad ending after the events covered in the play is speculatively explained by narrator Michael:

> Perhaps Agnes made the decision for both of them because she knew Rose wouldn't have got work there [at the new factory] anyway. Or perhaps, as Kate believed, because Agnes was too notionate to work in a factory. Or perhaps the two of them just wanted … away.
>
> (p. 59)

Pressing as the economic explanations are, it is the simple and vague desire of the last sentence that resonates with other parts of the play. A feeling of being trapped is notably expressed by both, in Agnes's riposte to Kate about the domestic labour that she and Rose do (pp. 23–4), and in Rose's escapades with Danny Bradley (pp. 5–6; p. 59).

5   Others: Other migrants are mentioned in the play, not quite characters
    but variously connected to the dramatis personae and, so to speak,
    out there: Danny Bradley's wife, Rose says, has left him and gone to
    England (p. 5); Maggie's friend Bernie O'Donnell reportedly married
    and settled in Stockholm (pp. 18–19); Michael observes that the
    search for Agnes and Rose involved 'neighbours who had a huge
    network of relatives all over England and America' (p. 60).

Only Kate, Chris and Maggie aren't or do not become migrants. They
experience at different points in the play feelings of oppression with
their circumstances in Ballybeg, but appear to be unable or unwilling to
try to escape them.

Migration is usually understood as departure from a 'home', where
'home' is a space of domicile or a space with regard to which some
rooted allegiance or notion of belonging is entertained. The dominant
critical convention at present is to think of such a 'home' as territorially
described, most often as a country (a nation or a state) from which
emigration happens or to which immigration takes place. Unsurprisingly,
therefore, the theme of migrations in *Dancing at Lughnasa* has been
critically engaged primarily in terms of the Irish nation: in terms of
movements related to the complex split between North and South, or
the Republic of Ireland (what was the Free State in 1936), or a
composite Irish nation and people, or sometimes specifically County
Donegal. The conflict, in this and other Friel plays, between allegiance
to Ireland (along any of those lines) as 'home' and emigration from
Ireland as 'home' has usually been accounted for by drawing attention
to Irish social history. Such an approach seems consistent with Friel's
Field Day and earlier plays, and indeed this is invariably a useful and
suggestive approach. Thus Declan Kiberd reads the play illuminatingly
as asking the question, 'who is to inherit Ireland?' (2001, p. 18), by
referring to the global migratory shifts of the 1930s:

In Ireland that shift meant, more often than not, a flight out of
the country itself; and this migration masked to some extent the
huge transformation that was taking place, as rural ways yielded to
urban living. What seemed like a crisis of overpopulation in the
'congested districts' of the west was really a failure to produce
goods and distribute food more efficiently. The manager of the
crisis invariably referred to it as a painful but challenging period of

transition. What it led to, in fact, was a growing sense of conflict between country and city. Power – cultural as well as economic – was wielded in the cities and it was there that the leaders of the emerging societies ran the business.

(Kiberd, 2001, p. 19)

At the same time, he keeps the social condition of Ireland when Friel penned the play in view:

Friel wrote his play at the close of a decade which had witnessed intense debate as to whether Ireland itself might be a Third World country. Economic stagnation and rampant unemployment reopened the question of whether the 'experiment' of political independence had been a success, or even a good idea. During every year up to 1988, over 40,000 people – most of them young – left Ireland for work overseas, as factories closed.

(Kiberd, 2001, p. 37)

An awareness of these contexts naturally clarifies the pressured environment of Ballybeg in 1936 depicted in the play, caught between the traditional rural lifestyle and the appearance of modernity (heralded by the radio and the glove factory). Interestingly, Kiberd also tries to articulate the postcolonial dimension of the play through the comparison between the nations of Uganda and Ireland offered through Jack's memories. He regards Jack as representing the

traditional notion of the Irish missionary seeking to found a spiritual empire for his people beyond the seas, [and observes that] [t]he Irish missionary campaign had no ulterior political imperial motive, such as disfigured other European efforts; and this meant that its exponents were more willing to identify with the struggles of native peoples for self-development. Both sides were involved, after all, in the attempt at decolonisation.

(Kiberd, 2001, p. 27)

This, however, is a more idealistic reading of Jack on Kiberd's part, reflecting an idealistic construction of Jack on Friel's part, than history permits. Studies of Irish missionaries in Africa suggest that Jack is, in his wholehearted adaptation to Kyangan ways, atypical among such missionaries. For instance, the historian of the Irish diaspora Tom Inglis observes:

> In Africa alone it is estimated that one-tenth of all missionaries (Catholic and Protestant) were Irish. The intention of the Irish missionaries was to help westernize indigenous people. Religion was taught within a classical curriculum based on language, mathematics, science and history. The Irish missionaries were often portrayed as ascetic, dour colonists who remained aloof from the indigenous people, who rarely learnt to speak the native language, eat the local food, or engage in local customs.
>
> (Inglis, 2007, p. 94)

This characterisation of Irish missionaries in Africa as reluctant to acclimatise themselves to the local way of life (in contrast to French missionaries) is also noted by Tim Pat Coogan (2001, pp. 504–5).

Similarly illuminating are attempts to understand the female Mundy household in terms of the position of women generally in 1930s Ireland. Thus, Helen Lojek has understood the variously expressed sense of limitations that the Mundy sisters suffer against the following background:

> In the independent state that emerged in the 1920s the image of suffering Mother Ireland joined the ideal of the 'sainted' Irish mother to become a hallmark of national patriarchal assumptions. The Republic's 1937 Constitution famously incorporated not only the tenets of conservative Catholicism, but also a romantic vision of Irish woman, a term that clearly meant 'wife and mother': her 'life' (not her work) within the home 'gives to the State a support without which the common good cannot be achieved.' Such legislative paternalism restricted women's roles outside the home and granted them less than equal citizenry. It was widely criticized at the time (usually by women) for its failure to preserve the promise of equality offered in both the 1916 Declaration and the 1922 Constitution.
>
> (Lojek, 2006, p. 78)

In a related way, Joan Fitzpatrik Dean usefully cites socially indicative statistics of Ireland to understand some of the gender issues that underpin the experience of characters in the play, noting that: Michael's illegitimacy was part of a larger reality (3.5 per cent of all births in 1933–4 were such (2003, p. 14)); the sisters' unmarried state was more common than not at the time (in 1936, 67 per cent of women and 89 per cent of women aged between 25 and 29 were unmarried in rural Ireland (p. 16)); and Rose and Agnes's emigration was part of a larger trend of female migration (female emigration exceeded male emigration in six out of ten decades from 1871 to 1971 (p. 16)).

Useful as such socio-historical backgrounds and details are for understanding the play, thinking of the theme of migration vis-à-vis Ireland as 'home' seems to me to go against the grain of the play. As observed above, *Dancing at Lughnasa* is deemed a departure from Friel's Field Day and earlier plays precisely in moving away from nationally defined agendas and the particularities of Irish history. The 'memory play' structure and studied disregard for Irish historical events and narratives here, the cosmopolitan evocations that are apparent, simply do not allow a sufficient sense of the Irish nation as the 'home' to and from which migrants move. The 'home' of the play is certainly *inside* the Ireland of 1936, but the 'home' is not Ireland *itself*. The 'home' is something more specific; it is no more than the Mundy household in Ballybeg in the few days of August 1936 that are etched in the narrator Michael's memory. This sense of 'home' is characterised by the specific memory of a time and place, where the 'homeliness' for Michael is defined by the unusual togetherness of all the characters then. Arguably, the 'home' from which Michael has emigrated is only formulated with photographic sharpness in the formal tableaux of all the characters together at the beginning and end of the play and the abstract memory of dancing in the last lines. If we wished to generalise from the play, we could, perhaps, say that migration is understood here in terms of what migrants recall as 'home' rather than of some objective territory – a region or nation – as 'home'.

Such an understanding of 'home', as migrant memory rather than country, gels with other aspects of the play. In Friel's Field Day and earlier plays (particularly *Translations*), the national and cultural formation of Ireland and the colonial/postcolonial nuances thereof were examined through a searching focus on language, spoken and written. The allegiances, slippages and power plays in language described the cultural and political conditions of Ireland's history and present. In

Dancing at Lughnasa a decisive shift occurs in Friel's diluting the focus on language and turning to expressions that are, so to speak, non-linguistic or more than linguistic – which are not conveyed in words but suggested through images, movements, music and their symbolic resonances.

Activity 5

Enumerate the moments in *Dancing at Lughnasa* where expressions appear through means other than or beyond words, that is, through image, music, movement and their symbolic resonances. Make brief notes on what significances can be attributed to such means of expression in the play.

Discussion

1   The Festival of Lughnasa: This is described minimally in Michael's opening narrative: 'in the old days August the First was *Lá Lughnasa*, the feast day of the pagan god, Lugh; and the days and weeks of harvesting that follow were called the Festival of Lughnasa' (p. 1). Rose gives an account of one of the bonfire rituals of the festival in which 'young Sweeney's trousers caught fire' (p .16), and Kate, from her devout Catholic perspective, gives a quite different account of the same incident (p. 35). What the Festival consists in remains ambiguously articulated through the play, but it casts an atmosphere – a charge of indescribable energy – at various moments in the play, and seems to provide an explanation for the other non-linguistic expressions that appear.

2   Dance: The dances provide a running thread through the play, and rise above verbal enunciations and social constraints. The climactic dance of the five sisters in Act 1 (pp. 21–2) is described in Friel's stage directions more as an expression of subconscious desires bursting forth than as a graceful performance ('*But the movements seem caricatured; and the sound is too loud; and the beat is too fast; and the almost recognizable dance is made grotesque*' (p. 21) – and it overcomes even Kate's Catholic reticence and propriety. Gerry's dances with Chris convey an immediate togetherness that runs deeper than words – the first time they dance the dialogues go:

> CHRIS: Gerry –
>
> GERRY: Don't talk.
>
> CHRIS: What are you at?
>
> GERRY: Not a word.

(p. 32)

And, of course, there are the last lines by Michael:

> Dancing as if language had surrendered to movement – as if this ritual, this wordless ceremony, was now the way to speak, to whisper private and sacred things … Dancing as if language no longer existed because words were no longer necessary …

(p. 71)

3   The radio: Music from the Minerva wireless set, christened Marconi in the Mundy household, has the ability to release pent-up and unspoken emotions and desires – as Michael says, 'I had witnessed Marconi's voodoo derange those kind, sensible women and transform them into shrieking strangers' (p. 2). As a theatrical prop, it presents an interesting combination of a modern mechanical instrument with an inexplicable life of its own, outside the sisters' control.

4   The boy's paintings on the kites: The effect of these atavistic stage images, first seen towards the end of the play, is described in Friel's stage directions: '*On each kite is painted a crude, cruel, grinning face, primitively drawn, garishly painted*' (p. 70). This effect is wholly unequal to the responsive dialogues that follow. The effect is purely visual in performance, gesturing towards a childish and yet somehow deeper and disturbing layer of consciousness.

5   Ryangan memories: Jack's various recollections of Ryangan life – rituals of yam and cassava and of exchange and of placating ancestral spirits, of attitudes to love-children – suggest *within* the Mundy house a curiously evocative, exotic and alternative world of the imagination. Jack's ethnographic descriptions do not quite capture the force of their evocation amidst the realities of Ballybeg.

These suggestive expressions without or beyond words in the play seem to push towards perceptions beyond the socially bound. They introduce a kind of uncertainty and fluidity into any territorially defined sense of 'home'. They also seem to provide a counterpart of let-outs and escapes *within* the Mundy household to the physical migrations that feature in the play – the escape or let-out of actually leaving.

Amidst the interstices of individual and collective memory and the migrations from the 'home' that are held by memory, there are expressions that cannot be put into words and which destabilise the space of 'home' and plough into deeper underpinnings of human society and consciousness. This is most cogently realised in the performance of, rather than through the words of, *Dancing at Lughnasa*.

In introducing this chapter I noted that the discussion above would exemplify an understanding of literary studies as involving heterogeneous and multiple perspectives, aptly thought of in terms of the plural 'literatures'. The various literary traditions and contending strands within a specific tradition (the Irish literary tradition) that feed into this play, the possible interpretations of the play and numerous debates that surround this play are outlined above in a spirit of embracing this pluralistic approach to studying literature. To those should be added the many different ways in which this play can be and has been performed at different times and in different places.

Language and performance in *Dancing at Lughnasa*

Anita Pacheco

We have already discussed several of the dramatic devices Friel employs to give vivid theatrical shape to his theme of memory: the tableaux that start and finish the play; the use of the adult Michael as a narrator; the convention of having the boy Michael as an 'absent-presence' on the stage, visible only to the characters. We have also considered Friel's use of props, like the radio and the kites, that take on a symbolic charge. The task of visualising what the play might look like on stage is made easier by Friel's long and detailed stage directions. In sharp contrast to an early modern play, where stage directions tend to be few and far between, *Dancing at Lughnasa* provides elaborate descriptions of how the play should be translated from the page to the stage. Friel starts out describing the set in some detail and then moves on to the actors' costumes. He tells us precisely the position of each character onstage during the opening and closing tableaux. Throughout, he provides directions for many of the actions taking place onstage; we have already seen, for example, that he describes with some care what each sister looks like as she dances to the music of the ceilidh band (pp. 21–2).

It will come as no surprise to learn that Friel is famously suspicious of theatre directors. Likening a play text to an orchestral score, he has insisted that it should be treated with a comparable level of respect, rather than cut or adapted in accordance with a director's whims (Lojek, 2006, p. 82). Friel would have nothing but contempt for the commonly held view that a play text is no more than a blueprint for performance.

Given the dramatist's detailed stage directions, are there any decisions left for a director of the play to make? In fact, Friel is considerably less interventionist with the script of the play – the words the actors are given to speak. So this is an area where decisions about performance would need to be taken.

Figure 7.3   *Dancing at Lughnasa*, dir. Patrick Mason (Phoenix Theatre, London, 1991). Photo: Photostage.

Activity 1

Let us consider the performance possibilities of one episode from Act 1: the exchange between Agnes, Rose, Chris and Kate about going to the harvest dance, from Agnes's line near the top of p. 12, 'Wouldn't it be a good one if we all went?', to the end of the stage direction at the top of p. 14. Reread this section, taking care first of all to glance through the previous pages to see what, according to Friel's stage directions, each sister is actually doing onstage. Then try to answer the following questions:

1   What are the sisters doing during this episode of the play?

2   How would you describe their language?

3 How does Friel use language to create character in this section of the play?

4 What clues about performance does the language provide?

Discussion

1 Friel's stage directions indicate that the four sisters are in the kitchen, doing the domestic chores that habitually occupy them: Chris is ironing; Kate, having just returned from Ballybeg laden with shopping, is sitting in a chair unpacking her bags; Agnes and Rose are knitting. All except Chris seem to be sitting down.

2 The sisters speak in a colloquial, everyday register. As they discuss whether they should all go to the harvest dance, the dialogue moves at a swift pace, the largely short, alternating lines creating a rapid interchange. The passage is remarkable for the number of questions it contains, from Agnes's opening 'Wouldn't it be a good one if we all went?' to Kate's 'What's come over you all?' near the bottom of p. 13. The short lines and proliferating questions convey not only the sisters' doubt and hesitation about going to the dance, but also their longing to do so and their mounting excitement at the prospect. The dialogue builds to a sort of climax when Kate, normally the voice of order and repression, comes close to relenting and agreeing to go. The unanimity is briefly signalled by Agnes's 'It's settled' and her repetition of Chris's short line, 'Like we used to' (p. 13). But the sight of Rose doing '*a bizarre and abandoned dance*' (stage direction, p. 13) leads Kate to panic and revert to her usual obstructive stance. The episode ends in silence until Maggie returns to the stage.

3 The similarities between the sisters' speech patterns do not obscure the differences between them. Kate clearly speaks more formally than her sisters, calling Agnes by her full name rather than by her nickname 'Aggie'. Her repetition of the word 'No' in the final section of the passage – 'No, no, we're going to no harvest dance' (p. 13) – encapsulates her role in the play. It also reasserts her authoritative position within the home, which in this passage, as at several other moments in the play, is challenged by Agnes, whose growing confidence and determination is signalled here by her interruption of Kate (p. 12) and by the fact that she comes to dominate the exchange linguistically, speaking noticeably

more than her sisters. Rose's speech, meanwhile, has a childlike quality to it, as she alone shows no hesitation about going to the dance and breaks into a spontaneous show of affection for Agnes: 'I love you, Aggie! I love you more than chocolate biscuits!' (p. 13).

4   Looking at language and characterisation in the excerpt tells us a good deal about its mood and tone and pace. The actors would need to convey the complex emotions of this episode through their delivery of the lines, their facial expressions and such body language as is allowed by their seated positions and/or engagement with their respective chores. We would expect to see the actor playing Agnes suggest a growing assertiveness as the scene progresses. In fact, Friel has prepared the ground for this a few lines earlier, with the stage direction '*AGNES had stopped knitting and is looking abstractedly into the middle distance*' (p. 11). As Kate begins talking about the harvest dance, Agnes apparently becomes lost in a reverie and stops working; this in itself would draw the audience's attention to her even before she begins speaking. The use of lighting could emphasise her pivotal role in this section of the play, as could the placing of her chair in a central position in the kitchen. By the same token, Kate's temporary loss of control might be signalled through her slumped, deflated posture in her chair. The relative lack of movement during the exchange works to intensify the visual impact of Rose's sudden eruption into song and dance, while Kate's reassertion of authority might be visually reinforced by increased movement – by having her stand up and move about the kitchen, for example. Any director would need to decide how long the final silence should last and what the sisters should do while it persists: one possibility is that they return to their chores, Agnes's bowed head communicating her anger and disappointment.

Figure 7.4 *Dancing at Lughnasa*, dir. Mick Gordon (Lyric Theatre, Dublin, 2007). Photo: Chris Hill/Lyric Theatre.

In addition to such passages of dialogue, you will have noticed that the play contains several long speeches or monologues, perhaps most notably those delivered to the audience by the adult Michael. Let us look now at the last of these.

Activity 2

Reread Michael's closing monologue in Act 2 on p. 71. How would you describe the language of the speech?

Discussion

The speech begins with the same sentence that opens the play as a whole: 'And so, when I cast my mind back to that summer of 1936, different kinds of memories offer themselves to me.' The verb 'offer' is interesting in that it ascribes to memory a kind of agency: memories 'offer' themselves to Michael, just as, a few lines later, the 'one memory' that forms the subject of the speech 'visits' him more often than any other. The metaphorical use of language here conveys the power of memory and contributes to the 'poetic' quality that characterises the speech as a whole. Michael goes on to say that the 'dream music' of his memory is 'both heard and imagined', 'both itself and its own echo; a sound so alluring and so mesmeric'. The repetitions and the careful balance of phrasing here ('both / and') give the language a distinctive, almost hypnotic rhythm, akin to that of the music Michael is describing. As we move through the speech, we find alliteration ('sweet sounds') and those two adverbs –'rhythmically, languorously' – that, with their combined eight syllables, seem to mimic the floating motion that dominates his memory. In the last nine lines of the speech, the word 'Dancing' appears four times, each time at the start of a sentence. Through the language of Michael's closing monologue, then, Friel foregrounds the non-verbal activity that lies at the heart of his play as the sentences build to a climactic statement of the transcendence of language: 'Dancing as if language no longer existed because words were no longer necessary ...'

Friel's stage business here – the closing tableaux, the just audible music and the slight swaying of the actors – helps to construct the charged atmosphere required by this climactic moment. But the language is crucial, too, and any actor playing Michael would need to keep the audience focused on him through a delivery of the speech attentive to its lyrical qualities and pronounced rhythms.

References

Boltwood, S. (2007) *Brian Friel, Ireland, and the North*, Cambridge, Cambridge University Press.

Chekhov, A. (1981 [1901]) *Three Sisters* (adap. B. Friel), Longcrew, Gallery Press.

Coogan, T.P. (2001) *Wherever Green Is Worn: The Story of the Irish Diaspora*, New York, Palgrave.

Csikai, Z. (2005) 'Brian Friel's adaptations of Chekhov', *Irish Studies Review*, vol. 13, no. 1, pp. 79–88.

Dean, J.F. (2003) *Dancing at Lughnasa*, Cork, Cork University Press.

Deane, S. (1984) 'Preface' in Friel, B., *Plays 1*, London, Faber and Faber, pp. 11–21.

Deane, S. (1991) *The Field Day Anthology of Irish Writing*, Derry, Field Day.

Friel, B. (1986) 'Introduction: important places' in McGlinchey, C., *The Last of the Name* (ed. and intro. B. Friel), Belfast, Blackstaff, pp. 1–6.

Friel, B. (1988) *Making History*, London, Faber and Faber.

Friel, B. (1990) *Dancing at Lughnasa*, London, Faber and Faber.

Heaney, S. (1993) 'For liberation: Brian Friel and the use of memory' in Peacock, A. (ed.) *The Achievement of Brian Friel*, Gerrards Cross, Colin Smythe, pp. 229–40.

Inglis, T. (2007) *Global Ireland: Same Difference*, New York, Routledge.

Kiberd, D. (2001) 'Dancing at Lughnasa', *The Irish Review*, vol. 27, pp. 18–39.

Lahr, J. (2000 [1991]) 'In *Dancing at Lughnasa*, due on Broadway this month, Brian Friel celebrates life's Pagan joys' in Delaney, P. (ed.) *Brian Friel in Conversation*, Ann Arbor, MI, University of Michigan Press, pp. 213–17.

Lojek, H. (2006) '*Dancing at Lughnasa* and the unfinished revolution' in Roche, A. (ed.) *The Cambridge Companion to Brian Friel*, Cambridge, Cambridge University Press.

MacNeill, M. (1962) *The Festival of Lughnasa: A Study of the Survival of the Celtic Festival of the Beginning of Harvest*, London, Oxford University Press.

Morash, C. (2002) *A History of Irish Theatre 1601–2000*, Cambridge, Cambridge University Press.

O'Connor, U. (2000 [1981]) 'Friel takes Derry by storm' in Delaney, P. (ed.) *Brian Friel in Conversation*, Ann Arbor, MI, University of Michigan Press, pp. 158–60.

O'Toole, F. (2003 [1990]) 'Review of *Dancing at Lughnasa*' in Furay, J. and O'Hanlon, R. (eds) *Critical Moments: Fintan O'Toole on Modern Irish Theatre*, Dublin, Carysfort, pp. 93–7.

O'Toole, F. (2000 [1993]) 'Making time: from *Making History* to *Dancing at Lughnasa*' in Peacock, A. (ed.) *The Achievement of Brian Friel*, Gerrards Cross, Colin Smythe, pp. 202–14.

Pine, R. (1990) *Brian Friel and Ireland's Drama*, London, Routledge.

Pine, R. (1999) *The Diviner: The Art of Brian Friel*, Dublin, University College of Dublin Press.

Richtarik, M.J. (2001 [1995]) *Acting Between the Lines: The Field Day Theatre Company and Irish Cultural Politics 1980–1984*, Washington, D.C., Catholic University of America Press.

Welch, R. (1999) *The Abbey Theatre 1899–1999: Form and Pressure*, Oxford, Oxford University Press.

Williams, T. (1988 [1945]) *The Glass Menagerie*, London, Penguin.

Further reading

Delaney, P. (ed.) (2000) *Brian Friel in Conversation*, Ann Arbor, MI, University of Michigan Press.

Friel, B. (1964) *Philadelphia, Here I Come!*, London, Faber and Faber.

Friel, B. (1974) *The Freedom of the City*, London, Faber and Faber.

Friel, B. (1980) *Translations*, London, Faber and Faber.

Friel, B. (1983) *The Communication Cord*, London, Faber and Faber.

Gagné, L.B. (2007) 'Three dances: the mystical vision of Brian Friel in *Dancing at Lughnasa*', *Renascence: Essays on Value in Literature*, vol. 59, no. 2, pp. 119–32.

McGlinchey, C. (1986) *The Last of the Name* (ed. and intro B. Friel), Belfast, Blackstaff.

McGrath, F.C. (1999) *Brian Friel's (Post)Colonial Drama: Language, Illusion and Politics*, Syracuse, NY, Syracuse University Press.

Peacock, A. (ed.) (1993) *The Achievement of Brian Friel*, Gerrards Cross, Colin Smythe.

Walsh, M.W. (2010) 'Ominous festivals, ambivalent nostalgia', *New Hibernia Review*, vol. 14, no. 1, pp. 127–41.

Chapter 8
W.G. Sebald, *The Emigrants*

Dennis Walder

Aims

This chapter will:

- introduce a modern German text in translation, W.G. Sebald's *The Emigrants*
- provide a European perspective on the nature of literary texts, especially narrative
- explore how the novel engages with memory, migration and nostalgia.

Introduction

The Emigrants (1996), like other narratives by the German author W.G. Sebald (1944–2001), can be exasperating when you first read it: long sentences, even longer paragraphs, and a digressive prose style that refers to numerous literary and historical figures, some of them quite obscure – not to mention the unexpected appearance of photographs that interrupt the text. But it is worth persevering. Sebald is a storyteller whose stories take time to grip you; once they do, it is hard to let go. There are good reasons why he writes the way he does, and why he has become one of the giants of contemporary literature, as you will see.

But first: who was he? Sebald was born to a working-class family in the small Bavarian town of Wertach im Allgäu on 18 May 1944. His father, who had risen to become an officer in the *Wehrmacht* during the Second World War, returned home from an Allied prisoner-of-war camp in 1947. Sebald senior was an austere man who never spoke about his wartime experiences. The same thing happened on a much larger scale throughout Germany. There was, in effect, a conspiracy of silence about the catastrophes of the recent past. In an interview conducted shortly before his untimely death in a car accident in 2001, Sebald recalled:

> Until I was 16 or 17, I had heard practically nothing about the history that preceded 1945. Only when we were 17 were we confronted with a documentary film of the opening of the Belsen camp. There it was, and we somehow had to get our minds around it – which of course we didn't. It was in the afternoon, with a football match afterwards. So it took years to find out what had happened. In the mid-60s, I could not conceive that these events had happened only a few years back.
>
> (Sebald quoted in Jaggi, 2001a, p. 4)

Realising more fully what had happened before and during the war, even in small backwaters like Wertach, Sebald grew disillusioned with his country, and went into self-exile in England where he lived for most of the rest of his life.

He first left his protected home environment in the Bavarian Alps to study German literature at Freiburg University, where the professors were 'dissembling old Fascists' (Sebald quoted in Bigsby, 2006, p. 33).

He then moved to Switzerland, before departing in 1966 for a spell as a language assistant at Manchester University. Unhappy about his own origins and culture, he returned to Switzerland as a schoolteacher, then left for Manchester once more, going on to pursue an academic career in England, where he eventually became Professor of European Literature at the University of East Anglia in Norwich. In his mid-forties he began writing in his native German the books that when translated into English were to give him an international reputation.

Sebald was the author of four major works of narrative prose, several books of literary criticism, essays and some poetry. His critical reputation and public success rest primarily on the works of narrative prose, which he called simply *Erzählungen* or stories: *Schwindel. Gefuehle, Die Ausgewanderten, Die Ringe des Saturn* and *Austerlitz* were all first published in German between 1990 and 2001, and eventually in English as *Vertigo, The Emigrants, The Rings of Saturn* and *Austerlitz*. They explore the relationship between the individual and the multiple pasts in which he (it is usually he) finds himself, through a unique mix of memoir, history, document, illustration and reportage. His narrators are all involved in a quest to find a stable vantage point from which to understand the people, events and landscapes they come across. The narratives are indirect and **allusive**, reflecting a struggle to find an acceptable or meaningful form for recalling the horrors of the twentieth century. They represent an unusual form of literature, hovering on the boundary between different fictional and non-fictional **genres**; some might question whether they are literature at all.

Die Ausgewanderten (1992) or *The Emigrants*, although the second of Sebald's narrative works, was the first to be published in English, in 1996. Until then, his literary work was known only in Germany, and to a small number of readers elsewhere. But in English translation *The Emigrants* proved a success, establishing his reputation beyond his homeland, in the UK and USA in particular. As a result, further translations and paperback publication of his other works soon followed. He was fortunate in his translators, Michael Hulse and Anthea Bell, with whom he collaborated closely. *The Emigrants*, while written in four distinct sections, has a consistent concern with various forms of migration and memory, which is why we study it here. Its manner of writing implies questions about how it represents the author's experiences, memories and history, and those of the figures who cross his path.

The edition of the text that is referred to in this chapter is the one published by Vintage in 2002, translated from the German by Michael Hulse.

You should now read the book, either in its entirety or at least initially the first narrative (i.e. up to p. 23) before continuing with the chapter and reading the rest of the book when you are directed to. In what follows I will be taking you through the text – at first in close detail, before speeding up as I consider the main themes. The first tale sets the tone and pattern for the rest of the book.

The Emigrants and genre

As you may have noticed, *The Emigrants* actually opens with a section title, 'DR HENRY SELWYN', beneath which there is an unattributed epigraph: *'And the last remnants memory destroys'*. How can memory destroy things? Usually, it is the 'remnants' of the past that memory retains. In fact, the epigraph is an inaccurate translation of the original motto in German: *'Zerstöret das Letzte / die Erinnerung nicht'*, which splits the verb and its negation in a way impossible in English, so that when you read the original only gradually do you realise that it is about *not* destroying the last or remaining bits of *'Erinnerung'* or memory. The issue of translation has immediately arisen. It looks as if readers in English have to take things on trust, while aware that what they are reading may not always reflect precisely what the author wrote. (I assume Sebald decided to leave the English version as it is.) The first line of the text itself bears this out: in German the place Norwich is referred to as an *'ostenglischen Stadt'* (literally, 'East English town') whereas in English this explanation of the city's location is omitted as unnecessary for English readers.

Keeping in mind that you are reading a translation is important; but the larger and more important issue is: what kind of writing do we have here? The first page of narrative begins with a photograph of what looks like an English country churchyard, dominated by a large yew tree, beneath which the text runs: 'At the end of September 1970, shortly before I took up my position in Norwich, I drove out to Hingham with Clara in search of somewhere to live' (p. 3) (see Figure 8.1).

We know – from the book jacket if nowhere else – that the author, born in Germany, was a teacher at the University of East Anglia. The narrator does not inform us that 'Clara' is his wife, or that 'Hingham' is

Ende September 1970, kurz vor Antritt meiner
Stellung in der ostenglischen Stadt Norwich,
fuhr ich mit Clara auf Wohnungssuche nach
Hingham hinaus. Über Felder, an Hecken ent-
lang, unter ausladenden Eichen hindurch, vor-
bei an einigen zerstreuten Ansiedlungen, geht

Figure 8.1   Yew tree and text from W.G. Sebald (1993) *Die
Ausgewanderten*, Frankfurt, Eichborn Publishers, p. 7 (p. 3 in your edition).

a market town in rural Norfolk, seventeen miles from Norwich – where
there is indeed an ancient churchyard with an immense yew tree. But is
the photograph of the same tree? This is the beginning of what is both
puzzling and enticing about the book. Are these details, including the
photograph, the 'remnants' of memory? And if so, what kind of writing
can we call this?

Activity 1

To help us decide what to make of it, let us consider the Selwyn narrative
in more detail. How would you describe the kind of narrator we meet
here? Is there a moment when his memories are suddenly rekindled,
apparently arbitrarily? When you have identified that moment, think about
and note what function memory seems to serve.

Discussion

1   There seems to me to be a *voice* here, and an observant eye, describing the opening scene in almost hallucinatory detail – a house 'hidden behind a two-metre wall and a thick shrubbery of hollies and Portuguese laurel' (p. 3), for example. This is a **first-person narrator** who seems to assume we know all about him – as if he were addressing a friend, or himself, as in an internal monologue, or a memoir.

2   Recalling 'the château in the Charente that I had once visited from Angoulême' (p. 4) is where the narrator begins to remember another time and place. The recall, however, does not interrupt the unhurried onward flow of the narrative.

3   Considering the textual details more carefully enables us to understand the function of memory: the impression of the 'dark mirror glass' (p. 4) of the windows of the house the narrator and his wife are looking at – but which shows no sign of life – is what specifically arouses recollection. The windows of the front of the château are, it seems, 'just as gleaming and blind' as those of the house (p. 4). Notice that the front of the château was false, a replica of the front of the palace at Versailles, 'utterly pointless' (p. 4) therefore, and suggestive of a kind of madness, or at least a confusion of illusion and reality. The function of the memory is to suggest how enigmatic or mysterious memories can be, and how, for all that this seems at first to be a **realist** narrative, it is also more than that, perhaps a reverie, or fantasy.

Like the quietness of the opening image of the yew tree, appearing to be rich with meaning, yet refusing to say more about what that meaning might be, the details of the house and its surroundings, and the memories brought to the narrator's mind, make this writing strange, even eerily fascinating. The details appear to be symbolic, but of what we are not sure.

As one of the first reviewers of the book, Gabriel Josipovici, put it:

> is this simply a careful description of a specific place visited by Sebald one day in September 1970, or is it, like Poe's *House of Usher*, heavily symbolic? The narrative refuses to come to rest on one side or the other: the fish-shaped knocker [on the door] may

be significant or it may not, the house may reflect the mind of its owner or of the narrator, or it may not.

(Josipovici, 1996/7)

Josipovici refers to the American Gothic author Edgar Allan Poe (1809–1849) whose story 'The Fall of the House of Usher' (1839) also begins with the narrator arriving at a suggestively crumbling house. The ambiguities of Sebald's writing are similarly what draw us in, creating a sense of dreamlike significance and anticipation, of symbolic resonance.

This sense of a borderline style of writing, neither firmly realist, nor purely symbolic, but hovering on the edge between, is further enhanced by the image in *The Emigrants* of the old man, 'head propped on his arm', seemingly 'absorbed in contemplation of the patch of earth immediately before his eyes', like 'a kind of ornamental hermit' (p. 5). This turns out to be Dr Henry Selwyn, the main focus of the first story. He looks like more than just an odd figure, perhaps even a mythic one – indeed, his pose is reminiscent of the traditional image of melancholy, such as that represented in Albrecht Dürer's famous engraving *Melancholia* (Figure 8.2). The image consists of a sad figure leaning on one arm, staring disconsolately down, accompanied by symbols of time, memory and mortality.

Another work of Sebald's, *The Rings of Saturn* (1998), refers explicitly to this engraving. But the most familiar literary example is probably Shakespeare's Hamlet, the melancholy Dane, often depicted similarly in a thoughtful or depressed posture, with ideas of death or suicide not far away. Not that you need to know all this to have a sense of the significance of the image of Selwyn, since its relevance for the outcome of Dr Selwyn's story soon becomes apparent. Selwyn himself, we learn, spends most of his time alone in a flint-built hermitage in a remote corner of the estate (see the photograph in *The Emigrants*, on p. 11).

A mythic, symbolic or fantasy element continues to hover about the narrative, for all its detailed realism, as if there were simultaneously a film playing in the narrator's head – suggested not only by Selwyn's posture when first discovered, and the visual imagery of cemetery, deserted tennis court and disused garden (see photographs on pp. 3, 6 and 7), but also by that reference at the end of the first paragraph on p. 8 to 'fairy-tale apples' that apparently tasted better than any the narrator has eaten since, and were called the 'Beauty of Bath'. Perhaps we are momentarily in that land of storytelling in which the wonderful

Figure 8.2   Albrecht Dürer, *Melancholia*, *c.*1514, engraving, 24 × 192 cm.
Photo: Mary Evans.

apples change one into some other being, or translate one onto another
level of reality? Or is this simply an aspect of how memory operates –
linking the unexpected, the distant and subjective in ways that are not
obviously logical or easily explicable? Certainly the narrative revels in
digression and the unexpected.

Most striking, however, and most unusual, in terms of the reader's
engagement with the text, are the visual elements inserted into it,

apparently without explanation, as if from a family album. A brief skim through the pages of the book reveals that there are a variety of images in it – photographs, drawings, newspaper clippings. This prompts the question: what purpose do these unusual insertions serve?

In a sense, it is the same as that of photographs in general, of evoking simultaneously the material survivals of the past, and the ephemerality of those survivals. These images, and their often apparently random, captionless placing in the text, highlight the importance of the visual in all remembering (as Suman Gupta suggested in Chapter 7 in relation to *Dancing at Lughnasa*); but it is an importance all the more telling in that for Sebald (as for many others), it was the visual record of the Holocaust that reverberated through memory, conjuring up a sense of horror, shame and guilt. For Sebald, as, perhaps, for many of the post-war generation, the first encounter with the recent past of Germany has been the viewing of a documentary film of the concentration camps, with imagery that remains in the consciousness and in what we might call the collective memory of European society.

Let us look now at the rest of the Selwyn narrative.

Activity 2

1   Try summarising the Selwyn story in a paragraph or so, and note how war, and specifically the Holocaust, feature in it.

2   What is the impact of Dr Selwyn's life story on the narrator?

Discussion

1   The narrator and his wife do not stay for long in the Selwyn house in which, apparently, the retired doctor is left alone by his wealthy Swiss wife as she goes on trips abroad. Their landlord invites them to dinner, during which Dr Selwyn recounts the story of his stay in Berne shortly before the First World War, and tells them of his great fondness for an Alpine guide, Johannes Naegeli, who disappeared, presumed to have fallen into a crevasse. After dinner Selwyn shows slides of a trip to Crete, one of which reminds the narrator of the Russian author Vladimir Nabokov (1899–1977), while another is a view recalled years later when he watches the German film *The Enigma of Kaspar Hauser* (1974). Once the narrator and his wife have moved out, Dr Selwyn continues to call on them, one day confessing to the narrator how homesick he is, before launching into his life story – about having left Lithuania as a child named Hersch Seweryn and growing up in London, before winning a scholarship to study medicine at Cambridge, when he changed his name. After this

came the visit to Berne, where he met his future wife, from whom he concealed his background for a long time. Later that summer the narrator learns that Selwyn has shot himself, with the gun he obtained while working as a doctor in India. Many years later the narrator comes across an item in a Swiss newspaper (reproduced on p. 22): Naegeli's body has been released by the glacier into which he had fallen seventy-two years earlier.

Selwyn was called up during the First World War; but of the Second, he says only that it 'and the decades after, were a blinding, bad time for me, about which I could not say a thing even if I wanted to' (p. 21). Thereafter, he says, he 'severed [his] last ties with what they call the real world' (p. 21). Clearly something appalling has happened to, or been witnessed by, Selwyn during and immediately after the Second World War; we do not know exactly what. He and his family were part of the pre-First World War 'exodus' (the resonant Biblical word itself is used) from Eastern Europe of Jews avoiding the pogroms (Russian for organised massacre). But, knowing about the Nazi 'cleansing' of Germany and then Eastern Europe, we suspect the source of his disaffection and depression, indeed the melancholy that finally leads to his suicide, to have its origins in that unspoken wartime experience, possibly to do with the concentration camps.

2   What we are given by the narrator is his reaction to the news of Dr Selwyn's suicide, 'a shock', but one he could overcome with 'no great difficulty'. 'But certain things, as I am increasingly becoming aware, have a way of returning unexpectedly, often after a lengthy absence' (p. 23). This refers to his visit to Switzerland in 'late July 1986', when a train journey reminds him, or perhaps he 'merely' imagined it, of 'the memory of Dr Selwyn' and his Alpine experience (p. 23). Later his eye is caught by the local newspaper item about the Swiss guide Naegeli's body re-emerging from the ice. 'And so they are ever returning to us, the dead' (p. 23). It is as if the memories of his erstwhile landlord are like the unavoidable remnants referred to in the ambiguous epigraph discussed earlier, apparently lost forever somewhere in the unconscious mind, yet also waiting to return, if prompted by the arbitrary event. The sentence itself has a curiously formal, emphatic ring, almost Biblical, that resonates for the reader, leaving us with the impression of a narrator who cannot help finding deeper meanings in the odd coincidences of life.

Now read to the end of the book, without pausing too long if you encounter any details that seem puzzling or obscure.

Memory, nostalgia and the return of the dead

I have dealt with the first story in some detail because all four stories follow a similar pattern, each of them in turn longer than its predecessor. *The Emigrants* consists of a series of connected, increasingly complex, first-person narratives or '*Erzählungen*' (the original German subtitle), revolving around four twentieth-century exiled Germans of Jewish descent who long consciously or unconsciously to return to their homeland. For various reasons to do with the rise and collapse of the Third Reich (*reich* is German for empire or state), this return is blocked, and their homes are lost. The symbolic structure of all the stories is fundamentally the same: migration, disturbance, travel, return, death.

The importance of the sense of a lost home, and the overwhelming desire for it, which leads to a sense of impossible yearning, affects all the characters to a greater or lesser extent. As we have seen, in the first story the narrator arrives in search of somewhere to live. If he is beset by a yearning for his own original home, this does not surface explicitly, but we are being prepared for its emergence in others – and, perhaps, for the numbness or sense of inadequacy that overtakes the narrator from time to time. The key to understanding this, it seems to me, is provided by the idea of nostalgia, which is not as straightforward as it may appear.

Consider, for example, when the retired doctor calls on the narrator to ask if he is ever homesick. 'I could not think of any adequate reply', he says, 'but Dr Selwyn, after a pause for thought, confessed (no other word will do) that in recent years he had been beset with homesickness more and more' (p. 18). Homesickness, or nostalgia, is what appears to lie behind Selwyn's increasing derangement. When the narrator asks where it is he feels drawn back to, Selwyn reveals his Lithuanian origins, a revelation prompted by a nostalgia which turns out to be fatal. But what exactly is meant by nostalgia? Can it be understood as an illness?

Activity 3

Look up the meanings of 'nostalgia', in a dictionary and/or online, and think about its relevance in 'Dr Henry Selwyn'. See if you can locate the derivation of the word, or its linguistic roots. Have you, perhaps, come across nostalgia elsewhere in twentieth-century writing?

Discussion

Nostalgia is, of course, a form of memory or remembering, usually thought of as an individual matter. According to the *New Oxford English Dictionary*, the current core sense of the term is 'a sentimental longing or wistful affection for the past, typically for a person or place with happy personal associations'. Additionally, it is 'the evocation of these feelings, especially in commercialised form', for instance, 'an evening of TV nostalgia'.

This strikes me as rather narrow, understanding nostalgia as little more than the inrush of sentimentality, or rose-tinted indulgence, when viewing the past. If you explore a little further you will find that the term derives from the Greek *nostos*, meaning 'return home', and *algos*, meaning 'pain' or 'yearning'. It was invented in the seventeenth century by a Swiss doctor to account for the sick longings for their native soil of lonely soldiers and servants employed abroad, and was seen as literally a disease, involving such disturbing symptoms as nausea, sleeplessness, loss of appetite, cardiac arrest and even suicide. This enables us to better understand Selwyn's derangement and self-inflicted death.

In fact, while the connection with displacement or migration from home continues into the present as part of the meaning of nostalgia, the clinical overtones have largely disappeared, and it has become more of a state of mind, which may or may not have a profound effect. In the great modernist writers such as Marcel Proust, James Joyce and Virginia Woolf, the return of the mind to specific times, places and experiences as a function of the remembering self brings a kind of truth of the past into the present, reviving not merely the past moment, but, in a sense, the experience of the past itself, an **epiphany** – examples of which can be seen in *Dubliners*, as you will recall.

But this is not what Selwyn's story brings: his suppressed wartime memories are never released; although his unexpected return to the narrator's imagination did release another memory – of the doctor's nostalgia for the time of supreme companionship with the guide Naegeli whose remains have been freed by the slow movement of the glacier. Perhaps that was a memory to be treasured, to be nostalgic about, not sentimentally or indulgently, but in a more fruitful sense.

In the next story, 'Paul Bereyter', about the narrator's schoolteacher, the key sentence is 'I had to get beyond my own very fond memories of him and discover the story I did not know' (p. 28). The narrator thus shoulders the burden of the other's past, unspoken and unknown though most of it is. This reflects back upon Selwyn's story too. The unhappy tale of Selwyn's attempted assimilation into British culture, including its empire (the India reference), suggests that survival is only possible or even desirable through the remembering of others, however difficult, even impossible that may on occasion turn out to be. The infinitely slow movement of the glacier that brought about the emergence of Naegeli's body and hence the end of his story, but the return of Selwyn's memories, suggests that this process is beyond the merely human scale, and depends upon ultimately unreachable natural forces. Throughout Selwyn's story nature has been depicted as powerful, but tending to decay; and that is also the case with the tales that follow.

'Paul Bereyter'

The theme of the return of the dead through chance event, involuntary memory but also nostalgic recall is reinforced by the tale of 'Paul Bereyter', which opens with another photograph (see Figure 8.3).

As you can see, this depicts a set of curving railway tracks from ground level, followed by the German words translated as:

> In January 1984, the news reached me from S that on the evening of the 30th of December, a week after his seventy-fourth birthday, Paul Bereyter, who had been my teacher at primary school, had put an end to his life.

(p. 27)

In actual fact, Sebald has stated that *The Emigrants* 'started from a phone call I got from my mother, telling me that my schoolteacher in Sonthofen had committed suicide' (quoted in Angier, 2007, p. 69). The news sends the narrator – whose biography is thus clearly interwoven with Sebald's – back to his home town in southern Germany, where he tries to reconstruct his teacher's life from a series of photographs that make him feel 'as if the dead were coming back, or as if we were on the point of joining them' (*The Emigrants*, p. 46).

These photographs are shown to him by Mme Landau, a friend of Bereyter's and herself a migrant from Germany, who reveals how the teacher was forced out of his post, and his family proscribed, because they were part Jewish, adding that she did not expect the narrator to be aware of:

the meanness and treachery that a family like the Bereyters were exposed to in a miserable hole such as S then was, and such as it still is despite all the so-called progress; it does not surprise me at all, since that is inherent in the logic of the whole wretched sequence of events.

(p. 50)

Im Januar 1984 erreichte mich aus S. die Nachricht, Paul Bereyter, bei dem ich in der Volksschule gewesen war, habe am Abend des 30. Dezember, also eine Woche nach seinem 74. Geburtstag, seinem Leben ein Ende gemacht, indem er sich, eine kleine Strecke außerhalb von S., dort, wo die Bahnlinie in einem Bogen aus dem kleinen Weidengehölz herausführt und das offene Feld gewinnt, vor den Zug legte. Der mit den Worten *Trauer um einen beliebten Mitbürger* überschriebene Nachruf im Anzeigeblatt, der mir zugleich geschickt worden war, nahm

Figure 8.3   Railway line and text from W.G. Sebald (1993) *Die Ausgewanderten*, Frankfurt, Eichborn Publishers, p. 41 (p. 27 in your edition).

Activity 4

Reread from 'And now, continued Mme Landau' on p. 48 to the end of the 'Paul Bereyter' narrative on p. 63. What is this 'whole wretched sequence of events' (p. 50), and how does it 'force' Bereyter's return (p. 57) and subsequent suicide? What do you think of the manner of his suicide? How might it link with the opening image of this section of the book?

Discussion

That 'whole wretched sequence of events' includes Bereyter's return to S after the war, having avoided deportation – ironically enough, since he is part Jewish – by being called up to serve in the *Wehrmacht*. What moved 'and even forced' him to return, according to Mme Landau,

> was the fact that he was a German to the marrow, profoundly attached to his native land in the foothills of the Alps, and even to that miserable place S as well, which in fact he loathed and, deep within himself ... would have been pleased to see destroyed and obliterated, together with the townspeople, whom he found so utterly repugnant.
>
> (p. 57)

It is not just that Bereyter's feelings about his home village are ambivalent, but that he is divided against himself, and most alienated when he is at home. It is a division he cannot live with, and so, on his final visit home, he lies down in front of a train. Mme Landau relates that she had an 'uncanny' premonition of this end, because 'Railways had always meant a great deal to him – perhaps he felt they were headed for death' (p. 61).

What we infer from this and her remark that Bereyter's end was 'the very image and symbol of Paul's German tragedy' (p. 61), is the railway's emblematic relation to the 'final solution' for German Jews. It was, after all, the railways that provided the logistics for control over large populations whether wanted or unwanted, from the nineteenth century onwards; and where the railways ended was, in a sense, where the concentration camps began.

This idea is reinforced elsewhere in Sebald's work, notably in his last major book, *Austerlitz* (2002), whose eponymous protagonist searches for his true – Jewish – identity by pursuing the railway tracks leading back to Central Europe and the extermination camps where his parents died.

'Ambros Adelwarth'

The third narrative of *The Emigrants*, 'Ambros Adelwarth', brings us yet
nearer to the narrator's own life, since it involves his great-uncle, an
émigré to the United States, and his great-uncle's companion, Cosmo
Solomon. Migration, trauma, madness, leading to silence and ending,
reflect the tendency of this, like the other narratives, towards what has
been aptly called a pattern of 'terrifying homecomings' (Zilcosky,
2004, p. 113). Why terrifying? Because of the increasing sense of
claustrophobia produced by the impact of memory, and the way in
which migration seems to involve a bewildering series of encounters
that end up going nowhere, or at least leading one back where
one started, with only the 'receding perspectives of time' left
(*The Emigrants*, p. 145).

Indeed, in Sebald's densely interwoven narrative trails, going away
always involves in some sense a return. During a series of disorienting
travels recorded in Ambros's pocket diary, he and Cosmo find
themselves in Constantinople (now Istanbul) in 1913 – that is to say, on
the brink of the First World War. The date suggests that last moment
before the arrival of the cataclysmic developments of the early twentieth
century. Every walk in the city brings Ambros and Cosmo alarm and
surprise:

> you turn down a gloomy back street that narrows and narrows till
> you think you are trapped, whereupon you take one last desperate
> turn round a corner and find yourself suddenly gazing from a
> vantage point across the vastest of panoramas.

(p. 131)

And this experience is heightened when they turn a corner in the
densely populated Jewish quarter and meet an unexpected view of
distant mountains, including 'the snowy summit of Olympus'; and
'For one awful heartbeat I imagine myself in Switzerland or at home
again …' (p. 131).

Activity 5

But where, then, does Ambros's homecoming take place? Reread from
'The whole house was always very neat and tidy' on p. 102 to 'with the
goose wing in the darkening air' on p. 116, and consider what we are

told happens to him, and how it echoes Dr Selwyn's story and hence relates to or develops the themes of memory and migration.

Discussion

Ambros's homecoming is neither to Switzerland nor to Germany: 'Have gone to Ithaca' he has scribbled on his visiting card (see the illustration on p. 103). This, we discover, is a sanatorium in Ithaca, in upstate New York, not, as it might have been, the Greek island of the same name that Ambros and Cosmo pass when they are en route to Constantinople (p. 129) – a place famous for its association with Homer's mythical wanderer, Odysseus, who spends ten years trying to get back to his home there. Instead, it is where Ambros finally migrates, becoming major-domo (butler or steward) to the wealthy, yet increasingly secluded Solomon family, whose downward trajectory into depression, paralysis and death he repeats in person, losing his memories as death approaches. The rather sinister figure of the head of the Ithaca sanatorium, Dr Abramsky, says he never met 'a more melancholy person' (p. 111). This reminds us of that earlier melancholy figure, Dr Selwyn, whom we met gazing at the grass beside his house in the first story. Here, in the chilling account of the administration of 'electrotherapy' or shock treatment for Ambros's melancholy (p. 111) – a treatment to which he willingly submits himself – we find that it is assumed to be a form of madness. It seems that the profound sadness created in migrants by their struggle with memories of a home they will never reach has led in Ambros Adelwarth's case to another form of suicide.

'Memory', the narrator's great-uncle reflects in a concluding postscript to the 'Ambros Adelwarth' story, 'often strikes me as a kind of dumbness. It makes one's head heavy and giddy, as if one were not looking back down the receding perspectives of time but rather down on the earth from a great height' (p. 145). There are several other **similes** or metaphors invoked through the text to try to capture the feelings associated with the return of memories; this one, however, seems particularly significant for Sebald. His first major work was called *Schwindel. Gefuehle* (in English, *Vertigo* (2002)), published in 1990, in which the narrator of (once again) four separate yet connected narratives experiences a sensation akin to 'vertigo' when contemplating memories that seem irrecoverable and yet which pull him down, as if towards the void.

This vertiginous sensation is the product of a profound sense of loss, of those remnants (remember the epigraph on p. 1 of *The Emigrants*) that will not return, the memories of the exterminated, which are lost because they have been denied, as they were in Sebald's village, and as they were also by the willed amnesia of his parents' generation in Germany. *The Emigrants* is centrally about the experiences of European Jews, not remembered by the narrator, but *remembered by those he remembers*. Their stories of endings are lost in the grim abyss of time, and are only partially recoverable through the traces that can still be written or rewritten, a process described elsewhere by Sebald as an art of 'palimpsests'; that is to say, like a parchment or piece of writing that is 'written over and over again, until I feel that a kind of metaphysical meaning can be read through the writing' (Sebald quoted in Bigsby, 2001, p. 60). Is this how the text of *The Emigrants* strikes you? Certainly there are moments, such as the strange illustration of Ambros Adelwarth's diary (p. 132), where the written entries do look literally overwritten, as if the writer were engaged in a futile struggle to decipher the meaning of his own life story – or perhaps this 'overwriting' is just a sign of that melancholy madness into which the journal writer finally descended, a loss of coherence induced by the downward pull of an incomprehensible past.

'Max Ferber'

The desire for a meaning beyond everyday realities, beyond what can be simply written down and recorded, reflects a further aspect of remembering that involves more than a yearning to recall people and places, but also a yearning for some indefinable, unreachable beyond. In a remarkable book entitled *The Future of Nostalgia* (2001), the Russian émigré historian Svetlana Boym has suggested that while nostalgia may be past-fixated and negative, there is also a more positive, creative aspect which, paradoxically, looks ahead, to the future. According to her, 'creative nostalgia', as she calls it, reveals the fantasies, the creative 'potentialities' of past time, which is where the future is born; 'One is nostalgic not for the past the way it was, but for the way it could have been', she argues (Boym, 2001, p. 351).

This is a tempting idea: re-creating the past as if it might have been perfect. Sebald's writing might seem a long way from such utopian notions. Yet if we pause for a moment and reflect upon the power of the unconscious yearning that underlies conscious recall, arguably the distress such yearning produces, which we are shown in such figures as Selwyn and Adelwarth, is the result of having an underlying conception of hope – that humankind can survive the appalling traumas that memory brings. Memory always begins with places and people, and yet, viewed with hope and compassion, the inevitable degeneration or destruction it brings can be understood more positively.

This possibility at any rate is what I take away from 'Max Ferber', the last of Sebald's four stories in *The Emigrants*, in particular, those passages in which the narrator first discovers the artist figure amidst the decaying outskirts of Manchester. The story has opened once again on a directly autobiographical note, as Sebald or his narrator – a distinction between author and narrator that again seems to disappear here – tells us about his first departure from home and arrival in England in 1966.

Activity 6

Reread from 'When one entered the studio' on p. 160 to 'a herd of deer headed for the night' on p. 169. Then reread the account of the return to Manchester in 1989 to revisit the artist after having by chance come across his work in the Tate Gallery (from 'Once I was out at the docks' on p. 179 to 'whose faces are both lovely and dreadful' on p. 181). Are there any clues in the writing to a more positive aspect of remembering for the narrator than has appeared in the preceding stories? Or is it entirely negative?

Discussion

At first, the image of the city appears as a memory as darkly negative as all the others: the overlapping migrations produced by successive empires are never-ending, while the empires themselves are always ending, sinking into a twilight like that which envelops Manchester as it appears when the narrator and Ferber first meet and the artist gives him a 'cursory' account of his life (p. 161). Manchester is now a post-industrial, post-imperial city of immigrants, including, for example, the Maasai chieftain who cooks in the Wadi Halfa transport café (p. 163). Yet if the metropolis first strikes the narrator as a place of emptiness, loss and displacement, of greatness past, it also presents new possibilities, as the work of the artist Ferber seems to suggest. He is, apparently, a man 'at home' in the midst of the debris he creates, his 'lines and shadows' escaping 'annihilation' as they figure forth 'a long lineage of grey, ancestral faces, rendered unto ash but still there' (pp. 161–2).

As if to underline this more positive impression – albeit in the midst of collapse and destruction – when the narrator revisits Ferber, he notices a picture clipped to an easel of 'a Courbet that I had always been especially fond of': 'The Oak of Vercingetorix', which is illustrated on the page, a massive and encouragingly leafy ancient oak. It suggests growth and survival, unlike the image of Germany as it strikes Ferber: 'a country frozen in the past' (pp. 180–1).

But things are not quite so straightforward. When the narrator later chances across a review of one of Ferber's paintings, he recalls the earlier encounter, while learning that in May 1939 when the fifteen-year-old Ferber fled Munich for London, his German Jewish parents were murdered by the Nazis. Prompted by this knowledge to return to Manchester and seek Ferber out, he hears Ferber recall his first impressions of the city in 1945:

> The most impressive thing, of course … were all the chimneys that towered above the plain and the flat maze of housing, as far as the eye could see. Almost every one of those chimneys … has now been demolished or taken out of use. But at that time there were still thousands of them, side by side, belching out smoke by day and night. … I can no longer say exactly what thoughts the sight of Manchester prompted in me then, but I believe I felt I had found my destiny.
>
> (pp. 168–9)

Ironically, the city reminded Ferber 'of everything I was trying to forget' (p. 191), his birthplace at the heart of an empire, because here at the heart of another empire he has found a home 'to serve under the chimney' (p. 192). Though this is a curious way of putting it, we can surmise that what he means is that extermination camps are, after all, not far away for him.

But, again, there is more to the second encounter than that. Ferber hands the narrator a brown paper package containing photographs, and his mother's handwritten memoirs of her early years in Steinach and Bad Kissingen, where three hundred years of Jewish culture once existed. These memoirs now seemed to Ferber:

> like one of those evil German fairy tales in which, once you are under the spell, you have to carry on to the finish, till your heart

breaks, with whatever work you have begun – in this case, the remembering, writing and reading.

(p. 193)

This discovery of what was forgotten leads the narrator to travel to Bad Kissingen to explore Ferber's origins for himself, so as to remember and write what we now read; the effect of which is to affirm the survival of these hidden ends of the Third Reich, although you could say they only survive as long as the spell lasts and the narrator pursues them.

Thus, terrible things are being hauled out of the dark past by these encounters with memory; but the suggestion is that there is nonetheless something of human significance in recording them. The fragility of memory is debilitating: 'I felt increasingly that the mental impoverishment and lack of memory that marked the Germans, and the efficiency with which they had cleaned everything up, were beginning to affect my head and my nerves' (p. 225). The narrator's anxiety about doing justice to the story of Ferber's family leads to doubt about 'the entire questionable business of writing' (p. 230). Nonetheless, his book lies before us. Nor does its existence deny the possibility of writing as a representation of reality, as some postmodernists insist: Sebald's kind of **postmodernism** – if it really is that – involves a dizzying plurality of perspectives, not a denial of any perspective at all or of the reality of experience.

Postmodernism and the butterfly man

Perhaps I should explain what I mean by postmodernism here, particularly since it relates to the discussion of genre, and indeed the idea of 'literature' more broadly, as that has developed in the twentieth century. Whereas modernism in a broad range of writers from T.S. Eliot (1888–1965) to Franz Kafka (1883–1924) involved abandoning traditional art forms and their underlying assumption of a direct representation of reality in favour of fragmented, experimental and more **self-reflexive** work, postmodernism foregrounds the disappearance of the real entirely, emphasising instead the 'intertextual' elements in art and literature, with an increased insistence on the way texts refer to one another, rather than to any external reality. Modernism, despite its rejection of tradition, can sometimes display nostalgia for the beliefs and attitudes that have disappeared; whereas postmodernism relishes the disappearance of the past, and views past achievements ironically, through parody, **pastiche** and allusion. There are aspects of Sebald's writing that imply a postmodernist outlook: in particular, the disorienting effect of his allusiveness, digressions, and ironic echoes of other writers and their work. But if that was all there was to it, there would be no reason for his pervasive emphasis upon documented people and events, which imply the importance of remembering historical reality as opposed to forgetting.

One quite striking example of the complexity of Sebald's outlook may be provided by that figure of the man with the butterfly net who, according to Ferber, stopped him from throwing himself down the mountain above Lake Geneva when he 'might really have done so had not a man of about sixty suddenly appeared before him' (p. 174). This is one of those mysterious figures whose significance only emerges after a rereading of the book.

Activity 7

In order to note the prominence and importance of the figure of the man with the butterfly net, try the following:

1 Read the rest of the description of this man on p. 174.

2 Then reread pp. 15–16, looking carefully at the photograph on p. 16.

3 Note the name of the writer mentioned on p. 43.

4 Then reread from 'The air was coming in from outside' to the end of the paragraph on p. 104.

5 Finally, note the allusion on p. 214.

What do you think the strange recurrence of this figure is meant to signify? If his name means nothing to you, try searching for it online and see what emerges. Is this merely postmodern **intertextuality**, that is, one writer referring to another, or might there be more to it, in the context of Sebald's themes in *The Emigrants*?

Discussion

The answers might not seem straightforward, but I am sure you will have observed the repeated allusion to the 'butterfly man', whose name is mentioned on p. 43, and whose photograph has already appeared in the first story: Vladimir Nabokov, the Russian émigré author (of, among other works, *Lolita* (1955) and an autobiographical memoir called *Speak, Memory* (1951)). The description on p. 174 continues:

> He was carrying a large white gauze butterfly net and said, in an English voice that was refined but quite unplaceable, that it was time to be thinking of going down if one were to be in Montreux for dinner.

Nabokov was well known for being a lepidopterist, or butterfly-collector, and for a long connection with Switzerland – where Sebald may have come across him when he was teaching there. More important, there is an uncanny coincidence of places between Nabokov's life history and that of Ambros Adelwarth, the narrator's great-uncle, who has, we have learned, worked at the Grand Hotel Eden in Montreux, where Nabokov spent the last twenty years of his life. Is this why, when Adelwarth is finally (according to the narrator's Aunt Fini) admitted to the Ithaca sanatorium where he dies, he obsessively recalls 'the butterfly man'? He cannot, it seems, rid himself of the image of 'a middle-aged man ... holding a white net on a pole in front of him and occasionally taking curious jumps' (p. 104). The image is both comical and poignant, in the context of Adelwarth's degenerating mind, suggesting the repeated motif of how memory sticks on certain images while losing others. This is more than merely postmodern intertextuality for the sake of it, one writer referring to another.

Sebald's interlinked narratives imply the intricate patterning of what is remembered and what is forgotten; and, in the final story, the difficulty for the artist of creating, or re-creating, images from the past. Repeated references to the Nabokov-figure give an added resonance to the significance of what happens. Thus the artist Ferber's encounter with the Nabokov-figure initiates a year-long quest to paint a portrait of the 'Man with a Butterfly Net', a quest that ends in despair with his failure to capture 'the strangeness of the apparition' (p. 174). Nabokov's final appearance in the text engages with the continuing theme of nostalgia as an aspect of memory: it is from Ferber's mother's diary, in which she remembers being proposed to 'just before the end of the 1913 season', a proposal she is moved to accept by her memory of a 'Russian boy' chasing butterflies in Bad Kissingen – 'I saw him as a messenger of joy' on that 'distant summer day', his beautiful butterfly specimens signalling 'my final liberation' (p. 214). But the First World War intervenes, her fiancé is killed and, the historical irony deepening, we learn with the narrator as he pursues his writing and 'researches' to the Jewish cemetery in Bad Kissingen, that Ferber's mother was 'deported, [her] fate unknown, in November 1941' (p. 225).

And so we return to the fate of all the major figures in the book, Jewish émigrés or exiles whose stories take them, and us, back to the Holocaust. More may be, and has been, made of this particular postmodern or intertextual dimension of the book (Curtin and Shrayer, 2005, pp. 258–83); what is clear is that the aim is to encourage us to ponder the way in which memory may overcome forgetting so as to bear witness to what happened in the dark past of Europe in the twentieth century.

The difficulties of remembering

It was in Manchester, where his landlord was a Jewish refugee, that the young Sebald apparently realised for the first time that the 'historical events' he had heard about 'had happened to real people':

> You could grow up in Germany in the postwar years without ever meeting a Jewish person. There were small communities in Frankfurt or Berlin, but in a provincial town in south Germany Jewish people didn't exist. The subsequent realisation was that they had been in all those places, as doctors, cinema ushers, owners of garages, but they had disappeared – or had been disappeared. So it was a process of successive phases of realisation.
>
> (Sebald quoted in Jaggi, 2001a, p. 4)

'Successive phases of realisation' are what Sebald's narrator takes us through as, prompted by a complex sense of the action of recall, he encounters the memories of others; memories that provoke moments of paralysing doubt, yet also increased awareness, as he begins (and we follow him) to realise the hidden connections they reveal.

When Sebald published a book on Austrian authors he called it *Unheimliche Heimat* (1991) or 'Unhomely Homeland'. '*Unheimliche*' also means 'uncanny', and it is often through the uncanny return of repressed memories that the present is disturbed, and past atrocity recalled. Looking back, Sebald remembered growing up in:

> quite an idyllic environment, at the same time the most horrendous things had happened in other parts of Europe. While I was sitting in my pushchair and being wheeled through the

> flowering meadows by my mother, the Jews of Corfu were being
> deported on a four-week trek to Poland. It is the simultaneity of a
> blissful childhood and those horrific events that now strikes me as
> incomprehensible. I know now that these things cast a very long
> shadow over my life.
>
> (Sebald quoted in Bigsby, 2006, p. 43)

The tension between the nostalgically remembered, idyllic childhood on
the one hand, and the later knowledge of what was happening in the
world on the other, is what drives Sebald's writing, creating an uneasy
sense of the past as the source of endless layers of destructive human
impulse that will and indeed must be remembered in the present. How
far remembering may redeem us is left open, just as the nature of time
remains an enigma.

At the very least, Sebald's apparently unique way of writing responds to
what he has witnessed travelling away from his German home – a
home that functions as the source of both yearning and despair,
because of the horrors with which it is complicit. Imprisoned in a
history he tries obsessively to understand and reconstruct, he cannot
ultimately recover his own past or origins; hence his repeated attacks of
anxiety and depression. But his aim is to suggest the importance of the
remembering that often begins in nostalgia for an earlier life, even if the
result is always partial.

This remembering is always grounded in real people and places
encountered or read about, experiences that, through hidden echoes and
connections, blur the boundary between the found and the made, fact
and fiction, history and literature. This can lead to difficulties: the
objections of the living artist Frank Auerbach to the name 'Auerach'
being used for the artist in the Manchester section in the original
German led Sebald to change it to 'Ferber'; and when Susi Bechhofer
discovered that Sebald's *Austerlitz* was in part based on her life story as
one of the 10,000 Jewish children rescued by the *Kindertransporten*, she
felt she had been robbed of her past. But Sebald, who 'didn't want
to make use' of the full horror of what happened to her, admitted
'I haven't the right. I try to keep at a distance and never invade'
(Clingman, 2009, pp. 193–5; Jaggi, 2001b, pp. 3, 8).

Clearly, Sebald was aware of the dangers of what he was trying to do in
representing the European Jewish past as a German. Confronting the
ethical and political difficulties of trying to make sense of the 'final

Figure 8.4   Human face from Sebald, W.G. (1993) *Die Ausgewanderten*, Frankfurt, Eichborn Publishers, p. 240 (omitted from the English version).

solution' also involved an artistic difficulty, which he thought he had found a way of resolving. He takes us a long way from some of the questionable interventions in the media today, such as the film version of Bernard Schlink's *The Reader* (2008), or Quentin Tarantino's *Inglourious Basterds* (2009) – and, as I write, there is widespread revulsion about a forthcoming film of the Holocaust made by a German film director known for his blood-soaked adaptations of video games (Connolly, 2010, p. 31).

As Sebald remarked in his last interview, writing about:

> the incarceration and systematic extermination of whole peoples and groups in society ... particularly for people of German origin, is fraught with dangers and difficulties ... you could not write directly about the horror of persecution in its ultimate forms, because no one could bear to look at these things without losing their sanity. So you would have to approach it from an angle, and by intimating

to the reader that these subjects are constant company; their presence shades every inflection of every sentence one writes.

(Sebald quoted in Jaggi, 2001a, p. 5)

This sense of every line being infused with the past creates his texts' characteristically formal, mesmeric quality, a way of writing that draws the reader ever deeper into a labyrinth, the end point of which is almost always something appalling, and from which it is difficult to look away – 'And so they are ever returning to us, the dead' (*The Emigrants*, p. 23).

But for Sebald we must follow where the remembered dead take us, while avoiding any direct account of the horrific events themselves. The deep affiliations between large historical events and individual histories are often obscure and indefinable, and can only be represented by means of indirection and implication; that is, a kind of literature that crosses the boundaries of memoir, document, photograph and fiction. This is how he creates an awareness of complicity with the histories of earlier generations, and a deeper understanding of their connectedness. He is aware of the risk involved in taking on the identities of those who suffered; but he offers a unique template for remembering histories mislaid or forgotten, using the yearnings and hidden, involuntary memories of travellers, migrants and exiles like himself. Yet he does not forget that for those who lost their families, anger, frustration, even a numbness in the face of the ultimate darkness, might override any urge to remember, much less to succumb to nostalgia.

References

Angier, C. (2007) 'Who is W.G. Sebald?' in Schwartz, L.S. (ed.) *The Emergence of Memory: Conversations with W.G. Sebald*, New York, Seven Stories Press, pp. 63–75.

Bigsby, C. (ed.) (2001) *Writers in Conversation*, vol. 2, Norwich, Pen & Inc Press.

Bigsby, C. (2006) *Remembering and Imagining the Holocaust*, Cambridge, Cambridge University Press.

Boym, S. (2001) *The Future of Nostalgia*, New York, Basic Books.

Clingman, S. (2009) *The Grammar of Identity; Transnational Fiction and the Nature of the Boundary*, Oxford, Oxford University Press.

Connolly, K. (2010) 'Holocaust film by "schlockmeister" causes outrage', *Guardian*, 13 November, p. 31.

Curtin, A. and Shrayer, M.D. (2005) 'Netting the Butterfly Man: the significance of Vladimir Nabokov in W.G. Sebald's *The Emigrants*', *Religion and the Arts*, vol. 9, nos 3–4, pp. 258–83.

Jaggi, M. (2001a), 'The last word' (interview), *Guardian G2*, 21 December, p. 4.

Jaggi, M. (2001b) 'Recovered memories', *Guardian*, 22 September [online], http://www.guardian.co.uk/books/2001/sep/22/ artsandhumanities/ (Accessed 31 July 2010).

Josipovici, G. (1996/7) 'The forces of memory', *Jewish Quarterly*, vol. 43, no. 4 [online], http://sebald.wordpress.com/2010/03/23/gabriel-josipovici-on-w-g-sebalds-the-emigrants/ (Accessed 2 July 2010).

Sebald, W.G. (2002 [1996]) *The Emigrants* (trans. M. Hulse), London, Vintage. First published in German as *Die Ausgewanderten*, 1993.

Zilcosky, J. (2004) 'Sebald's uncanny travels' in Long, J.J. and Whitehead, A. (eds) *W.G. Sebald – A Critical Companion*, Seattle, WA, University of Washington Press, pp. 102–20.

Further reading

Aciman, A. (1998) 'Out of Novemberland', *New York Review of Books*, vol. 45, no. 19, pp. 6–7.

Schlant, E. (1999) *The Language of Silence: West German Literature and the Holocaust*, London, Routledge.

Sebald, W.G. (1998) *The Rings of Saturn* (trans. M. Hulse), London, Harvill. First published in German as *Die Ringe des Saturn*, 1995.

Sebald, W.G. (2002) *Austerlitz* (trans. A. Bell), London, Penguin. First published in German, 2001.

Sebald, W.G. (2002) *Vertigo* (trans. M. Hulse), London, Vintage. First published in German as *Schwindel. Gefuehle*, 1990.

Walder, D. (2010) *Postcolonial Nostalgias: Writing, Representation, and Memory*, New York and London, Routledge.

Conclusion to Part 2

Sue Asbee

It is evident from the texts we have studied in this part of the book that creativity is one major consequence emerging from the disruption, dislocation and crisis of migration. John Brannigan says that the canon of English literature 'is constantly unstable and hotly contested in every period' but goes on to suggest that 'it could be argued that for the period since 1939 no canon has ever been established' (quoted in Poplawski, 2008, p. 643). One reason for this is the proliferation of writers, like the five we have studied here, none of whom were born or bred in England, but each of whom has written in – or had their work translated into – English. Many other writers have responded to the experience and effects of mass movements of people around the globe, each in their own individual way, but collectively they have definitively changed any earlier notion of 'English literature' to 'literatures in English'.

Each of the texts we have studied contributes something distinctive to developing ideas of 'literatures': significantly these new voices do not fit comfortably into conventional forms. Selvon's anecdotal, episodic experiment with dialect voices was so innovative that the critics who dismissed *The Lonely Londoners* in 1956 would be taken aback to discover its reissue as a Penguin Classic in 2006. Bishop employs old poetic forms – ballad and sestina – but also introduces new ones, like her Brazilian sambas, while *The Emigrants* also challenges canonical expectations of genre. What kind of text is it? A novel, biography, autobiography, history? Is it fact or fiction? We have no way of knowing whether the inclusion of photographs, indecipherable diary entries and other ephemera which *might* provide documentary evidence are authentic. In *Dancing at Lughnasa*, Brian Friel experiments with the 'memory play', using the device of the narrator Michael whose childhood self is invisible to the audience but not to the other characters.

Raising a central question about what 'home' means to emigrants, Bishop asks in her poem 'Questions of Travel', 'Should we have stayed at home and thought of here?'. James Berry's powerful phrase 'hating the place we loved', referring to the homeland which he believed could offer nothing to his generation, is echoed by the narrator of Sebald's 'Paul Bereyter', 'profoundly attached to his native land' at the same time

303

as 'he loathed' that 'miserable place'. In *Dancing at Lughnasa*, Ballybeg is no longer home for Jack, returning from Africa, and it can no longer provide economic support for Rose and Agnes. Displacement – whether of an individual like Bishop, or of people en masse – will always mean memories of what has been left behind, whether for better or for worse.

The five texts we have studied in this part of the book have shown that memory is not straightforward: Friel's Michael sums up the complexities when he concludes that what fascinates him about a particular memory is 'that it owes nothing to fact' (*Dancing at Lughnasa*, p. 71). The border between recollection and imagination becomes blurred, occupying a liminal space; migrants' similarly ambiguous status, poised between different worlds and cultures, has resulted in texts like these which both elude, and also splendidly redefine, conventional genre classifications.

Reference

Poplawski, P. (2008) *English Literature in Context*, Cambridge, Cambridge University Press.

Glossary

allegory

A narrative that has a sustained parallel meaning; an extended metaphor in the form of a story.

alliteration

An example of the patterning of sound in poetry, alliteration occurs when words that appear in close proximity to one another begin with the same letter or sound.

alliterative

see **alliteration**.

allusion

With allusion a literary text invokes another, older literary text or author. Often this is done by direct quotation, correct or incorrect, and with or without attribution.

allusive

see **allusion**.

ballad stanza

A four-line stanza, rhyming *abxb*, with simple three-beat lines that are usually end-stopped.

canon

see **canonical**.

canonical

A literary work is canonical if it belongs to the literary canon, the collection of works traditionally thought to be the most deserving of study on the grounds of their superior artistic merit.

characterisation

The techniques a writer uses in creating a character in a dramatic or narrative work.

diction

The specific choice of words used by a writer. The term 'diction' is also used to describe the type of language that characterises a particular literary work.

epiphany

This term (from the Greek for 'manifestation') primarily relates to the feast commemorating the appearance of the infant Christ to the Magi, which is observed on 6 January. It also denotes a more general manifestation of God's presence in the world. James Joyce adapted it for literary use, where it signifies a moment at which a character experiences a sense of sudden radiance and revelation while contemplating an ordinary, everyday object.

first-person narrator

A first-person narrative has 'I' or 'We' as the originator of the narrative. It is useful to think of the first-person narrator as a character who is actually telling the story, as in 'The Sisters', the first story in James Joyce's *Dubliners*.

flâneur

A French word meaning a (male) wanderer, stoller, but also an observer.

flâneuse

The female equivalent of a *flâneur*.

focalisation

A narrative technique whereby, while the third-person narrator remains the 'speaker' in a novel or story, a particular character becomes the 'focaliser': the character through whose eyes and perceptions the narrative is mediated.

free indirect style

A style of narrative employing focalisation, in which a character's speech and/or thoughts are conveyed by the narrator but free of any narrator's tags such as 'she thought'.

free verse

Poems with no regular metre or rhyme are known as 'free verse'.

genre

The French word for 'kind', a genre is a category or type of art work with its own form and conventions.

half-rhyme

A rhyme in which the paired words fail fully to match one another, as in Elizabeth Bishop's pairing of 'parlor' with 'Arthur' in her poem 'First Death in Nova Scotia'.

iambic pentameter

A line of ten syllables that falls into five measures of two syllables each, in which one unstressed syllable is followed by one stressed syllable.

intertextuality

The interconnecting relationship that a given text might have with other texts, in terms of influences or common reference points between texts.

leitmotif

German for 'guiding motif', which when used as a literary term denotes a recurrent theme or verbal phrase within a single work.

lexicon

The vocabulary of a particular person, class, activity or literary work.

malapropism

Humorous misuse of words, named after 'Mrs Malaprop', a character in Richard Sheridan's play *The Rivals* (1775), who habitually used polysyllabic words incorrectly.

metaphor

A type of figurative language that establishes an identity between two apparently dissimilar things.

mock-epic

A form of satire, usually associated with poetry, but also applicable to other literary forms, which involves the inappropriate employment of elevated or grandiose language to describe events usually regarded as trivial.

monologue

In drama a monologue is a long speech made by a character, either to address others, or with others present but as if alone. Monologues also feature in prose fiction, appearing as extended representations of a character's thoughts.

motif

A prominent idea, theme or image in a work of literature.

narrator

The voice which tells the story in any written narrative.

oeuvre

A French word used to refer to the whole body of a writer's work.

parody

An imitation which mocks another well-known text.

pastiche

Whereas parody is usually designed to mock an existing text, pastiche is more usually an imitation designed to pay tribute to the original.

pastoral

A literary genre with a history dating back to classical times, pastoral involves poems, plays or novels set in the countryside. The conventional assumption of pastoral is of a rural innocence or purity that provides a moral reference point for the corruption, greed and decadence of cities.

pathos

Emotionally moving qualities in a literary work that appeal to or provoke feelings of pity or sorrow in the reader for characters.

plot

A plot may conveniently be defined in opposition to a story. A story is a narrative of events told in the order in which they happened. A story turns into a plot when it is told in a particular way, with a stress on cause and effect (why things happened), and with any number of emphases and distortions: a plot need not be chronological, for example. A writer normally seeks to structure the plot in such a way as to arouse curiosity in the reader or spectator.

point of view

Point of view refers to the perspective from which a particular story is told. In first-person narratives the point of view tends to be that of the first-person narrator; in third-person narratives, the point of view may shift from one character to another, though third-person narrators normally privilege the points of view of one or a few of the principal characters.

postmodernism

Whereas modernism involved abandoning traditional art forms in favour of a representation of reality as fragmented and discontinuous, postmodernism foregrounds the intertextual elements in art and literature, emphasising the ways in which texts refer to one another rather than to an external reality.

protagonist

The chief character in a literary work.

realism

The term used to describe literary works characterised by their author's interest in representing human life and experience 'as they really are'. The term is often opposed to Romantic fiction, which tends to represent human existence as we might like it to be.

realist

see **realism**.

register

A register is a particular type or style of language associated with a particular context.

screenplay

A work written for film, which includes the dialogue, directions for actions and movements of characters as well as instructions for types of shot.

self-reflexive

Literary works that self-consciously reflect on their own composition.

sestina

A sestina is an elaborate poem constructed of six-line stanzas (or sixains) followed by a final three-line tercet.

shot

In filmmaking, an uninterrupted run of the camera to expose a series of frames. In the finished film, an uninterrupted framed image.

simile

A comparison of two apparently dissimilar things that uses either 'like' or 'as' to enforce the comparison.

sonnet

A fourteen-line lyric poem in iambic pentameter with a complex rhyme scheme.

spondaic

see **spondee**.

spondee

A metrical foot which in ancient Greek and Latin verse contains two consecutive long syllables. In accentual languages like English, 'spondaic' describes the effect of consecutive stressed, rather than long, syllables.

symbolism

The use of symbolic elements in a literary work, whereby sometimes ordinary everyday objects become a representative sign or mark, or stand for, or denote, something else.

tercet

A set or group of three lines, usually printed together.

third-person narrator

In contrast to the first-person narrator ('I'/'we'), who is a character in the story telling the story, the third-person narrator is not a character but tells the story from outside/above the characters and events. Whereas 'I'/'we' abound in first-person narration, in third-person narration all the characters are described in the third person (she/he/they). Many third-person narrators are endowed with omniscience, that is, they know everything about the story they are telling.

Acknowledgements

Grateful acknowledgement is made to the following sources:

Readings 4.1, 4.2, 4.3, 4.4, 4.9, 4.10, 4.11, 4.13, 4.14, 4.15, 4.16, 4.17

Rampersad, A. (ed.) (1994) *The Collected Poems of Langston Hughes*, New York, Alfred A Knopf/Vintage Books. Permission granted on behalf of Langston Hughes Estate by David Higham Associates (UK) and Random House in New York.

Readings 4.6, 4.7, 4.8

McKay, C., 'When Dawn comes to the City', 'Subway Wind' and 'The Tropics in New York' © Claude McKay Estate.

Reading 4.12

Kerouac, J. (1950) *The Town and the City*, published by Harcourt Brace, New York and republished by Penguin Books in 2000.

Chapter 5

Berry, J., 'To Travel this Ship', 'Empire Day' and 'Reminiscence Voice' © James Berry.

Chapter 6

Bishop, E., 'Sandpiper', 'Brazil, January 1, 1502', 'Questions of Travel', 'The Burglar of Babylon' and 'Sestina' © Elizabeth Bishop Estate.

Index